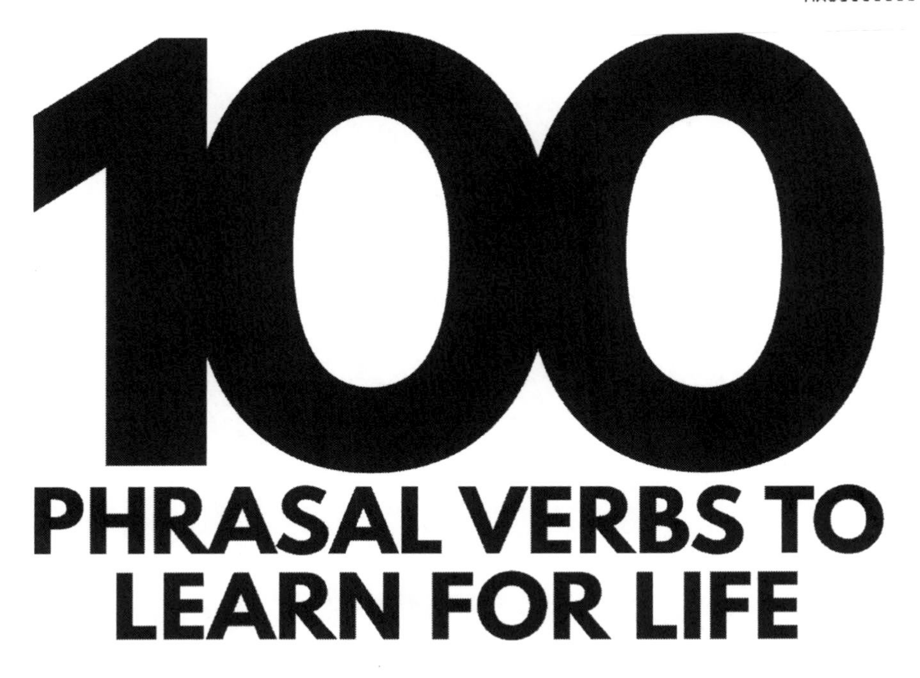


# PHRASAL VERBS TO LEARN FOR LIFE

VOCABULARY EXPANSION FOR HIGH-INTERMEDIATE AND ADVANCED STUDENTS

A1 A2 B1 B2 C1 C2

LUIZ OTÁVIO BARROS

EDITOR: DEBORAH GOLDBLATT

ISBN: 978-65-00-13481-0 (Paperback edition)

Editor: Deborah Goldblatt
Cover art: Eduardo de Freitas
End matter: Natália Guerreiro
Additional proofreading: Nelson Bueno
Inside images: unsplash.com and shutterstock.com

# CONTENTS

# IS THIS BOOK RIGHT FOR YOU?

Thanks for your interest in *100 Phrasal Verbs to Learn for Life.* With so many titles on the market, we know how hard it can be to pick the right one. So, here's some information to help you decide whether *100 Phrasal Verbs* is the book you're looking for... or maybe the one you didn't know you needed!

**Level**

*100 Phrasal Verbs* was written for **high-intermediate (B2) to advanced (C1)** students of English as a **second or foreign language**. You're probably at the right level for this book if you've completed an intermediate (B1) course or higher, but, to be sure, take a look at the first few lessons. They will help you get a feel for the book and make the right decision. Tip: On Amazon, the Kindle version lets you preview more lessons than the paperback edition.

**Scope**

There are literally thousands of phrasal verbs in English, and some of them have dozens of meanings. *100 Phrasal Verbs*, as is evident from the title, **focuses on a limited number of verbs and their most common uses**. Our less-is-more approach allows us to provide, on average, 15 examples of each phrasal verb so you can understand how it works and use it with confidence.

**Kinds of examples**

*100 Phrasal Verbs* contains over **1,500 examples** adapted from authentic sources, such as TV shows, newspapers, magazines, blogs, and essays. These are real-world examples, which will teach you how to express yourself naturally using phrasal verbs.

**Teaching philosophy**

When it comes to phrasal verbs, linguistic terminology can sometimes do more harm than good. Terms like "type 1-4" and "separable/inseparable" can make phrasal verbs seem more complicated than they actually are. For this reason, *100 Phrasal Verbs* keeps jargon to a minimum so you can focus on **what really matters: the words and grammatical patterns that different phrasal verbs tend to attract in everyday use**. For example, *carry out* is often (1) followed by words like *research, investigation, orders, attacks*, and (2) preceded by phrases expressing ability, such as *be able/unable to*. We believe that it's this kind of information that will help you *really* learn how to use phrasal verbs to communicate.

But don't take our word for it. Look at the first few lessons so you can decide for yourself whether *100 Phrasal Verbs to Learn for Life* is the right book for you.

**Welcome aboard!**

# THIS BOOK IN A NUTSHELL

If you are looking at this book, you probably already know (a) what phrasal verbs are, (b) how common they are, and (c) how important it is to learn how to use them. So, rather than discuss a–c at length, we have created a short, to-the-point introduction that will allow you to dive right into the actual lessons more easily. Here's a brief Q&A to help you learn more about the book:

▶ *Can I use this book without a teacher?*

Yes. *100 Phrasal Verbs* is essentially a reference book, ideal for self-study. However, if you are a teacher, you might find it a useful addition to your main textbook, for use as supplementary material.

▶ *How are the phrasal verbs organized?*

The 100 verbs are grouped by topic and spread over 17 sections. At the end of each section, you will find a series of exercises (with answers) to help you check your progress. If you'd like to do the exercises online, you can scan the QR codes provided.

▶ *Do I have to follow the lessons sequentially?*

No. The lessons don't get progressively harder, so you can start, say, from section 10, move on to section 13, and then go back to section 2. The lessons within each section can also be done in any order, though it's probably best to complete all of them and do the suggested exercises before starting a new section.

▶ *What does a typical lesson look like?*

Every lesson is divided into five different parts. Here's a quick overview of each one:

1. *What it means*: The first part of the lesson defines the phrasal verb using simple English and easy-to-process examples. Unlike dictionaries, which present multiple meanings of each verb, we usually focus on one, sometimes two. This means more examples, more relevant information, and less confusion.
2. *How it works*: Here we present some of the grammar behind the new phrasal verb: Can you separate the particle from the verb? If the object is a noun, where does it go? Can you use this phrasal verb in the passive voice? The rules are clear, easy to remember, and light on terminology.
3. *How you use it in real life*: This part contains examples adapted from real-life sources and organized by subthemes. Words in bold highlight common word combinations (also known as *collocations*) and grammatical patterns so they are easy to spot.
4. *Related meaning(s)/More real-life data:* In some lessons, part 4 explores meanings that are related to the main definition presented at the beginning of the lesson. In others, it highlights useful collocations and patterns that appear frequently in authentic examples of each phrasal verb.
5. *Conversation tip.* Here you will find sentences illustrating how you can use the new phrasal verbs at work, at school, or when talking to friends and family members.

▶ *Some phrasal verbs have lots of definitions! Where can I find the ones not taught in the lesson?*

Additional definitions are listed at the back of the book for reference only. They won't be tested in the *check your progress* exercises.

▶ *How were the phrasal verbs in this book selected?*

The initial selection was based on the University of Nottingham's *PHaVE list*, which contains the 150 most frequent phrasal verbs in English based on data from the one-billion-word Corpus of Contemporary American English (COCA). Each phrasal verb was then checked against Cambridge's *English Profile* to ensure it was within the B1-C2 range. The final step was a corpus analysis of phrasal verbs typically taught in B2/C1 textbooks, with the most relevant ones being added to the final list.

▶ *What do you mean by "corpus"?*

A corpus (plural *corpora*) is a collection of written/spoken texts stored in a computer database. Corpora are used to investigate how languages are used, as opposed to how we *think* they are. Take the phrasal verb *carry out*, for example. The collocations *carry out attacks* and *carry out murders* are both correct, but COCA suggests that *carry out attacks* is far more common. This kind of information helped us decide what to include in the lessons, what to leave out, and which collocations to flag as extremely common:

▶ *Do you have any study tips?*

1. When you read the examples in this book, pay close attention to the bold/underlined words that are near each phrasal verb. Memorizing these "partner words" will make it easier for you to use the new phrasal verbs in real life.
2. As you read the examples, find a way to "bring them to life." In other words, try to visualize the scenes, hear the sounds, and feel the emotions described. Engaging the senses like this has the potential to enhance the learning experience.
3. Try underlining or circling your favorite examples from each lesson and "playing" with them. You could, for example, read a sentence out loud, look away, say it from memory, and modify it to talk about people and places you know. Vocabulary that is processed more deeply is easier to remember.
4. The more you hear a phrasal verb being used in real life, the more likely you are to remember it. Here's a useful tool that allows you to hear examples of any word in English: youglish.com. Just type in a phrasal verb and click to watch hundreds of videos. You can then jot down any interesting collocations or sentences you hear.
5. Another useful strategy is to create mind maps to help you remember the new phrasal verbs. You can put the verb in the center, with your favorite collocations branching out. More information here: bit.ly/3lMu68I.
6. Space out your study sessions and revisit the lessons regularly. So, instead of completing one section per week, you could do a lesson on Monday, review it on Tuesday, watch a few youglish.com videos on Wednesday, and, say, start another lesson on Thursday. However you plan your schedule, keep in mind that a little each day goes a long way, especially in language learning.

We hope you enjoy using this book!
100phrasalverbs@gmail.com

# 1 CARRY OUT

## 1 WHAT IT MEANS

**1 When you carry out a task, you do it:**

▶ They need to carry out further research and collect more data.

= They need to do more research and get more information.

**2 *To carry out* also means to do something that you have said you will do or have been told to do:**

▶ Will the mayor carry out her promises?

= Will the mayor do what she says she will do?

## 2 HOW IT WORKS

**1 *Carry out* takes an object (i.e., what you carry out). If the object is a noun, it usually goes at the end:**

☑ They need to carry out further research.

**2 If the object is a pronoun, it always goes in the middle:**

☑ They need to carry it out.

☒ They need to ~~carry out it~~.

**3 *Carry out* is often used in the passive voice:**

☑ Who was the research carried out by?

## 3 HOW YOU USE IT IN REAL LIFE

carry out research

**1 *Carry out* + words related to data collection:**

▶ With your help, we can **carry out research*** that will help cancer patients worldwide.

▶ The **study** was **carried out** to compare three premium brands of pens.

▶ Archaeologists are currently **carrying out tests** to determine the identity of the remains.

*As you use this book, pay close attention to the word combinations in **bold**.

▶ The museum was cordoned off as police **carried out** an **investigation**.

▶ Developing customer satisfaction programs [UK: programmes**] is not just about **carrying out surveys**.

2 ***Carry out*** **+ words describing things we are required to do or committed to doing:**

▶ Staff members are expected to **carry out** their **duties** honestly and responsibly.

▶ People with computer skills are usually more efficient at **carrying out tasks** that could otherwise be too time-consuming.

▶ The president still relies on a shrinking number of military loyalists to **carry out** his **orders**.

▶ As assistant manager, Ann Palmer always **carried out** her **responsibilities** with the utmost degree of honesty, loyalty, and integrity.

▶ The Red Cross relies on the support of the American people to **carry out** its **mission**.

▶ You can't stop Lisa. She's determined to **carry out** her **plan** at any cost.

3 ***Carry out*** **+ words related to war:**

▶ Last week's attack has the markings of Al-Qaeda, which has **carried out** similar **operations** before.

▶ Since ISIS emerged in the mid-2010s, the group has tried to **carry out attacks** in the West in line with its official propaganda.

## 4 MORE REAL-LIFE DATA

***Carry out*** **often attracts words and expressions describing ability:**

▶ We are looking for someone who **is able to carry out** multiple tasks successfully.

▶ Seek medical attention if you **are unable to carry out** your usual daily activities.

▶ The mine was closed down in 2017 to **enable** the company **to carry out** maintenance work.

## 5 CONVERSATION TIP

**Imagine you are giving a talk about a study you conducted. Here's how you can describe its aim:**

**This study was carried out in order to [...].**

**Relevant differences between American and British English are signposted throughout the book.

***A collocation is a common word combination. *Top collocation* = the most frequent word combination we identified by looking at huge amounts of real-life data.

# 2 COME UP WITH

## 1 WHAT IT MEANS

1 **When you come up with a plan or idea, you think of it and suggest it:**

▶ She came up with a great idea for the campaign.

= She had a great idea for the campaign and suggested it.

2 **After you finish this lesson, turn to page 243 for an additional meaning of *come up with**.**

## 2 HOW IT WORKS

***Come up with* takes an object (i.e., what you come up with). The object always goes at the end, whether it is a noun or a pronoun, so never separate the verb (*come*) from the particles (*up, with*):**

☑ She came up with an idea.

☑ She came up with it.

☒ She ~~came up an idea with~~.

☒ She ~~came it up with~~.

## 3 HOW YOU USE IT IN REAL LIFE

1 ***Come up with* tends to attract words related to solutions, ideas, and plans:**

▶ This is unlike anything we have ever experienced, but I'm sure we'll be able to **come up with** a **solution**.

▶ Your novel has a fascinating premise. How did you **come up with** the **idea** for the book?

▶ There's no time to waste, so the sooner the two of you **come up with** a **plan**, the better.

▶ European leaders held emergency meetings today to **come up with ways** to stop the virus from spreading.

*We have limited the number of meanings per lesson so you don't get confused. The meanings listed at the end of the book are an added bonus, NOT the main learning objectives.

- ▶ The EU demands that the UK pass a deal or **come up with** an **alternative** by April 12.
- ▶ To prepare for the interview, first we **came up with** a **list** of questions.
- ▶ Wow! Congratulations! I can't believe how quickly you **came up with** the **answers** to these questions.
- ▶ These men are smart, so it's hard to believe they could not **come up with** better **names** than they did.
- ▶ Henry couldn't **come up with** an **explanation**, but he did have several new questions.
- ▶ I find myself **coming up with excuses** all day long whenever I plan to exercise after work.
- ▶ In tonight's episode, Rebecca **comes up with** a brilliant **strategy** to protect Ian's family business.
- ▶ Which scientist **came up with** the **concept** of a periodic table that included all the known elements?

2 ***Come up with* is often followed by *something* (+ adjective):**

- ▶ I had no time to prepare the speech, so I'll have to **come up with something** on the plane.
- ▶ The username I wanted was taken, so I had to **come up with something else**.
- ▶ Google never fails to amaze its users and always **comes up with something new** and **creative**.

## 4 MORE REAL-LIFE DATA

***Come up with* often attracts words and phrases describing effort and ability, *try* being the most frequent:**

- ▶ Both parties are **trying to come up with** a deficit-cutting plan of $1.2 trillion over 10 years.
- ▶ I **tried hard to come up with** a creative message, but all I could think of was "happy birthday."
- ▶ I had a lot to say, but I found myself really **struggling to come up with** a coherent response.
- ▶ Using this method, the scientists **were able to come up with** a formula that could be used for a variety of purposes.

## 5 CONVERSATION TIP

**Imagine you are giving an employee feedback on a project you are not impressed with. Here's what you can say:**

> **This is not bad, but I'm sure you can come up with something better.**

# 3 GO AHEAD (WITH)

## 1 WHAT IT MEANS

**1 When you go ahead with something you have planned, promised, or asked permission to do, you start to do it:**

▶ The government intends to go ahead with its plans to build nuclear reactors.

= The government had plans to build nuclear reactors, and now it wants to start building them.

**2 When something previously planned goes ahead, it happens:**

▶ The meeting will go ahead as planned.

= A meeting had been planned, and it will take place.

## 2 HOW IT WORKS

1 ***Go ahead with*** **takes an object (i.e., what you go ahead with). The object always goes at the end, whether it is a noun or a pronoun, so never separate the verb (*go*) from the particles (*ahead, with*):**

☑ The government will go ahead with its plans.

☑ The government will go ahead with them.

☒ The government will ~~go ahead its plans with~~.

☒ The government will ~~go them ahead with~~.

2 ***Go ahead*****, without *with*, takes no object. You simply say that something goes ahead:**

☑ Things will go ahead as planned.

## 3 HOW YOU USE IT IN REAL LIFE

***Go ahead with*** **can be used with a lot of different words, but the following word combinations are especially common:**

▶ I'm still hoping senior management doesn't **go ahead with** this stupid **plan**, but it seems like logic is not always their strong suit.

▶ The prime minister is risking a trade war if he **goes ahead with plans** to impose steep tariffs on steel and aluminum imports.

▶ The team **went ahead with** the **project** despite the cost involved and all the opposition it faced.
▶ If you'd been aware of the risks, would you have **gone ahead with** the **surgery** anyway?
▶ When my fiancé resisted the idea of **going ahead with** the **wedding**, it made me wonder if the lockdown had actually changed his feelings about me.
▶ The mayor said she is **going ahead with** a **lawsuit** against the blogger, who has allegedly been spreading fake news.
▶ As an inexperienced journalist, I suspected the leaked documents might be fake, but I **went ahead with** the **story** anyway.
▶ Once the decision had been made to **go ahead with** the **program** [UK: programme], there was no turning back.
▶ Despite threats of sanctions, India has **gone ahead with** the **deal**.

## 4 MORE REAL-LIFE DATA

**1 You can use *go ahead* to give someone permission to do something or to let them speak before you:**
▶ "Do you mind if I turn on the AC?" "No, **go ahead**. It really is hot in here, isn't it?"
▶ "Can I just finish my last thought?" "Sure, **go ahead**. Sorry to interrupt you."

**2 The phrase *go ahead and...* followed by verbs to express encouragement, permission, or urgency is very common. These are some of the most frequent verbs:**
▶ If you haven't changed your LinkedIn password yet, **go ahead and do** it now.
▶ The sooner you get tested, the better. Just **go ahead and get** it over with!
▶ The issue with the article is that it might encourage people to **go ahead and have** unsafe sex.
▶ Why are you acting so weird? I wish you'd just **go ahead and say** what's on your mind.

## 5 CONVERSATION TIP

**Imagine a friend who wants a new phone is hesitating because it is expensive. Here's what you can say:**

**Just go ahead and buy it! Life's too short!**

# 4 OPEN UP

## 1 WHAT IT MEANS

1 ***To open something up*** **means to make it possible, available, or accessible:**

▶ An MBA will open up all kinds of new job opportunities for you.

= If you have an MBA, you will have new job opportunities.

2 **After you finish this lesson,** **turn to page 243** **for additional meanings of *open up*.**

## 2 HOW IT WORKS

1 ***Open up*** **can be used with or without an object (i.e., what you open up). You can simply say that something opens up:**

☑ New opportunities will open up.

2 **If you use an object, and the object is a noun, it usually goes at the end:**

☑ An MBA will open up new opportunities.

3 **If the object is a pronoun, it always goes in the middle:**

☑ An MBA will open them up.

☒ An MBA will ~~open up them~~.

## 3 HOW YOU USE IT IN REAL LIFE

1 ***Open up*** **+ words describing future prospects. Notice the frequent use of the adjective *new*:**

▶ When you join our team, you **open up** exciting **new opportunities** for development in an innovative company with an international focus.

▶ With 5G, all kinds of **new possibilities open up**, and it's up to business owners to come up with ways to make the most of them.

▶ The proliferation of fake news has **opened up new directions** for research on social media habits.

2 *Open up* + **figurative use of words describing access. Notice the highlighted prepositions (e.g., *for, of*):**

▶ If you have the right attitude, I'm sure that many **doors** will **open up for** you.

▶ Screening children as young as two or three years old **opens up** a **window of** opportunity to identify vision loss at a young age.

▶ New treatments for autoimmune diseases, cancer, and pain could be available within a decade as venom toxins **open up** whole new **avenues of** research.

▶ Policies and laws that **open up pathways for** women's empowerment are critically important.

3 *Open up* + **words describing communication. Again, notice the prepositions:**

▶ I hope that my book will **open up** a **dialogue with** both parents and young teens on the topic of Internet safety.

▶ The governor's comments have **opened up** a national **conversation about** race relations.

## 4 MORE REAL-LIFE DATA

1 **Notice the use of *myself, yourself*, etc. followed by *to*:**

▶ As the new year begins, it is time to **open yourself up to** new ideas and strategies.

▶ When a company has a strong social media presence, it is **opening itself up to** feedback.

2 **Notice the pattern with *open up* + *for…to…*:**

▶ Remember: Letting go **opens up** opportunities **for** new experiences **to** happen.

▶ The initiative certainly **opened up** pathways **for** young talent **to** rise to the top of the corporate ladder.

## 5 CONVERSATION TIP

**Imagine you are in a job interview. You want to talk about an eye-opening experience. Here's something you can say:**

**(Living abroad) opened up a whole new world to me.**

# 5 SET UP (1)

## 1 WHAT IT MEANS

**When you set something up, you create it or start it:**

▶ I've always wanted to set up my own business.

= I've always wanted to start a business.

## 2 HOW IT WORKS

1 ***Set up* takes an object (i.e., what you set up). If the object is a noun, it usually goes at the end:**

☑ I want to set up a business.

2 **If the object is a pronoun, it always goes in the middle:**

☑ I want to set it up.

☒ I want to ~~set up it~~.

3 ***Set up* is often used in the passive voice:**

☑ Many new businesses have been set up this year.

## 3 HOW YOU USE IT IN REAL LIFE

1 ***Set up* + words describing business ventures:**

▶ It looks as if China will continue to encourage local companies to **set up businesses** in Afghanistan.

▶ As far as I know, this company was the first global giant to **set up operations** in India.

▶ The new bill aims to stop multinational companies from **setting up headquarters** in low-tax EU countries.

▶ In order to avoid losing profits, some companies **set up offices** in countries where tax laws are less stringent.

▶ In 1980, Stan Lee moved to Los Angeles to **set up** an animation **studio**.

▶ Japan will make manufacturers of electric vehicles responsible for **setting up facilities** to collect and recycle used batteries.

2 *Set up* + **words describing non-profit and government initiatives:**

▶ An **evacuation center** [UK: centre] was **set up** at San Diego's Qualcomm Stadium, where hundreds of residents stayed overnight.

▶ My wife and I have decided to **set up** a **foundation** aimed at providing assistance to single mothers.

▶ The pope has announced plans to **set up** a special **commission** for the protection of minors and vulnerable people.

▶ In North Carolina, new advisory **committees** have been **set up** to examine medication errors in nursing homes.

▶ Malala Yousafzai announced she would continue her campaign for universal education by **setting up** the Malala **fund**.

3 **Common expression –** ***set up shop*****:**

▶ Several chain stores have announced plans to **set up shop** (= start a business) in the new mall [UK: shopping centre].

## 4 RELATED MEANING

*Set up* **also means to arrange something:**

▶ I suggest **setting up** a **meeting** with your child and the teacher so you can identify the key issues.

▶ Click on the link below to **set up** an **appointment** so we can learn about your needs and discuss your options.

▶ Once an employer identifies a prospect for an open position and **sets up** an **interview**, another great challenge arises: how to conduct the interview effectively.

## 5 CONVERSATION TIP

**Imagine a friend has been fired. You think this person should start a business. Here's what you can say:**

**Why don't you set up your own business?**

# 6 SET UP (2)

## 1 WHAT IT MEANS

1 ***To set something up* also means to get it ready to use:**

▶ It's relatively easy to set up a Wi-Fi network.

= It's relatively easy to get a Wi-Fi network ready to use.

2 **After you finish this lesson, turn to page 243 for additional meanings of *set up*.**

## 2 HOW IT WORKS

1 ***Set up* takes an object (i.e., what you set up). If the object is a noun, it tends to go at the end:**

☑ It's easy to set up a network. (more common)

☑ It's easy to set a network up. (less common)

2 **If the object is a pronoun, it always goes in the middle:**

☑ It's easy to set it up.

☒ It's easy to ~~set up it~~.

3 ***Set up* is often used in the passive voice:**

☑ When was the network set up?

## 3 HOW YOU USE IT IN REAL LIFE

1 **This meaning of *set up* tends to attract words related to technology:**

▶ Professional **cameras** are **set up** on each cart to capture the action, and the production staff then edits the videos.

▶ I know from experience that **setting up** a **server** takes some time and a lot of technical know-how.

▶ The boy's family and local authorities searched everywhere. They even **set up** a **website** for tips.

▶ Production assistants ran in circles, while the crew quickly **set up** the **equipment**.

▶ To avoid confusion, remember to **set up** your guest **network** with a different login and password.

- One of my self-appointed tasks was **setting up** a computer **program** [UK: programme] to take lunch orders.
- Our goal was to make the entire process automated, so once you **set up** the **system**, you just press "start," and that's it.
- Remember to keep your students busy while you are **setting up** the **equipment**.
- Once your customer has the app and **sets up** an **account**, you can exchange secure messages.

2 **You can use *set up* with some of the words from the previous page when there is no technical meaning:**

- One solution is for college students to **set up** an **account** with a local bank that offers better rates and fewer fees.
- The LifeLine Assistance **program** was **set up** in the 1990s to help low-income families with their monthly landline bills.
- Good management identifies problems early and **sets up systems** to tackle them.

## 4 RELATED MEANING

***To set someone up for something*** **means to put them in a situation that will have an unexpected outcome, often related to success or failure:**

- Diets that severely restrict calories will **set you up for failure**. (= make it less likely that you will manage to lose weight)
- If you pick the right business partner, you **set yourself up for success** at the outset.
- I already know how this story ends, so I'm not going to **set myself up for disappointment** this time around.

## 5 CONVERSATION TIP

**Imagine you are struggling to create a second social media account. Here's how you can ask a friend for help:**

**How do you set up a second (Instagram) account?**

# CHECK YOUR PROGRESS 1

**A Write the phrasal verbs in the box next to their meanings.**

| carry out | come up with | go ahead with | open up | set up (x 2) |
|---|---|---|---|---|

1 They intend to ______________________ (do) an extensive study.
2 We have decided to ______________________ (proceed with) the wedding.
3 The company will ______________________ (start) operations in Brazil.
4 How do I ______________________ (create) a new Wi-Fi network?
5 An MBA will ______________________ (make available) good job opportunities.
6 We need to ______________________ (think of) a better plan.

**B Which phrasal verb from exercise A completes all the sentences in each group? The first one is done for you.**

**group 1:** *open up*

• These findings will ___ new avenues of research.
• The new law will ___ a conversation about tax reform.
• New opportunities ___ when you learn a second language.

**group 2:** ______________

• Scientists should ___ more research on nanotechnology.
• ISIS has threatened to ___ more attacks.
• The police will ___ a thorough investigation.

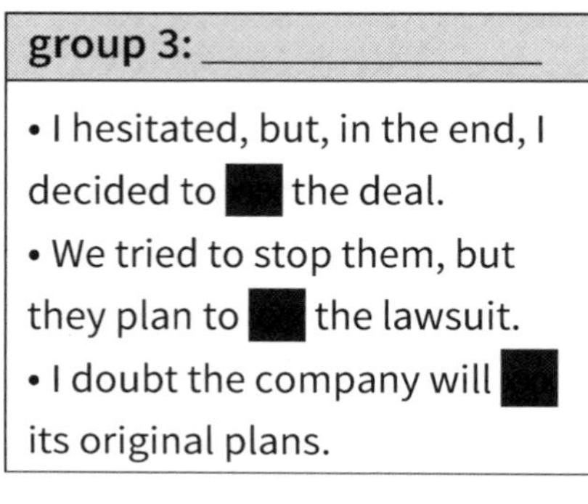

**group 3:** ______________

• I hesitated, but, in the end, I decided to ___ the deal.
• We tried to stop them, but they plan to ___ the lawsuit.
• I doubt the company will ___ its original plans.

**group 4:** ______________

• The company has ___ an office in Paris.
• I'd like to ___ my own business one day.
• I ___ an appointment for Thursday morning.

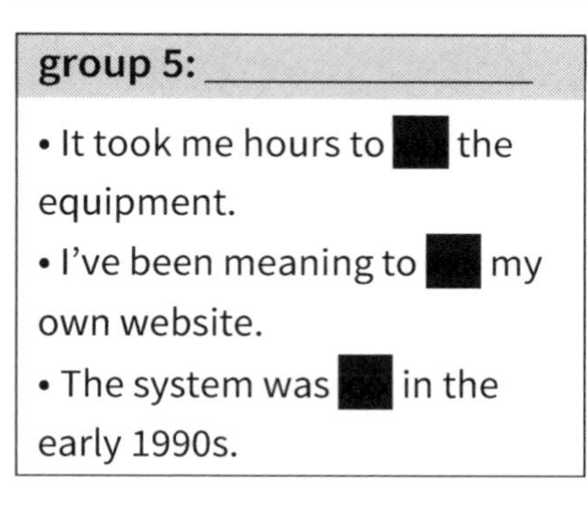

**group 5:** ______________

• It took me hours to ___ the equipment.
• I've been meaning to ___ my own website.
• The system was ___ in the early 1990s.

**group 6:** ______________

• How exactly did you ___ the idea for this song?
• I don't like this title, but I can't ___ something better.
• We need to ___ a better strategy to succeed.

**C Some of the sentences below have an extra word that is grammatically wrong. Cross it out.**

1 You should open yourself up to new and fresh ideas.
2 The project will go it ahead as planned.
3 Setting it up the printer was more complicated than I expected.
4 If you act like this, you're setting yourself up for failure.
5 A similar operation was carried it out in 2019.
6 They came it up with a brilliant strategy.

**D EXTRA CHALLENGE! Choose the correct options.**

1 Many new businesses ___ up in the city last year.

A was set B has been set C were set D have been set

2 ___ up the printer is not as easy as it seems.

A Set B Setting C Sets D To setting

3 Would you have ___ ahead with the wedding if you'd known about his past?

A go B went C gone D going

4 Investing in the developing world ___ up new horizons for economic development.

A open B opening C opens D have opened

5 She's the kind of employee who keeps ___ up with good ideas.

A come B coming C comes D to come

6 A number of studies ___ out, but there is no conclusive evidence yet.

A was carried B have been carrying C were carrying D have been carried

Answer key:

Exercise A

1 carry out
2 go ahead with
3 set up
4 set up
5 open up
6 come up with

Exercise B

group 2: carry out
group 3: go ahead with
group 4: set up
group 5: set up
group 6: come up with

Exercise C

Sentences 1 and 4 are correct. In sentences 2, 3, 5, and 6, the extra word is *it*.

Exercise D

1 C
2 B
3 C
4 C
5 B
6 D

# 7 CARRY ON

## 1 WHAT IT MEANS

1 **When you carry something on, you continue to do or be involved in it:**

▶ My grandmother used to play the piano, and I want to carry on the tradition.

= I want to play the piano, just like my grandmother used to do.

2 **After you finish this lesson, turn to page 244 for additional meanings of *carry on.***

## 2 HOW IT WORKS

1 **This meaning of *carry on* takes an object. If the object (i.e., what you carry on) is a noun, it tends to go at the end:**

☑ I want to carry on the tradition. (more common)

☑ I want to carry the tradition on. (less common)

2 **If the object is a pronoun, it always goes in the middle:**

☑ I want to carry it on.

☒ I want to ~~carry on it~~.

3 ***Carry on* + verb is more common in British than American English. Remember to put the verb in the *-ing* form:**

☑ You'll have an accident if you carry on driving (= keep driving) like that.

## 3 HOW YOU USE IT IN REAL LIFE

***Carry on* tends to attract words that describe the act of continuing what someone else started:**

▶ The original Beetle* was always ahead of its time, and the 2019 model proudly **carries on** that **tradition**.

▶ As my mother's successor, I am more determined than ever to **carry on** the **work** that she started.

▶ Bill Jenkins had always wanted a grandson to **carry on** the **family name**, but he died before Glen was born.

*The Beetle, now discontinued, was a popular car model.

▶ After Marc's death, Rebecca vowed to keep the family strong and **carry on** his **mission** to educate people about endangered wildlife.
▶ Julia adored her father and is committed to **carrying on** his **legacy**.

## 4 RELATED MEANINGS

1 **When you carry on something/with something, you take part in it for a period of time:**
▶ Reading Julia's writing is like **carrying on** a **conversation** with an old friend who knows you well.
▶ People resent the fact that their local government is **carrying on with business** as normal, without community input.
▶ As long as employees have laptops, they can **carry on with** their **work** as usual, no matter where they are.

2 **You can also use *carry on*, without an object, to talk about overcoming obstacles. Notice the underlined words, which express a *no matter* idea:**
▶ It was a daunting task, and we thought about giving up, but we wanted to **carry on**, no matter what.
▶ She was a strong woman who held her head high and **carried on**, regardless of the many losses and hardships she had endured.
▶ Placing trust in a team to **carry on** without you for a while can help you identify strong candidates for succession.

## 5 CONVERSATION TIP

**Imagine you are learning another language, and a friend asks how well you can speak it. Here's what you can say:**

**Oh, I can carry on a simple conversation, and that's about it.**

# 8 HOLD ON TO

## 1 WHAT IT MEANS

**1 When you hold on to something important or beneficial to you, you continue to have it:**

▶ The president is expected to hold on to power after a tight race.

= The president will probably win a competitive election and get reelected.

**2 When you hold on to someone, you try to stop them from leaving you:**

▶ Parents can't hold on to their children forever.

= Parents can't expect their children to live with them forever.

**In both cases, notice the connection to the basic physical meaning of *hold on to*, which is to hold something tightly so you do not drop it.**

## 2 HOW IT WORKS

***Hold on to* takes an object (i.e., what or who you hold on to). The object always goes at the end, whether it is a noun or a pronoun, so never separate the verb (*hold*) from the particles (*on, to*):**

☑ She will hold on to power.

☑ She will hold on to it.

☒ She will ~~hold on power to~~.

☒ She will ~~hold it on to~~.

## 3 HOW YOU USE IT IN REAL LIFE

**1 *Hold on to* + *power* and other related words, especially in politics:**

▶ "It is clear he will stop at nothing to **hold on to power**," the Republican candidate said at a Las Vegas rally Friday.

▶ With almost 60 percent reporting, Democrat Bill Nelson is projected to **hold on to** his **seat** as Florida senator.

▶ As Congressional races ended, Republicans were able to **hold on to** their **majority** in the Senate.

2 *Hold on to* + **words describing values and expectations:**

▶ José continued to take courses in computer electronics, **holding on to** the **hope** that he could someday get a better job.

▶ Even in the face of rising global COVID-19 cases and deaths, many people **hold on to** the **belief** that the pandemic is nearly over.

3 *Hold on to* + **words describing emotions and feelings:**

▶ If we feel that someone has wronged us, it can last forever. For some reason, we sometimes **hold on to** the **anger**, unable to release it.

▶ When my wife left me, I'd spend hours trying to convince myself I was strong enough to survive and **hold on to** my **sanity** until the feeling went away.

4 *Hold on to* + **words indicating a past idea:**

▶ **Holding on to memories** of the past can shape your future in many important ways.

▶ First-generation South Asians migrating to the UK have **held on to** their **traditions** and culture in order to retain their connection to their identity and origin.

5 **Common expression –** ***hold on to your hats*****:**

▶ **Hold on to your hats** (= get ready for what is about to happen). We're in for a bumpy ride.

## 4 MORE REAL-LIFE DATA

***Hold on to*** **often attracts words and phrases expressing ability and difficulty:**

▶ I really admire the way the Japanese have **been able to hold on to** their values and their culture.

▶ The stock market **managed to hold on to** modest gains heading into the afternoon.

▶ The play tells the story of a middle-aged writer desperately **trying to hold on to** his youth.

▶ The Democrats lost the Senate and **could barely hold on to** the House (of Representatives).

▶ With this economy, a lot of people are **struggling to hold on to** their homes.

## 5 CONVERSATION TIP

**Imagine a friend who went through a divorce last year asks your advice. Here's what you can say:**

**It's no use holding on to the past. You have a whole life ahead of you!**

# 9 HOLD UP

## 1 WHAT IT MEANS

**1 When something holds up, it continues in the same condition without losing accuracy, logic, strength, or effectiveness:**

▶ Gold prices held up well during the recession.

= The recession did not affect gold prices, which remained stable.

**2 After you finish this lesson, turn to page 244 for additional meanings of *hold up*.**

## 2 HOW IT WORKS

**This meaning of *hold up* takes no object. You simply say that something holds up (in a certain way):**

☑ Prices have held up.

☒ Prices ~~have held themselves up~~.

☒ They ~~have held prices up~~.

## 3 HOW YOU USE IT IN REAL LIFE

**1 You can use *hold up* with a relatively wide range of nouns. It often attracts words related to the economy:**

▶ While many leading **stocks** are **holding up** OK, some have shown signs of stress this past week after the president's interview.

▶ While the labor [UK: labour] **market** was **holding up** well in October, after December's election, job openings fell to nearly 800k last month.

▶ Investors tend to prefer utility **companies**, which carry high dividends and **hold up** relatively well during periods of turmoil.

▶ Our **currency** seems to have **held up** well compared to some other emerging markets.

**2 *Hold up* often attracts words describing things that can be logically argued:**

▶ I hear what you're saying, but I'm not sure that **hypothesis holds up** quite as well as you think it does.

▶ The storm, if the **predictions hold up**, will not hit Berlin as hard as it hit Frankfurt.

▶ Einstein's **theory** of relativity **holds up** not because Einstein said so, but because it has been confirmed experimentally.

▶ We're going through a crisis, I know, but the Watergate **analogy** doesn't **hold up**. You're blowing things out of proportion.

3 **Common expression – *hold up to scrutiny*:**

▶ Clearly, your argument does not **hold up to scrutiny** (= make sense when it is investigated carefully) and sinks under the weight of your political bias.

## 4 MORE REAL-LIFE DATA

***Hold up* often attracts adverbs like the ones in bold:**

▶ If your two-year-old iPhone is **holding up nicely**, why not keep it another year or so?

▶ As the election has evolved, Jackson's polling has **held up well** in Florida, which put him four points ahead.

▶ For a movie [UK: film] that came out in the late 1980s, I think *Dirty Dancing* still **holds up remarkably well**.

▶ *Sea Around Us* does feel a bit dated at times, but it still **holds up surprisingly well** as a solid read.

## 5 CONVERSATION TIP

**Imagine you are on a conference call, trying to reassure foreign clients who are worried about the economy. Here's what you can say:**

I can assure you that markets are holding up remarkably well.

# 10 KEEP UP

## 1 WHAT IT MEANS

**1 When you keep something up, you continue doing or providing it at the same (usually high) level:**

▶ Activist groups will keep up the pressure until the government changes the law.

= Supporters of a certain cause will continue putting pressure on the government until it changes the law.

**2 After you finish this lesson, turn to page 244 for an additional meaning of *keep up*.**

## 2 HOW IT WORKS

**1 *Keep up* usually takes an object (i.e., what you keep up). If the object is a noun, it tends to go at the end:**

☑ They will keep up the pressure. (more common)

☑ They will keep the pressure up. (less common)

**2 If the object is a pronoun, it always goes at the end:**

☑ They will keep it up.

☒ They will ~~keep up it~~.

**3 In some cases, you can simply say that something keeps up, without using an object:**

☑ The pressure will keep up.

## 3 HOW YOU USE IT IN REAL LIFE

**1 *Keep up* + words describing things that require perseverance:**

▶ Grandma was truly a remarkable woman. She **kept up** her charity **work** even after she got cancer.

▶ This is a good **fight**, and we need to **keep** it **up** until we can pass comprehensive health-care reform.

▶ No matter what happens, never give up. You've got to keep fighting, and you've got to **keep up** your **strength**.

▶ With 2020's *Future Nostalgia*, Dua Lipa not only **kept up** the **momentum** of her debut album, she exceeded all expectations.

2 ***Keep up** + **appearances*** **and other related words:**

▶ It's no use **keeping up appearances** with neighbors [UK: neighbours]. They know what kind of car you drive and have probably heard you yell at your children once or twice.

▶ This **charade** is getting tired. How long do you think you can **keep** it **up** before people know who you really are?

▶ Things are tough, but I'm still trying to **keep up** the **pretense** [UK: pretence] that I'm OK.

3 **Common expression –** ***keep up the good work*:**

▶ You've been doing an amazing job. **Keep up the good work**! (= continue doing the good work that you are doing)

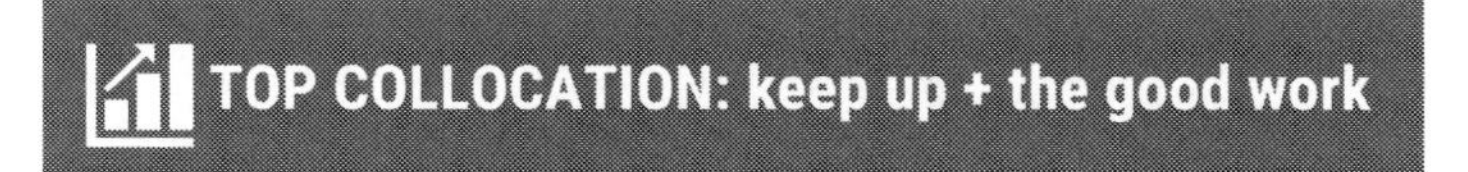


## 4 RELATED MEANINGS

1 **Common expression -** ***keep your spirits up*:**

▶ When you're having a terrible day, do you succumb to negativity, or do you try to **keep your spirits up**? (= stay cheerful)

2 ***Keep up*** **also means to prevent something from going down. In this case, when the object is a noun, it usually goes in the middle:**

▶ A sudden increase in demand has **kept prices up**.

▶ The pool is not heated, but it has a nighttime cover that **keeps the temperature up** overnight.

## 5 CONVERSATION TIP

**Imagine you want to praise an employee who is doing an excellent job. Here's what you can say:**

**Keep up the great work you've been doing.**

# 11 STICK TO

## 1 WHAT IT MEANS

**1 When you stick to something, you continue doing, using, or following it. You don't change your mind:**

▶ Martha was determined to stick to the original plan.

= Martha was determined to follow the plan she had made.

**2 You can use *stick to* when describing things people say or talk about:**

▶ I said I'd help you, and I'll stick to my promise.

= I promised to help you, and that's exactly what I intend to do.

## 2 HOW IT WORKS

**1 *Stick to* takes an object (i.e., what you stick to). The object always goes at the end, whether it is a noun or a pronoun:**

☑ She wanted to stick to the original plan.

☑ She wanted to stick to it.

☒ She wanted to ~~stick the original plan to~~.

☒ She wanted to ~~stick it to~~.

**2 Verbs are relatively rare after *stick to*, but if you do use a verb, put it in the *-ing* form:**

☑ Stick to writing about something you understand well.

## 3 HOW YOU USE IT IN REAL LIFE

stick to a strict diet

**1 *Stick to* + words related to habits and previous arrangements:**

▶ I'm having trouble **sticking to** a strict **diet** and an exercise **routine**.

▶ Do your best to **stick to** the original **plan** and the **budget** you'd agreed on.

▶ During the first few months after my son was born, I tried to **stick to** a sleep-wake-feed-play **schedule** every three hours or so.

2 ***Stick to*** **+ words related to truth and objectivity:**

▶ **Stick to facts, stick to the truth**, and move away from conspiracy theories, as they will only affect your credibility.

▶ This **story** is obviously not true. I don't think it is wise to **stick to** it.

▶ When debating her opponents, Dana always **sticks to the issues** and stays away from negative personal attacks.

▶ Why do people give such long answers on the Quora website instead of just **sticking to the point**?

3 ***Stick to*** **+ words indicating instructions:**

▶ To keep her job, Francis fought his basic instincts, kept his profile low, and **stuck to the rules**.

▶ Bob read the **script** and really **stuck to** it. He didn't improvise at all.

▶ China claims it **sticks to** a **policy** of "non-interference" when offering financial aid to developing countries.

4 ***Stick to*** **+ words related to personal beliefs:**

▶ I think you deserve a lot of credit for **sticking to** your **principles** and doing what you think is right.

▶ If your **convictions** are wrong, there is no point **sticking to** them.

5 **Common expression –** ***stick to your guns*** **(informal):**

▶ Despite harsh criticism, he's **sticking to his guns** (= won't change his mind) on this issue.

## 4 MORE REAL-LIFE DATA

***Stick to*** **often attracts the modal verb** ***should*****:**

▶ In the interest of time, we **should** try to **stick to** the topic at hand.

▶ It was my fault. I **should have stuck to** the original plan.

## 5 CONVERSATION TIP

**Imagine you are conducting a meeting, and people are losing focus. Here's what you can say:**

**We're running out of time. Can we stick to the point, please?**

# CHECK YOUR PROGRESS 2

**A What do the sentences in italics mean? Choose the correct option.**

1 *I want to carry on the work that my father started.*
I want to [continue doing / change] the work that my father started.

2 *You can carry on with your work now.*
You can [get back to work / stop working] now.

3 *It's no use holding on to those memories.*
You should [keep / let go of] those memories.

4 *Democrats were able to hold on to their Senate seats.*
Democrats [lost / won] the race for the Senate.

5 *Stocks are holding up well despite the economic crisis.*
The stock market has [gone up / remained stable].

6 *A sudden spike in demand has kept prices up.*
Because of the high demand, prices have [suddenly gone up / remained high].

7 *You should stick to the original plan.*
You [should / should not] improvise.

**B Each box has three logical ways to continue the sentences on the left. Match boxes A–E to sentences 1–5. The first one is done for you.**

1. I am determined to carry on [ B ].
2. She's trying to hold on to [ ].
3. It seems that [ ] has held up well.
4. He's trying to keep up [ ].
5. I really think you should stick to [ ].

| A |
|---|
| • a strict exercise routine<br>• the budget we'd agreed on<br>• your guns |

| B |
|---|
| • my mother's legacy<br>• this tradition<br>• Dr. Murray's mission |

| C |
|---|
| • our currency<br>• this hypothesis<br>• the market |

| D |
|---|
| • power<br>• the hope that things will be OK<br>• her sanity |

| E |
|---|
| • the good fight<br>• appearances at work<br>• momentum |

**C Choose the correct words.**

1 Mary was determined to carry on, regardless [by / of] all the setbacks that came her way.
2 I'm going to carry on my father's mission, [don't / no] matter what.
3 Hold on to [the / your] hats. You're all in for quite a surprise.
4 This comparison is weak and doesn't really hold up [for / to] scrutiny.
5 I know things are tough, but try to keep [all / your] spirits up.
6 Wow! Congratulations! Keep up [a / the] good work.
7 Stick to [a / the] point, please. We don't have all day!

**D EXTRA CHALLENGE! Match the first part of each sentence to the correct way to continue it a–c. There is one extra choice in each group.**

1 Since my father passed away, I
2 After my father passed away, I

a [ ] carry on his work.
b [ ] carried on his work.
c [ ] have carried on his work.

3 The president will have trouble
4 The president will struggle

a [ ] hold on to power.
b [ ] to hold on to power.
c [ ] holding on to power.

5 Last month, the stock market
6 This month, the stock market

a [ ] held up surprisingly well.
b [ ] holds up surprisingly well.
c [ ] has held up surprisingly well.

7 It's no use
8 You won't manage

a [ ] keep up appearances.
b [ ] to keep up appearances.
c [ ] keeping up appearances.

9 You ought
10 You should have

a [ ] stick to the facts.
b [ ] to stick to the facts.
c [ ] stuck to the facts.

Answer key:

Exercise A
1 continue doing
2 get back to work
3 let go of
4 won
5 remained stable
6 remained high
7 should not

Exercise B
2 D
3 C
4 E
5 A

Exercise C
1 of
2 no
3 your
4 to
5 your
6 the
7 the

Exercise D
1 C
2 B
3 C
4 B
5 A
6 C
7 C
8 B
9 B
10 C

# 12 CATCH UP ON

## 1 WHAT IT MEANS

**When you catch up on an activity that you have not had time to do recently, you spend time doing it:**

▶ All I want to do this weekend is catch up on my reading.

= This weekend, I want to read all the things I haven't had time to read.

## 2 HOW IT WORKS

1 ***Catch up on*** **takes an object (i.e., what you catch up on). The object always goes at the end, whether it is a noun or a pronoun, so never separate the verb (*catch*) from the particles (*up, on*):**

☑ I want to catch up on my reading.

☒ I want to ~~catch up my reading on~~.

☑ I want to catch up on it.

☒ I want to ~~catch it up on~~.

2 **If you mention the activity earlier in the sentence, you can simply say *catch up*, without an object:**

☑ There's so much I want to read. I hope I can catch up this weekend.

## 3 HOW YOU USE IT IN REAL LIFE

1 ***Catch up on + sleep*:**

▶ If you think a long flight is a good way to **catch up on sleep**, think again. Studies show that it is not.

2 ***Catch up on*** **+ words related to staying informed:**

▶ Safari now stores the content from web pages in your reading list so you can **catch up on** your **reading** even when you're offline.

▶ I need at least two solid hours of uninterrupted time to **catch up on** hundreds of **emails**.

▶ I like to **catch up on** the local **news** on my way to work.

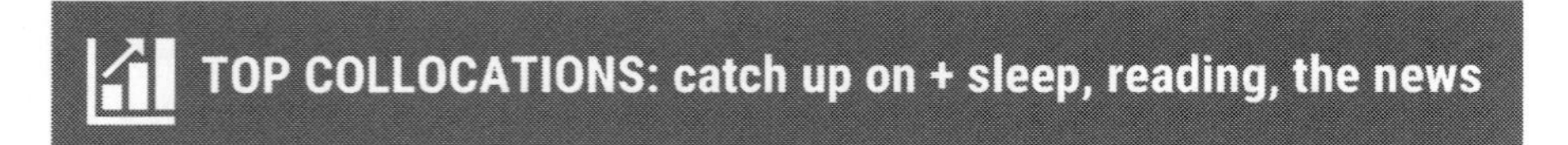

trying to catch up on her paperwork

3 *Catch up on* + **words describing prior commitments:**

▶ I have two reports to write, so I'm working late tonight to **catch up on** my **paperwork**.

▶ "The Den" is a place where our students can hang out with friends or **catch up on homework**.

▶ Among those who responded to the survey, 47% said they will need at least four months to **catch up on** late **payments**.

4 *Catch up on* + **phrases with** ***missed*****:**

▶ A primary benefit of our app is that it offers students the opportunity to **catch up on missed lectures**. (*missed* as an adjective)

▶ I would love to go back to Istanbul and **catch up on what I missed**. (*missed* as a verb)

5 **Common expressions:**

▶ I'll leave you two alone now as you probably **have a lot of catching up to do**. (= news to share)

▶ In today's episode, Sam and Katy **catch up on old times**. (= reminisce about the past)

## 4 MORE REAL-LIFE DATA

***Catch up on*** **is often followed by the words** ***all*****,** ***some*****, and** ***the latest*****:**

▶ I can't think of anything more useful to do right now than **catch up on some** laundry.

▶ I'm a new subscriber, and I'm currently **catching up on all** your past videos. What a great YouTube channel!

▶ The new screen is perfect for you to **catch up on the latest** episode of your favorite [UK: favourite] series without too much eye strain.

## 5 CONVERSATION TIP

**Imagine a friend asks about your plans for the weekend. You want to stay home. Here's what you can say:**

**I think I might just stay home and catch up on my reading.**

# 13 CATCH UP WITH

## 1 WHAT IT MEANS

**1 *To catch up with someone or something* means to reach the same level or standard that they have achieved:**

▶ If you miss a lot of classes, it'll be hard to catch up with the other students.

= If you miss a lot of classes, it'll be hard to have the same level of performance as the other students.

**Notice the connection to the basic physical meaning of *catch up with*, which is to try to reach someone who is ahead of you by moving faster.**

## 2 HOW IT WORKS

**1 *Catch up with* takes an object (i.e., what or who you catch up with). The object always goes at the end, whether it is a noun or a pronoun, so never separate the verb (*catch*) from the particles (*up, with*):**

☑ It'll be hard to catch up with the other students.

☑ It'll be hard to catch up with them.

☒ It'll be hard to ~~catch up the other students with~~.

☒ It'll be hard to ~~catch them up with~~.

**2 If the sentence provides enough context, you can simply say *catch up*, without an object:**

☑ I missed a lot of classes, but I'm trying to catch up.

## 3 HOW YOU USE IT IN REAL LIFE

**1 *Catch up with* + phrases with *(the) other(s)* and *the rest of*:**

▶ Not for the first time in the current crisis, the UK government has found itself trying to **catch up with other** countries.

▶ Even though she had never studied Portuguese before, Michel soon **caught up with the others**.

▶ "**Catching up with the rest of** the world in terms of education and health care should be our top priority," the senator said.

trying to catch up with competitors

2 ***Catch up with + peers, competitors,* and other related words:**

▶ The app is trying to **catch up with** its **competitors** with a plan to release a host of new features.

▶ Studies have shown that students living in poverty before they start school have a more difficult time **catching up with** their **peers**.

▶ Having trailed behind the rest of Europe at first, Italy has been **catching up with** its **neighbors** [UK: neighbours] with substantial investment in electric cars.

▶ In order to **catch up with** its **rivals** from Germany, the company has unveiled a brand new UK model.

3 **Other common word combinations:**

▶ Facial recognition is one of those areas where laws have not **caught up with technology** yet, so no one really knows what is legal or illegal.

▶ A spokesperson for the company said it will probably take a few more weeks before supply **catches up with demand**. (= There is enough supply to meet the demand.)

▶ Times have changed, and our idea of digital privacy must **catch up with reality**. (= update itself in order to remain useful or relevant)

## 4 RELATED MEANINGS

1 **When something catches up with you, it starts to affect you, usually in a negative way:**

▶ I think my lack of sleep is finally **catching up with me**. I'm so tired I can barely move!

▶ Don't try to hide your past. It will **catch up with you** eventually, and the truth will come out sooner or later.

2 ***To catch up with* also means to talk with someone you have not seen for some time and get up to date:**

▶ More and more people are turning to video conferencing platforms to conduct business and **catch up with friends** and **family**.

## 5 CONVERSATION TIP

**Imagine a friend invited you to dinner. Later that evening, you send an audio message to say thank you. Here's what you can say:**

**It was great catching up with you. Dinner was amazing.**

# 14 FALL BEHIND

## 1 WHAT IT MEANS

**When you fall behind, you fail to do something well enough, fast enough, or on time. *Fall behind* implies that there is some competition or ranking involved:**

▶ Reinaldo is falling behind all the top players on the team.

= Reinaldo is not playing as well as the top players on the team.

## 2 HOW IT WORKS

1 ***Fall behind* can be used with or without an object (i.e., what or who you fall behind). You can simply say that someone falls behind:**

☑ He's falling behind.

2 **If you use an object, it always goes at the end, whether it is a noun or a pronoun:**

☑ He's falling behind the top players.

☑ He's falling behind them.

☒ He's ~~falling the top players behind~~.

☒ He's ~~falling them behind~~.

## 3 HOW YOU USE IT IN REAL LIFE

1 ***Fall behind* + words describing people or things belonging to the same category:**

▶ These figures illustrate how far British teenagers have **fallen behind** their **peers** in countries such as China and South Korea.

▶ Some experts say New Zealand is **falling behind other** developed countries in the treatment of breast cancer.

▶ Experts warn Australia's Internet speeds risk **falling behind the rest of** the world unless more money is invested in fiber-optic [UK: fibre] networks.

2 ***Fall behind* + words and phrases related to competition:**

▶ In recent years, the company has been **falling behind** its German **rivals** in the luxury-car race.

▶ The once dominant gaming company has **fallen behind** its **competitors** in the past five years or so.

▶ A new report suggests that Toronto is **falling behind in the race** to grab a slice of the 5G market.

3 **Common expression – *fall behind schedule*:**

▶ If you're **falling behind schedule** (= failing to do something by the time agreed on), get in touch with your supervisor right away and negotiate a new deadline.

## 4 RELATED MEANING

**You can use *fall behind* to talk about financial and work commitments. In this case, it is usually followed by *on*. *With* is often used in British English:**

▶ I'm aware that I'm **falling behind on** my **deadlines**, but, trust me, I'm doing my very best to catch up.

▶ This year, borrowers are **falling behind on** their **payments** at a rate faster than in other economic downturns.

▶ A recent study found that 30 percent of residents in flooded areas had **fallen behind on** their **mortgage**.

## 5 CONVERSATION TIP

**Imagine you are a student who wants some advice on time management. Here's what you can ask your teacher:**

**I keep falling behind schedule. What should I do?**

# 15 KEEP UP WITH

## 1 WHAT IT MEANS

**When you keep up with something that is happening or changing fast, you manage not to stay behind:**

▶ The company was able to keep up with the demand for the product.

= The company had enough of the product to meet the demand.

## 2 HOW IT WORKS

1 ***Keep up with*** **takes an object (i.e., what you keep up with). The object always goes at the end, whether it is a noun or a pronoun, so never separate the verb (*keep*) from the particles (*up, with*):**

☑ The company kept up with the demand.

☑ The company kept up with it.

☒ The company ~~kept up the demand with~~.

☒ The company ~~kept it up with~~.

2 ***Keep up with*** **can be followed by a *wh-* word, most commonly *what*:**

☑ I'm trying to keep up with what's happening.

3 **If the sentence provides enough context, you can simply say *keep up*, without an object:**

☑ Things are changing fast, and it's hard to keep up.

## 3 HOW YOU USE IT IN REAL LIFE

keep up with technology

1 ***Keep up with*** **+ words describing developments:**

▶ Gone are the days when you could delegate the job of **keeping up with technology** to your IT staff. Today, it is *your* responsibility.

▶ As a student of journalism, she probably **keeps up with news** and **current events** much more than the average person.

▶ Is Canada going to have to legalize [UK: legalise] drugs in order to **keep up with** the recent **changes** in U.S. laws?

▶ A well-qualified person five years ago is almost worthless today unless they've **kept up with** the latest **trends**.

2 ***Keep up with*** **+ words related to money and business:**

▶ Over the past year, earnings have risen a scant 1.4% – hardly enough to **keep up with inflation**.

▶ Miranda lost her job and ended up using her credit card to **keep up with** her mortgage **payments.**

▶ More and more companies need to sell online to **keep up with the competition**.

▶ Will our county's infrastructure **keep up with** the economic **growth** of the past year?

3 ***Keep up with*** **+ *pace* and *speed*. Notice the use of the preposition *of*:**

▶ Those who couldn't **keep up with the pace** and amount **of** work required were advised to quit.

▶ These companies have had something of a challenge to **keep up with the speed of** globalization [UK: globalisation].

4 **Common expressions:**

▶ As long as Google is innovating and **keeping up with the times** (= staying current), it will continue to make plenty of money.

▶ "**Keeping up with the Joneses**" (= trying to show you are as rich as other people) is at a whole new level thanks to social media.

## 4 RELATED MEANING

**When you keep up with other people, you manage to do something as fast or as well as them:**

▶ I had to work extra hard to **keep up with** the other **students**. (= I had to work harder to do as well as the other students.)

## 5 CONVERSATION TIP

**Imagine you need to borrow money from a friend. Here's how you can explain why:**

**I'm having trouble keeping up with (my mortgage payments).**

# 16 MISS OUT (ON)

## 1 WHAT IT MEANS

**1 When you miss out on something useful or enjoyable, you fail to benefit from it because you are not involved in it:**

▶ Am I coming to the party? Of course! I don't want to miss out on all the fun.

= I'm sure the party will be fun, so I'm coming because I want to enjoy myself.

## 2 HOW IT WORKS

**1 *Miss out on* takes an object (i.e., what you miss out on). The object always goes at the end, whether it is a noun or a pronoun, so never separate the verb (*miss*) from the particles (*out, on*):**

☑ I don't want to miss out on the fun.

☑ I don't want to miss out on it.

☒ I don't want to ~~miss out the fun on~~.

☒ I don't want to ~~miss it out on~~.

**2 Verbs are relatively rare after *miss out on*, but if you do use a verb, put it in the *-ing* form:**

☑ I don't want to miss out on having fun.

**3 *Miss out*, without *on*, takes no object:**

☑ I'm sure the party will be great. You don't want to miss out.

## 3 HOW YOU USE IT IN REAL LIFE

**1 *Miss out on* can be followed by a relatively wide range of words. The bold words below are especially common:**

▶ My grandma always said, "Don't **miss out on something** that could be great just because it could also be difficult."

▶ Our culture has become obsessed with not **missing out on anything** fun that is going on, no matter the cost to our physical and mental health.

▶ This is the offer of a lifetime. It would be a sin to **miss out on** such an **opportunity**!

- At university, I **missed out on** a lot of **experiences** because I was worried about getting A-pluses on my assignments.
- I'll never forgive myself for **missing out on** the **chance** to become a professional DJ. Now it's too late, I suppose.
- When we simply exist, instead of living each day as if it were the last, we **miss out on** lots of **fun** and squander our full potential.
- A person who avoids negativity **misses out on** the **benefits** of being "whole" – in other words, someone who can take advantage of both positive and negative emotions.
- Hit the subscription button below so you never **miss out on** our weekly **updates**.

**2 The adjectives in bold are common, too:**

- More than 25% of UK companies are **missing out on valuable** online sales by keeping away from e-commerce, a new study reveals.
- Don't **miss out on the latest** car news. Sign up for our newsletter.
- If you don't return emails or phone calls, you may be **missing out on potential** sales.
- I feel kind of sorry for all the U2 haters out there. They're **missing out on** some **incredible** music.

## 4 MORE REAL-LIFE DATA

**The bold verb and verb phrases below are often used before *miss out on*:**

- Make your reservation now! You **don't want to miss out on** all the action!
- Sometimes I **feel** I'm **missing out on** what should be the best time of my life.
- The growing trend towards a dairy-free diet **means** we may be **missing out on** calcium.
- Our city simply **can't afford to miss out on** the benefits of electric vehicles.

## 5 CONVERSATION TIP

**Imagine you are on vacation** [UK: holiday]**. You text a friend who couldn't join you. Here's what you can say:**

**You have no idea what you're missing out on.**

# 17 SET APART (FROM)

## 1 WHAT IT MEANS

**If a quality or characteristic sets people or things apart, it makes them different from, and usually superior to, others in its class. *Set apart* is usually used with *from*:**

▶ This phone has several features that set it apart from the competition.

= This phone has several characteristics that make it different from and better than similar models.

## 2 HOW IT WORKS

**1 *Set apart* takes an object. The object (i.e., what or who you set apart) always goes in the middle, whether it is a noun or a pronoun:**

☑ What sets this phone apart from the competition?

☑ What sets it apart from the competition?

☒ What ~~sets apart this phone from~~ the competition?

☒ What ~~sets apart it from~~ the competition?

**2 Reflexive pronouns (e.g., *myself, herself*) can be used as objects:**

☑ She sets herself apart from the crowd because of her people skills.

## 3 HOW YOU USE IT IN REAL LIFE

**You can use a wide range of nouns with *set apart* (e.g., *set the models apart, set Joe apart, set these companies apart*). *Set apart from* is often followed by the words in bold:**

▶ One of the things that **sets** *Friends* **apart from other** shows available for streaming is the heavy dose of nostalgia that comes with it.

▶ The review says that LG's latest 8K model **sets** itself **apart from others** in its class because of its powerful speakers.

▶ Perhaps what **sets** superachievers **apart from the rest** of us is their ability to make things happen.

▶ My mentor gave me a lot of pointers on how to **set** myself **apart from** everyone **else** at work.

▶ The carefully selected ingredients **set** Joe's Pasta **apart from** its **competitors**.

▶ The company was able to maintain its relevance and **set** itself **apart from the crowd** (crowd = other companies) by focusing on user experience.

▶ To **set** themselves **apart from** their **peers**, Chinese car companies have been striving to reduce costs.

## 4 MORE REAL-LIFE DATA

***Set apart* tends to attract clauses with *what* and *that*:**

1 *What + set apart (from) + be*:

▶ The breadth of our portfolio is unparalleled, but **what** truly **sets** us **apart is** our customer service.

▶ **What set** Coco Chanel **apart from** her peers **was** her rejection of everything that was previously considered luxurious.

2 *Be + what + set apart (from)*:

▶ Ian has only been with us for about a month, but I can tell that his drive **is what sets** him **apart from** the other interns.

▶ A follow-up email after the interview **could be what sets** you **apart from** other job applicants.

3 *It + be + that + set apart (from)*:

▶ **It is** the raspiness of Rod Stewart's voice **that sets** him **apart from** most of his contemporaries.

▶ Back in the day, **it was** Chaplin's heartfelt performances **that set** him **apart**.

## 5 CONVERSATION TIP

**Imagine you are interviewing someone for a job. You want to know what makes them special. Here's what you can ask:**

**What do you think sets you apart from other applicants?**

# 18 STAND OUT (FROM)

## 1 WHAT IT MEANS

**1 When something stands out, it is superior to or more noticeable than other things of the same kind:**

▶ Find a way to make your Instagram feed stand out so you can attract more followers.

= Find a way to make your Instagram feed more noticeable than the rest so that more people follow you.

**2 People can stand out, too:**

▶ Most of the candidates were good, but three stood out from the crowd.

= Most of the candidates were good, but three were clearly better than the others.

## 2 HOW IT WORKS

1 ***Stand out*** **takes no object. You simply say that something or someone stands out:**

☑ Three candidates stood out.

2 ***Stand out from*** **takes an object (i.e., what or who you stand out from). The object always goes at the end, whether it is a noun or a pronoun, so never separate the verb (*stand*) from the particles (*out, from*):**

☑ Three candidates stood out from the rest.

☒ Three candidates ~~stood out the rest from~~.

## 3 HOW YOU USE IT IN REAL LIFE

1 ***Stand out from*** **tends to attract words that express the idea of otherness:**

▶ Gallup has studied millions of employees around the world to find out why some workplaces **stand out from the rest**.

▶ In some career paths, the use of photos in a résumé [UK: CV] can help the applicant **stand out from the competition**.

▶ The recent poll numbers indicate that Miller **stands out from** his **peers**, but in a surprisingly negative way.

▶ *Time* magazine says that *Game of Thrones* **stood out from other** works of fantasy because of its feminism.

▶ Personal branding is not about money; it is all about establishing yourself and **standing out from the others.**

2 **Common expression – *stand out from the crowd*:**

▶ In today's episode, we look at practical ways to help your business **stand out from the crowd**. (*crowd* = other businesses of the same kind)

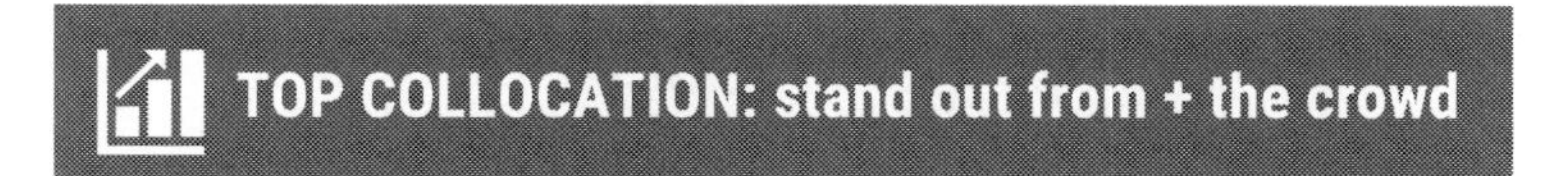


## 4 MORE REAL-LIFE DATA

1 **You can use *stand out + as* to talk about a distinguishing characteristic:**

▶ She was praised after the debate for **standing out as the most** mature among the candidates.

▶ Denmark **stands out as an example** in the fight against domestic violence.

2 ***Stand out + above/among*, although not as common as *stand out + from*, is also possible:**

▶ Two of the cars we tested **stood out among the rest**: the Civic and the Focus.

▶ There's a magic to *Final Fantasy IV* that **stands out above all** the **other** games.

3 ***Stand out + against* is often used to talk about contrasting colors** [UK: colours]**:**

▶ Notice how prominently yellow **stands out against** the dark **background**.

4 ***Make someone or something stand out* is a very common pattern:**

▶ To **make** your brand **stand out**, don't be afraid to try different fonts and graphics.

▶ When you think back to last conference you went to, what exactly **made** it **stand out**?

## 5 CONVERSATION TIP

**Imagine you are telling a friend about your school days. Here's something you can say:**

**My mother always said I stood out from the crowd.**

# CHECK YOUR PROGRESS 3

**A Look at the photo and complete the sentences. You can repeat numbers.**

1 Number _____ is falling behind the others.
2 Number _____ is trying to catch up with the others.
3 Numbers _____ and _____ are trying to keep up with each other.

**B Match each sentence 1–7 with the most logical way to continue it a–g.**

1 Of course I'm going to Ann's party. [ ]
2 I haven't seen Ben in a while. [ ]
3 Vicky needs an extension. [ ]
4 You should increase production. [ ]
5 I can't go out tonight. [ ]
6 Tom's good at multitasking. [ ]
7 I'm not surprised you got promoted. [ ]

a I'd love to catch up with him some time.
b Otherwise, you won't keep up with the demand.
c I've got to catch up on some paperwork.
d You've always stood out from the rest.
e Otherwise, she might fall behind schedule.
f I don't want to miss out on all the fun.
g That's what sets him apart from his peers.

**C Choose the correct words.**

1 Julia and I haven't seen each other in years, so, naturally, we have a lot of catching up to [do / have].
2 I'm dying to get home so I can catch up [on / to] the latest episodes of *This is Us*.
3 Greg lost his job three months ago, so now he's falling behind [at / on] his mortgage payments.
4 Is your doctor keeping up with [all / the] times and learning about the best treatment options for you?
5 [That / What] sets the Mazda 3 apart from other cars is its refined handling.
6 It is Mary's willpower [that / who] sets her apart from most of her peers.
7 When you create an Instagram business account, you need to make it stand out from [a / the] crowd.
8 In a time when people are so divided, Mr. Tolle stands out [as / from] an example of kindness and understanding.

**D EXTRA CHALLENGE! Choose the correct options.**

1 In his free time, Ethan enjoys ___ up on the latest music news.
A catch B catching C to catch D catches

2 ___ up with the competition should be the company's top priority.
A Catch B Catching C Caught D To catching

3 Since the merger, the company ___ behind its key competitors.
A fall B falls C fell D has fallen

4 You're speaking too fast! I'm having trouble ___ up with you.
A keep B keeping C to keep D to keeping

5 What ___ this product apart from the crowd is ___ slick design.
A sets / its B sets / it's C set / its D set / it's

6 In this course, you will learn how to write a résumé [UK: CV] that ___ out from the pack.
A stand B stands C standing D stood

Answer key:

| Exercise A | Exercise B | Exercise C | Exercise D |
| --- | --- | --- | --- |
| 1 34 | 1 f | 1 do | 1 B |
| 2 34 | 2 a | 2 on | 2 B |
| 3 6 and 90 or 90 and 6 | 3 e | 3 on | 3 D |
| | 4 b | 4 the | 4 B |
| | 5 c | 5 What | 5 A |
| | 6 g | 6 that | 6 B |
| | 7 d | 7 the | |
| | | 8 as | |

# 19 BUILD UP

## 1 WHAT IT MEANS

**1 When you build up something, you cause it to increase or become greater over a period of time:**

▶ I use a lot of techniques to help me build up my self-confidence.

= I use a lot of techniques to help me feel more self-confident.

**2 After you finish this lesson, turn to page 244 for additional meanings of *build up*.**

## 2 HOW IT WORKS

**1 *Build up* takes an object (i.e., what you build up). If the object is a noun, it usually goes at the end:**

☑ I'm trying to build up confidence.

**2 If the object is a pronoun, it always goes in the middle:**

☑ I'm trying to build it up.

☒ I'm trying to ~~build up it~~.

## 3 HOW YOU USE IT IN REAL LIFE

build up confidence

**1 *Build up* + words describing positive qualities:**

▶ First, try to establish a few easily achievable goals so you can **build up confidence**.

▶ You'd think that a good way to help people **build up** their **self-esteem** is to constantly praise them, but it's not.

▶ Try not to spam your audience. You need to **build up trust** and provide them with quality content.

▶ Jamie's is a well-established wine bar brand in London, having **built up** a **reputation** for delivering quality and value.

**2 *Build up* + *community* and other related words:**

▶ When you **build up** an online **community**, people will engage with you and your posts. If you don't respond, your community will slowly die.

▶ The next step is to promote your blog on the Internet and **build up** a **network** of readers and subscribers.

▶ Jeff live tweets a lot of political events and has **built up** a strong **following** among other journalists as a result.

▶ Congratulations to all of you in the audience who have succeeded in **building up** a strong client **base**.

3 *Build up* + **words related to physical strength:**

▶ The program [UK: programme] allows people with disabilities to exercise, **build up strength**, and enjoy themselves in their own way.

▶ Jane **built up muscle mass** by gradually increasing the weights she used in her workouts.

▶ Del Potro needs to **build up** his **stamina** if he is to challenge the world's top tennis players.

▶ This is a great article, and it describes different ways in which you can **build up** your **immune system**.

## 4 RELATED MEANING

**With negative ideas, *build up* is often intransitive (i.e., no object):**

▶ **Pressures** have been **building up**, and the government can't pretend everything is as usual for much longer.

▶ The **anger** kept **building up**, and yet I couldn't express it.

▶ Ann's **frustration** and the **tension** in her body **built up**, begging for a release. No wonder she blew up at me!

▶ When you drink heavily, certain **toxins build up** in your system and cause many of the symptoms associated with a hangover.

▶ Take a twenty-minute break to let go of the **stress** that's been **building up** over the course of the day.

## 5 CONVERSATION TIP

**Imagine a friend who is having trouble finding a job asks your advice. Here's something you can say:**

**First, you've got to build up a professional network.**

# 20 PICK UP

## 1 WHAT IT MEANS

1 **When something picks up, it improves, increases, or grows stronger:**

▶ It looks as if the economy is starting to pick up.

= Apparently, the economy is starting to improve.

2 **After you finish this lesson, turn to page 245 for additional meanings of *pick up*.**

## 2 HOW IT WORKS

1 ***Pick up* can be used with or without an object (i.e., what you pick up). You can simply say that something picks up:**

☑ The economy is picking up.

2 **If you use an object, it always goes at the end:**

☑ The economy is picking up momentum.

☒ The economy is ~~picking momentum up~~.

## 3 HOW YOU USE IT IN REAL LIFE

pick up speed

1 ***Pick up* tends to attract the words *speed, pace,* and *steam*:**

▶ Her foot hit the accelerator, and the car quickly **picked up speed**.

▶ The book **picks up steam** (= gets more exciting) as it goes along, and each chapter is more exciting than the one preceding it.

▶ Brookdale's **pace picked up** in the second half, and they won the game.

2 **Notice how you can use *pick up* + *speed*, *pace*, and *steam* to talk about trends and the economy:**

▶ A new report out this morning indicates that the Australian economy is **picking up speed**.

▶ Over the past few centuries, the **pace** of change has **picked up**, and today new technologies are coming faster than ever.

- The <u>video</u> quickly **picked up steam** over the weekend, and, as of Monday morning, it had been viewed more than two million times.
- The general consensus is that the <u>recovery</u> will **pick up pace** in the third quarter, regardless of who gets elected.
- As global <u>markets</u> **pick up steam**, our experts have some great investment ideas for you.

3 ***Pick up* can be used to talk about the weather:**

- **Winds** are expected to **pick up from** five miles per hour **to** about nine later today.
- Tom stood in the doorway, looking out. The **breeze** had **picked up**, and the temperature was falling rapidly.
- The National Hurricane Center report indicates that **Hurricane** Sandy is now starting to **pick up speed**.

## 4 MORE REAL-LIFE DATA

1 ***Pick up* often attracts the following adverbs:**

- Media coverage of the wildfires has **picked up considerably** in the U.S., I think.
- While online sales have **picked up significantly** for many merchants, the gains don't come close to replacing the business they lost during the pandemic.
- My small business is **slowly picking up**, so I'm considering dropping out of college.
- Things are **picking up quickly**, so we'd better move faster.

2 **Notice the use of *my, your*, etc. before *pace*:**

- I tried to **pick up my pace** (= run faster) but failed miserably because of dehydration and lack of energy.
- She saw him approaching and nervously **picked up her pace**.

## 5 CONVERSATION TIP

**Imagine you have a small shop that almost went out of business. A friend asks how things are going. Here's what you can say:**

> **The worst is over, and things are slowly picking up.**

# 21 SLOW DOWN

## 1 WHAT IT MEANS

1 **When something slows down, it starts to happen or move more slowly:**

▶ The economy slowed down a bit in the first quarter.

= There was slightly less economic activity in the first three months of the year.

2 ***Slow down* also means to cause something to happen or move more slowly:**

▶ The lockdown slowed down the economy in a lot of countries.

= Because of the lockdown, there was less economic activity in a lot of countries.

## 2 HOW IT WORKS

1 ***Slow down* can be used with or without an object (i.e., what you slow down). You can simply say that something slows down:**

☑ The economy slowed down.

2 **If you use an object, and the object is a noun, it tends to go at the end:**

☑ The lockdown slowed down the economy. (more common)

☑ The lockdown slowed the economy down. (less common)

3 **If the object is a pronoun, it always goes in the middle:**

☑ The lockdown slowed it down.

☒ The lockdown ~~slowed down it~~.

## 3 HOW YOU USE IT IN REAL LIFE

1 ***Slow down* + words describing biological processes:**

▶ To relax, **slow down** your **breathing** and imagine air moving in and out of your body while you breathe from your diaphragm.

▶ When you starve yourself, your body responds by **slowing down** your **metabolism**.

▶ Study after study shows that the best way to **slow down** the aging [UK: ageing] **process** is to sleep well and stay in good shape.

2 *Slow down* + *speed* **and other related words:**

▶ Embedding a lot of YouTube videos can significantly **slow down** the loading **speed** of your web site.

▶ There is ample evidence that social distancing was effective in **slowing down** the **rate** of infection.

▶ There are a lot of characters in the book, and the **pace** does **slow down** a bit in the second half.

3 *Slow down* + *progress* **and other related words:**

▶ Research shows that a more traditional approach **slows down** students' **progress**.

▶ Politics can either promote economic **growth** or **slow** it **down**.

▶ Dark matter **slows down** the **expansion** of the universe, while dark energy speeds it up.

4 *Slow down* + **words related to traffic and vehicles:**

▶ Eastbound **traffic slowed down** at around 1:30 p.m. on State Route 44.

▶ My husband's **car slowed down** and came to a complete stop, but the SUV kept going and drove into it.

5 **Common expression** – *show (...) signs of slowing down*:

▶ Now in her 80s, Jane Fonda **shows no signs of slowing down**. (= is likely to remain as active as ever)

▶ In May, the housing market **showed few signs of slowing down**. (= remained reasonably active)

## 4 RELATED MEANING

**When someone slows down, they become less busy or active than they usually are:**

▶ I was having panic attacks, so the doctor told me to **slow down** and take up a hobby.

## 5 CONVERSATION TIP

**Imagine you are worried about a close friend who is under a lot of stress. Here's what you can say:**

**You'd better slow down or you'll have a heart attack.**

# 22 SPEED UP

## 1 WHAT IT MEANS

1 **When something speeds up, it starts to happen or move faster:**
▶ With the new system, the registration process will speed up.
= With the new system, the registration process will be faster.

2 ***Speed up* also means to cause something to happen or move faster:**
▶ The team developed a new system to speed up the registration process.
= The team developed a new system to make the registration process faster.

## 2 HOW IT WORKS

1 ***Speed up* can be used with or without an object (i.e., what you speed up). You can simply say that something speeds up:**
☑ The process will speed up.

2 **If you use an object, and the object is a noun, it tends to go at the end:**
☑ The new system will speed up the process. (more common)
☑ The new system will speed the process up. (less common)

3 **If the object is a pronoun, it always goes in the middle:**
☑ The new system will speed it up.
☒ The new system will ~~speed up it~~.

## 3 HOW YOU USE IT IN REAL LIFE

1 ***Speed up* can be used with a relatively wide range of words. Phrases with *process* are very common:**
▶ I've heard that translation agencies often use translation memory software to **speed up** the **process**.
▶ Exfoliation helps **speed up the process of** cell regeneration.
▶ The police department is working with Facebook to **speed up the process of** finding missing children.

2 **Other common word combinations:**

- ▶ A new study suggests that Taekwondo training **speeds up** the **development** of balance and sensory functions in adolescents.
- ▶ Lemon water is said to be a natural way of **speeding up** your **metabolism**, but there is little scientific evidence to support this claim.
- ▶ It's long been thought that shaving **speeds up** hair **growth**, making it thicker and fuller. Is this fact or fiction?
- ▶ In an increasingly competitive market, it is critical for companies to **speed up** the **pace** of product development.
- ▶ The development of information technology has **sped up** the **production** of digital news media.
- ▶ In offering policies to **speed up** economic **recovery**, the president often highlighted the role of start-ups and small businesses.
- ▶ Scientists have developed a new gel patch that could **speed up** the **healing** of a skin wound while reducing the formation of scars.

## 4 MORE REAL-LIFE DATA

***Speed up* is often used along with *slow down*:**

- ▶ I wasn't sure if I should **slow down or speed up**, so I just slammed on the brakes. Guess what, a red car drove into me!
- ▶ Experts say that a car **slowing down and then speeding up** is bad for air pollution.
- ▶ My father always says that the key to having a more fulfilling life is to **slow down, not speed up**.

## 5 CONVERSATION TIP

**Imagine you are at a business meeting, and you want to make a suggestion. Here's something you can say:**

> **We need to find a way to speed up (our hiring process).**

# 23 TAKE OVER

## 1 WHAT IT MEANS

***To take over* means to take control, management, or possession of something, often by replacing the previous system, user, owner, etc.:**

▶ K-pop artists are slowly taking over the world.

= K-pop artists are becoming extremely popular worldwide.

## 2 HOW IT WORKS

**1 *Take over* takes an object (i.e., what you take over). If the object is a noun, it usually goes at the end:**

☑ They're taking over the world.

**2 If the object is a pronoun, it always goes in the middle:**

☑ They're taking it over.

☒ They're taking ~~over it~~.

**3 *Take over* can be used in the passive voice:**

☑ The company was taken over by a competitor.

**4 You can use *take over* without an object. Notice the use of *from* and *as*:**

☑ Ann took over from Dale as CEO. (= Ann, not Dale, is the new CEO.)

## 3 HOW YOU USE IT IN REAL LIFE

**1 *Take over* is often used in sentences describing cultural, economic, and political dominance:**

▶ Many years before Apple **took over the world**, Steve Jobs used to tell people about the importance of being "insanely great."

▶ The blogosphere, I believe, is simply **taking over the role** that second-tier newspapers used to play in most small towns.

▶ "The American dream was stolen by the wealthiest 4%, who **took over the government** and created laws to benefit them," the senator said.

▶ Maybe we deserve the kind of government we have allowed to **take over** our **country**, but our children deserve better.

▶ Conservatives, for the most part, have **taken over the party**, and there are fewer and fewer moderates.

2 *Take over* **+ words related to careers, businesses, and logistics:**

▶ I know a lot of you feel that I'm an outsider who **took over** a **job** that should have gone to a local, but please give me a chance.

▶ Ben's idea was that, after a six-year apprenticeship and a little experience, his son would **take over** the **business**.

▶ Well, it looks as if your little plan to sideline me and **take over** my **company** has failed.

▶ The project was initially planned as a public-private partnership, but the state eventually **took over operations**.

▶ Chrysler was forced into the arms of Fiat, which eventually **took over management** of the company.

## 4 MORE REAL-LIFE DATA

***Take over*** **often attracts the adjectives** ***whole*** **and** ***entire*****:**

▶ A tower of smoke grew and **took over the whole** room.

▶ Training for the Olympics can **take over your whole** life.

▶ Misery has spread unabated, and drug lords have **taken over entire** communities.

▶ My grandfather was a mob boss who had ambitions to **take over the entire** Southeast territory.

▶ I knew university was going to be tough. What I hadn't anticipated was the way it would **take over my entire** existence.

## 5 CONVERSATION TIP

**Imagine you are a student. You are not happy about some of the changes in your school. Here's something you can say:**

> **Things have changed for the worse since (Mr. Ford) took over.**

# 24 WEAR OFF

## 1 WHAT IT MEANS

**1 When the effect of something wears off, it slowly disappears:**

▶ The painkillers will wear off after a couple of hours.

= The painkillers will gradually stop working, and, after a couple of hours, they will have no effect on your body.

**2 You can also use *wear off* to talk about emotions and sensations:**

▶ The initial excitement wore off quickly.

= I was excited at first, but soon the excitement was gone.

## 2 HOW IT WORKS

***Wear off* takes no object. You simply say that something wears off:**

☑ The excitement wore off.

☒ The excitement ~~wore it off~~.

☒ ~~I wore off the excitement~~.

## 3 HOW YOU USE IT IN REAL LIFE

**1 Words related to enthusiasm + *wear off*:**

▶ Honeymoons don't last forever. Eventually, the **newness wears off**, and married life doesn't seem as fun anymore.

▶ Although I've been teaching for 30 years, the **thrill** has not **worn off**.

▶ After a while, the **adrenaline** began to **wear off**, and Anna realized [UK: realised] the imminent danger she had put herself in.

▶ Chris Hemsworth turned down the next *Star Trek* sequel because he wasn't sold on the script and felt that the **magic** had **worn off**.

▶ The initial **euphoria** seems to have **worn off**, and the 2020s are tempered by a new sense of realism.

▶ Experts claim that once the **novelty** of the new mall [UK: shopping centre] **wears off**, shoppers will return to the convenience of local stores [UK: shops].

**TOP COLLOCATION: novelty + wear off**

2 *Medication* **and other related words +** *wear off*:

▶ Unfortunately, as soon as the **medication wore off**, the delusions returned, and we had to sedate the patient again.

▶ Still drowsy and confused, I sat in the armchair watching for signs that the **sedative** was **wearing off**.

▶ Don't worry! You'll be able to speak normally in a couple of hours when the **anesthetic** [UK: anaesthetic] **wears off**.

▶ The **effects** of the drug usually **wear off** in about six hours, although sometimes it will happen overnight.

## 4 MORE REAL-LIFE DATA

***Wear off* often attracts the words *after*, *once*, and *until*. Notice the use of the underlined <u>tenses</u>, which can go with any of these time expressions:**

▶ Oh, no! What have I done? I'll just go and hide somewhere **until** my **embarrassment** <u>wears off</u>! (simple present)

▶ I really admire your will power. How do you keep going **once** the initial **enthusiasm** <u>has worn off</u>? (present perfect)

▶ I felt incredibly relieved **after** the initial **shock** <u>had worn off</u>. (past perfect)

## 5 CONVERSATION TIP

**Imagine you are telling a close friend about a failing relationship. Here's what you can say:**

**It feels as if the magic is wearing off, you know.**

# 25 WEAR OUT

## 1 WHAT IT MEANS

**When something wears out or you wear it out, it becomes damaged or useless because you used it a lot or for a long time:**

▶ I wore out three pairs of shoes last year.

= Last year, I wore the same three pairs of shoes so often that they eventually became useless.

## 2 HOW IT WORKS

**1 *Wear out* can be used with or without an object (i.e., what you wear out). You can simply say that something wears out:**

☑ My shoes wore out fast.

**2 If you use an object, and the object is a noun, it can go in the middle or at the end:**

☑ I wore out my shoes.

☑ I wore my shoes out.

**Notice that longer objects tend to go at the end:**

☑ I wore out three pairs of shoes. (more common)

☑ I wore three pairs of shoes out. (less common)

**3 If the object is a pronoun, it always goes in the middle:**

☑ I wore them out.

☒ I ~~wore out them~~.

## 3 HOW YOU USE IT IN REAL LIFE

***Wear out* often attracts words belonging to the following categories:**

**1 Clothes and fabrics in general:**

▶ These are the most comfortable **shoes** ever. Last week I bought my second pair after **wearing out** the first one.

▶ I've always wanted to know if dry-cleaning a cotton **shirt** will make it last longer or **wear out** faster.

▶ **Carpets wear out** over time and have to be replaced, even if they have been properly taken care of.

2 **Machinery:**

▶ **Tires** [UK: tyres] will **wear out** long before your car does, so be sure to check the tread wear regularly.

▶ When the original model was designed, the engineers made sure that, as **parts wore out**, they could be replaced easily.

▶ The new operating system has a hidden feature that keeps your **battery** from **wearing out** too fast.

3 **The body:**

▶ As we age, our **bodies** start to **wear out** and fall apart, which may result in limited mobility.

▶ The heavier you are, the more weight your **hips** have to bear, and the faster they'll **wear out**.

▶ For your knee to work properly, all parts must remain in balance. If one element is misaligned, the whole **joint** begins to **wear out** faster.

4 **Common expression – *wear out your welcome*:**

▶ After staying with my sister for a week, I felt I had **worn out my welcome** (= stayed longer than I was welcome for), so I decided to book a room in a hotel.

## 4 RELATED MEANING

***To wear somebody out*** **means to make them feel very tired:**

▶ These puppies are so full of energy they're really **wearing me out**. I can hardly keep my eyes open.

▶ Try not to go too fast at the beginning. If you **wear yourself out**, you won't be able to race at the end.

## 5 CONVERSATION TIP

**Imagine you are shopping with a friend. You are trying to persuade them not to buy a cheap rug. Here's what you can say:**

**This one will wear out pretty quickly, don't you think?**

# CHECK YOUR PROGRESS 4

**A Complete the sentences with the correct phrasal verbs. You can use the same particle more than once, and there is one extra particle. The first one is done for you.**

| build | pick | slow | speed | take | wear |
|---|---|---|---|---|---|

| down | off | out | over | up |
|---|---|---|---|---|

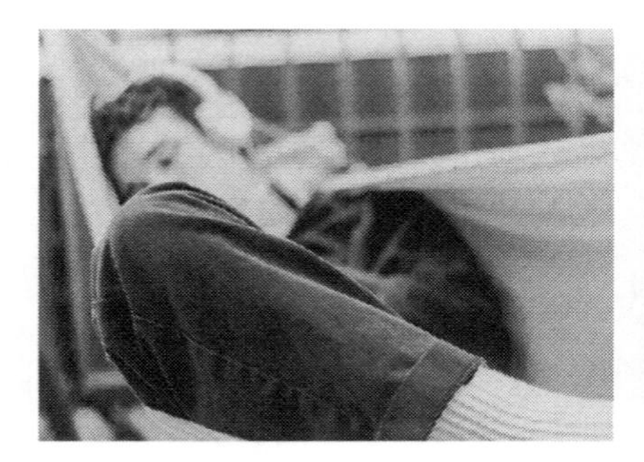

He's trying to (1) *speed up* the learning process.

She wants to (2) ______________ muscle mass.

Economic activity is expected to (3) ______________.

He will (4) ______________ as CEO on March 23.

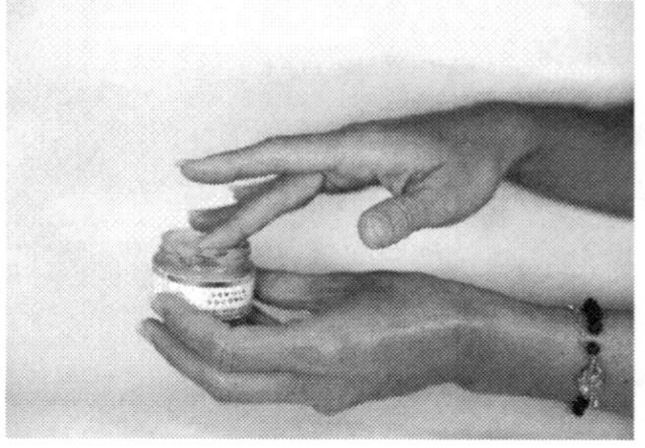

She's trying to (5) ______________ the aging [UK: ageing] process.

The thrill is starting to (6) ______________.

**B Complete the sentences with *off* or *out*.**

1 When the adrenaline wore ______, I knew I was in deep trouble.
2 Sales will probably drop once the novelty wears ______.
3 If you wear this scarf every day, you'll wear it ______.
4 Sometimes I feel my body is starting to wear ______!
5 As soon as the medication wore ______, I was in pain again.
6 I think I've worn ______ my welcome. Maybe I should look for a hotel.
7 I love my students, but they're so active that they wear me ______ sometimes.
8 As I watched the sequel, it was clear that some of the magic had worn ______.

**C Some of the sentences below have either an extra word or a mistake in word order. Correct the mistakes. Ignore the sentences that are correct.**

1 Tina's company has built up a solid reputation.

______________________________

2 The economy is finally picking steam up.

______________________________

3 Self-confidence can speed up your progress, while anxiety can slow down it.

______________________________

4 Hanna took the business over when her father died.

______________________________

5 The initial euphoria has been worn off, and now we can see things clearly.

______________________________

**D EXTRA CHALLENGE! Complete the second sentence in each pair so that it means the same as the original sentence. Use a phrasal verb from exercise A in the correct tense and form.**

1 When you get good feedback, you become more self-confident.
Good feedback *builds up* your self-confidence.

2 There has been a significant increase in online sales this year.
Online sales ______________ significantly this year.

3 The play was good, but things happened more slowly in the second half.
The play was good, but the pace ______________ in the second half.

4 Is there a way of making the process faster?
Is there a way of ______________ the process?

5 Margaret has become the new vice president.
Margaret ______________ as the new vice president.

6 I'm not as excited about the job as I once was.
My excitement about the job ______________.

Answer key:

Exercise A
2 build up
3 pick up
4 take over
5 slow down
6 wear off

Exercise B
1 off
2 off
3 out
4 out
5 off
6 out
7 out
8 off

Exercise C
1 Correct
2 ...finally picking up steam.
3 ...anxiety can slow it down.
4 ...took over the business when...
5 ...euphoria has worn off, and...

Exercise D
2 have picked up
3 slowed down
4 speeding up
5 has taken over
6 has worn off

# 26 ACCOUNT FOR

## 1 WHAT IT MEANS

**1 When something accounts for a fact or situation, it explains why it happens.** ***Account for*** **is a relatively formal phrasal verb:**

▶ Sue's dedication to her clients accounts for her success.

= Sue is dedicated to her clients, and this explains her success.

**2 After you finish this lesson, turn to page 246 for additional meanings of *account for*.**

## 2 HOW IT WORKS

***Account for*** **takes an object (i.e., what something accounts for). The object always goes at the end, whether it is a noun or a pronoun:**

☑ Her dedication accounts for her success.

☑ Her dedication accounts for it.

☒ Her dedication ~~accounts her success for~~.

☒ Her dedication ~~accounts it for~~.

## 3 HOW YOU USE IT IN REAL LIFE

***Account for*** **can be followed by a relatively wide range of abstract nouns. It tends to attract words describing variation, especially in academic writing. Notice the use of the preposition** ***in*****:**

▶ Differences in laboratory methods and control of variables may **account for** the **difference in** the findings.

▶ Findings from this study suggest that the family context significantly **accounts for variation in** children's early school success.

▶ Some of the factors which have **accounted for** the **decline in** fertility in Europe may also apply to developing countries.

▶ Significant differences in analytical methods **accounted for** the **disparity in** results among the three laboratories.

▶ Governor DeSantis told reporters on Saturday that testing alone does not **account for** the **increase in** COVID-19 cases in the state of Florida.

## 4 RELATED MEANING

***Account for* also means to form part of a total. It tends to attract the words in bold below, which express quantity and amount. Notice the use of the preposition *of* and the underlined adjectives/adverbs, which are very common, too:**

▶ In 2016, suicides **accounted for the** vast **majority of** gun deaths in Washington.

▶ Books aimed at children ages 7-14 **account for the bulk of** the company's sales.

▶ Together, Indonesia and India **account for** almost **a quarter of** the world's population.

▶ The use of wind and solar power has steadily increased, and, by 2035, it will **account for** approximately **one-third of** our country's **total** electricity output.

▶ Compared to the United States, Japan's spending on education **accounts for** a relatively small **proportion of** its gross national product.

▶ In 1978, according to an inflation-adjusted study, LP sales **accounted for** $9 **billion of** the country's $15 billion music sales revenue.

▶ Renewable energy currently **accounts for** a small **percentage of** U.S. energy generation.

▶ First-time buyers **accounted for** roughly 30 **percent of** home purchases in July. (= About 30 percent of home purchases in July were made by first-time buyers.)

## 5 CONVERSATION TIP

**Imagine you are at a sales meeting. You want to describe your key markets. Here's what you can say:**

**(Paris) currently accounts for (70) percent of our sales.**

# 27 BRING ABOUT

## 1 WHAT IT MEANS

**When you bring about something, you make it happen, especially in a way that is gradual and causes changes in a situation:**

▶ Globalization [UK: globalisation] has brought about many changes in the way the world economy works.

= Globalization has caused the world economy to work in a different way.

## 2 HOW IT WORKS

1 ***Bring about*** **takes an object (i.e., what you bring about). If the object is a noun, it usually goes at the end:**

☑ Globalization has brought about changes.

2 **If the object is a pronoun, it always goes in the middle:**

☑ Globalization has brought them about.

☒ Globalization has ~~brought about them.~~

3 ***Bring about*** **is often used in the passive voice:**

☑ Many changes were brought about by globalization.

## 3 HOW YOU USE IT IN REAL LIFE

1 ***Bring about*** **+ words describing changes with positive outcomes. In the first two examples, notice the prepositions in bold, too:**

bring about improvements

▶ A recent report suggests that exercise can **bring about improvements in** 13 different conditions, from diabetes to dementia.

▶ In this latest book, Ray Kurzweil depicts a utopia that will **bring about** the **end of** disease and poverty.

▶ The candidate promised to **bring about reforms** that would pull the economy from its worst recession in decades.

▶ The iPhone was a game changer, and it **brought about** a **revolution** at Apple, turning it into one of the world's richest companies.
▶ Our mission is to **bring about justice** and **peace** in our world.
▶ The president stated that the media has a key role to play in **bringing about** social **change**.

2 *Bring about* + **words describing painful transitions. Notice the use of the preposition *of*:**
▶ Pundits believe that the political difficulties created by the Information Age will **bring about the demise of** democracy.
▶ My father says that the government has **brought about the destruction of** British healthcare as we know it.
▶ In many important ways, World War I **brought about the collapse of** the monarchies of Austria-Hungary and Germany.

## 4 MORE REAL-LIFE DATA

**The following adjectives are commonly used with *bring about*:**
▶ In yesterday's interview, Alan Robbins laid bare the details of the crimes that **brought about** his **political** downfall.
▶ Structural adjustment has not yet **brought about social** and **economic** recovery on the continent.
▶ Most people feared that the government's proposal would **bring about real** chaos in the region.
▶ That kind of rhetoric will not **bring about** any **positive** results.
▶ The task force that was implemented last November has helped **bring about** a **significant** drop in crime.
▶ Nano technology has **brought about fundamental** changes in medicine.

## 5 CONVERSATION TIP

**Imagine you are giving a school presentation on important inventions of the 21st century. Here's something you can say:**

**The (smartphone) has brought about important changes in our lives.**

# 28 COME DOWN TO

## 1 WHAT IT MEANS

**When a situation or a decision comes down to something, that is the single most important factor it is influenced by:**

▶ I'm not surprised she took such a stressful job. In the end, it all comes down to money, I guess.

= She probably took a stressful job because money is usually the most important thing.

## 2 HOW IT WORKS

1 ***Come down to*** **takes an object (i.e., what something comes down to). The object always goes at the end, whether it is a noun or a pronoun, so never separate the verb (*come*) from the particles (*down, to*):**

☑ It all comes down to money.

☑ It all comes down to it.

☒ It all ~~comes down money to~~.

☒ It all ~~comes it down to~~.

2 **If you use a verb after *come down to,* put it in the *-ing* form:**

☑ It all comes down to making more money.

3 ***Come down to*** **can be followed by a *wh-* word (i.e., *what, why, how,* etc.):**

☑ It all comes down to how much money you expect to make.

## 3 HOW YOU USE IT IN REAL LIFE

***Come down to*** **can be followed by a relatively wide range of words. The following word combinations are especially common:**

1 ***Come down to*** **+ *wh-* words and *whether*:**

▶ There are very few rules. It really **comes down to what** works for you as an individual.

▶ I've been making records for a long time, and there's no secret formula to a hit. It really **comes down to how** much work you put in, I think.

▶ Both players were good, but, in the end, it **came down to who** was well-conditioned physically.

▶ Ultimately, your success will not **come down to whether** you can have a good idea; it will **come down to whether or not** you can execute it.

2 *Come down to* **+ phrases with** ***question*****:**

▶ When all is said and done, it all **comes down to** one **question**: How strong is the economy?

▶ The case is expected to **come down to the question of whether** the murder was premeditated.

3 *Come down to* **+ words indicating choice:**

▶ Deciding between one phone and the other really **comes down to** personal **preference**.

▶ This election **comes down to** a **choice** between chaos and stability.

▶ It's a tight election, and, in the end, it's going to **come down to** a few hundred **votes**.

4 *Come down to* **+** ***simple*** **and other related adjectives:**

▶ In the end, it all **comes down to** a **simple** question: Is Facebook a tech or a media company?

▶ A lot of what Americans disagree on **comes down to** the **basic** tension between big, strong government and small, limited government.

▶ When I asked why I'd been fired, the guy from HR said it **came down to** a "**fundamental** lack of alignment with the company's values," whatever that means.

## 4 MORE REAL-LIFE DATA

**To add emphasis, people often use** ***what*** **to introduce the main idea. Notice the underlined patterns:**

▶ There are pros and cons, but **what it** really **comes down to is** <u>the question of whether</u> the pros outweigh the cons. **(*what* + *it* + *come down to* + *be* + <u>noun phrase</u>)**

▶ I have mixed feelings about this method. Maybe **what it comes down to is** <u>that it works</u> for others, but not for me. **(*what* + *it* + *come down to* + *be* + <u>clause</u>)**

## 5 CONVERSATION TIP

**Imagine you have a friend who is learning a new skill but making little progress. Here's how you can give this person some advice:**

**I think it all comes down to this: You need to work harder.**

# 29 LIE IN

## 1 WHAT IT MEANS

**1 *To lie in* something means to be caused by it:**

▶ Lucy's success lies in her ability to communicate effectively.

= Lucy is successful because she is an effective communicator.

**2 After you finish this lesson, turn to page 246 for an additional meaning of *lie in*.**

## 2 HOW IT WORKS

**1 *Lie in* takes an object (i.e., lie in what). The object always goes at the end, whether it is a noun or a pronoun:**

☑ Her success lies in her ability to communicate.

☑ Her success lies in it.

☒ Her success ~~lies her ability to communicate in~~.

☒ Her success ~~lies it in~~.

**2 If you use a verb after *lie in*, put it in the *-ing* form:**

☑ Her success lies in knowing how to communicate.

## 3 HOW YOU USE IT IN REAL LIFE

**1 Words describing problems + *lie in*:**

▶ Perhaps our biggest HR **problems lie in** understanding our workforce.

▶ In the experiment, 3D technology showed good results in some classrooms, but the **challenge lay in** finding enough 3D-friendly content. (*lay* = past of *lie*)

▶ When children fail to learn in schools, the **fault** often **lies in** outdated methods of instruction.

▶ Internships usually pay off in terms of future employment, but the **difficulty lies in** finding a paid one in your field.

**2 Words describing solutions + *lie in*. Notice the prepositions in bold:**

▶ If you're looking for a faster machine, the **solution to** your problem may **lie in** software rather than hardware.

▶ This is an important **question**, the **answer to** which might **lie in** the nature of politics itself.

▶ The **key to** the product's enduring popularity **lies in** its simplicity.

▶ The **success of** these discussion groups **lies in** the members' involvement.

**3 Words describing positive characteristics + *lie in*. Again, notice the prepositions:**

▶ The **strength of** this book **lies in** the author's ability to focus on the inner workings of the federal government.

▶ The **power of** a brand **lies in** its ability to evoke emotion from consumers.

▶ The **beauty of** the book **lies in** Applegate's nuanced descriptions of the characters.

▶ Much of the play's **appeal lies in** Michael Ball's flawless performance.

## 4 RELATED MEANING

**In the expressions below, *lie in* means *exists* or *can be found*:**

▶ The solution **lies in our hands** (= is up to us), but many of us refuse to accept it.

▶ Her research **interests lie in** (= she is interested in) the field of modernist literature.

▶ When faced with two opposite positions, remember that **the truth lies** in the middle.

▶ Cell phone carriers [UK: mobile phone providers] would like you to believe that **the future** of broadband **lies in** the 5G networks they have built.

▶ The problem **lies in the fact that** many people do not see depression as a biological disorder, but as a failure of will.

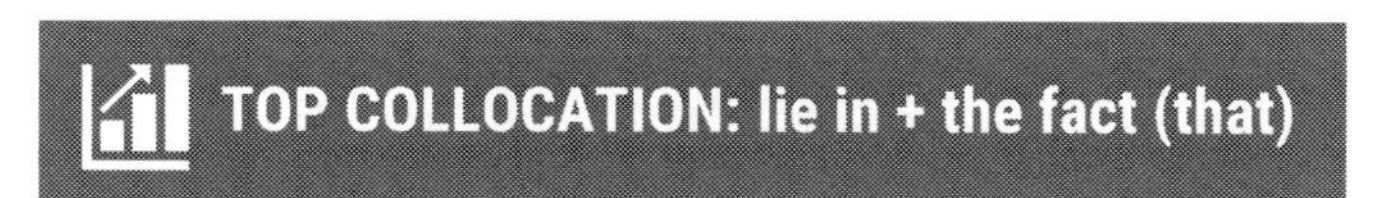


## 5 CONVERSATION TIP

**Imagine you are giving a school presentation on an influential celebrity. Here's something you can say:**

**I believe (Madonna)'s success lies in (her courage).**

# 30 RULE OUT

## 1 WHAT IT MEANS

**1 When you rule something out, you stop considering it a possibility:**

▶ I'm surprised they ruled out the first option.

= I'm surprised they no longer think the first option is a possibility.

**2 You can also use *rule out* when referring to people:**

▶ They ruled out all candidates.

= They didn't select any of the candidates.

## 2 HOW IT WORKS

**1 *Rule out* takes an object (i.e., what or who you rule out). If the object is a noun, it tends to go at the end:**

☑ They ruled out this option. (more common)

☑ They ruled this option out. (less common)

**2 If the object is a pronoun, it always goes in the middle:**

☑ They ruled it out. ☒ They ~~ruled out it~~.

**3 If you use a verb after *rule out*, put it in the *-ing* form:**

☑ She doesn't rule out running for mayor.

**4 *Rule out* is often used in the passive voice:**

☑ No options should be ruled out.

## 3 HOW YOU USE IT IN REAL LIFE

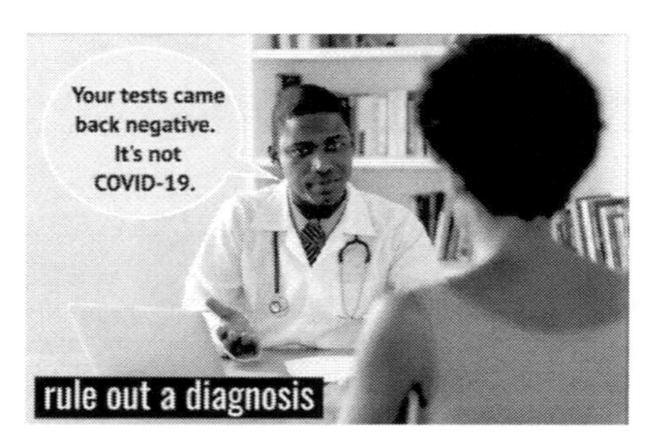


**1 You can use *rule out* with a lot of different words. It is commonly used in medicine, politics, and law:**

▶ "Doctors should not use testing as the sole basis for **ruling out** a COVID-19 **diagnosis**," Anderson added.

▶ Iran's supreme leader has again **ruled out** any **negotiations** with the U.S., amid heightened tensions.

- Law enforcement officials have **ruled out** any **connection** between the two deaths.

2 *Rule out* + **words indicating possibility:**

- By all accounts, the president has not **ruled out** the **possibility** of preemptive military action at a later date.
- Once you have **ruled out** obvious **potential** sources of interference, your next step is to move your router.

3 *Rule out* + *cause* **and other related words:**

- Subsequent testing **ruled out** any underlying physical **causes**, such as a brain tumor or stroke.
- Robertson and her team spent two years validating their findings, and all possible alternative **explanations** were **ruled out**.
- While these preliminary findings certainly do not **rule out** my **theory**, they suggest that more evidence is needed.

## 4 MORE REAL-LIFE DATA

**The adverbs below are commonly used with** ***rule out*****:**

- This is not a bad phone, but the battery life **completely rules** it **out** for me.
- In the interview, Chelsea Clinton did not **entirely rule out** a future run.
- The prime minister **effectively ruled out** the opposition's ideas for a compromise plan.
- During the debate, the candidates **explicitly ruled out** any cuts to Social Security benefits.

## 5 CONVERSATION TIP

**Imagine a friend asks if you would consider moving abroad. You think it might be a future possibility. Here's something you can say:**

**I wouldn't rule it out. Maybe when (the kids are older).**

# 31 STEM FROM

## 1 WHAT IT MEANS

1 ***Stem from* means to develop as a result of something else:**

problems stemming from childhood

▶ Most of Ted's problems stem from his difficult childhood.
= Most of Ted's problems were caused by his difficult childhood.

2 **You can also use *stem from* to talk about something you have inherited from another (usually older) family member:**

▶ Some of my emotional issues stem from my father.
= My father is responsible for some of my emotional issues.

## 2 HOW IT WORKS

1 ***Stem from* takes an object (i.e., stem from someone or something). The object always goes at the end, whether it is a noun or a pronoun:**

☑ Ted's problems stem from his childhood.
☑ Ted's problems stem from it.
☒ Ted's problems ~~stem his childhood from~~.
☒ Ted's problems ~~stem it from~~.

2 **Verbs are relatively rare after *stem from*. If you do use a verb, put it in the *-ing* form:**

☑ Ted's problems stem from his having been neglected as a child.

## 3 HOW YOU USE IT IN REAL LIFE

1 ***Stem from* + negative words:**

▶ Bullying based on religious beliefs usually **stems from** a **lack of** understanding and tolerance.
▶ The company's problems **stemmed from** its **inability to** keep pace with the ever-changing footwear landscape.
▶ Unfortunately, you may run into people at work who will treat you unfairly because of your bipolar disorder. Their behavior [UK: behaviour] often **stems from ignorance**.

- If you dig deep, you'll find that your social anxiety **stems from** your **fear of** disapproval.
- The difficulties some children encounter in school can **stem from** their **failure to** pay attention in class.

2 ***Stem from* + words describing beliefs and attitudes. Notice the use of *that* and *to*:**

- The CEO's legendary work ethic **stems from** a **belief that** the work itself, rather than the money it produces, is the true reward.
- Gender inequality in marriage seems to **stem from** people's **tendency to** regard women as the default parent.
- Many of our internal struggles **stem from** our **desire to** control things.
- Legalizing [UK: legalising] same-sex marriage is not a question of granting a group of people a privilege. Rather, it **stems from** the **conviction that** everyone should have the same rights.

3 *Stem from + the fact (that)*:

- My lack of assertiveness **stems from the fact that** I tended to avoid conflict as a child.

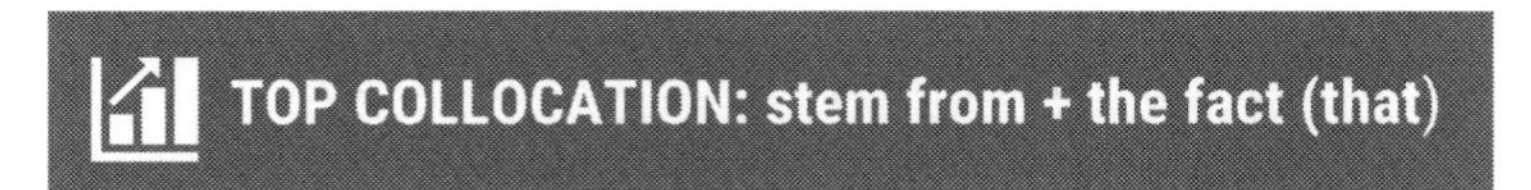


## 4 MORE REAL-LIFE DATA

***Stem from* often attracts words expressing possibility and probability:**

- Differences in behavior **may stem from** differences in cultural values.
- The shooting **may have stemmed from** an argument over a parking space.
- Authorities said the incident **likely stemmed from** ongoing gang conflict in the area.

## 5 CONVERSATION TIP

**Imagine you are talking to a group of foreigners about a problem facing your country. Here's something you can say:**

**Our (inequality) stems from a lack of (investment in education).**

# CHECK YOUR PROGRESS 5

**A What do the sentences in italics mean? Choose the correct option.**

1 *High interest rates account for the strength of the dollar.*
A The dollar is strong because interest rates are high.
B Interest rates are high because the dollar is strong.

2 *The Internet has brought about massive changes in society.*
A The Internet has changed because of society.
B Society has changed because of the Internet.

3 *In the end, the choice comes down to how much you want to spend.*
A The cost will determine your choice.
B Your choice will determine the cost.

4 *Her success lies in her vast network of business associates.*
A She is successful because she has a vast network of business associates.
B She has a vast network of business associates because she is successful.

5 *He hasn't ruled out running for president.*
A He is definitely running for president.
B He might run for president.

6 *Your anxiety stems from your lack of sleep.*
A You are not getting enough sleep because you are anxious.
B You are anxious because you are not getting enough sleep.

**B Each box has three logical ways to continue the sentences on the left. Match boxes A–E to sentences 1–6. One box will be used twice.**

1. This line of products accounts for [ ].
2. The new legislation has brought about [ ].
3. That kind of behavior [UK: behaviour] stems from [ ].
4. There's no right or wrong. It all comes down to [ ].
5. After the lab experiment, scientists ruled out [ ].
6. Basically, the problem lies in [ ].

| A |
|---|
| • key economic reforms |
| • a massive wave of protests |
| • major social changes |

| B |
|---|
| • roughly 40% of the total |
| • about half of our revenue |
| • the bulk of our sales |

| C |
|---|
| • what your priorities are |
| • your personal preference |
| • the simple question of cost |

| D |
|---|
| • his sheer ignorance |
| • her lack of willpower |
| • the fact that he is lazy |

| E |
|---|
| • this particular explanation |
| • such a possibility |
| • any external causes |

**C EXTRA CHALLENGE! Rewrite the sentences without changing the meaning. Use the bold words to create phrasal verbs. The first two are done for you.**

1 He is determined to do what he planned no matter what difficulties are involved.
**CARRY**
He is determined to *carry out his plan at* any cost.

2 They didn't let the pandemic stop them from getting married.
**WENT**
Despite the pandemic, they *went ahead with the* wedding.

3 It is up to us how to solve this problem.
**LIES**
The solution to this ________________________________________ hands.

4 We took all suggestions into consideration at the meeting.
**RULED**
No ________________________________________ at the meeting.

5 In the United States, about half of the population is made up of women.
**ACCOUNT**
In the United States, ________________________________________ of the population.

6 Medicine will change drastically because of nanotechnology.
**BRING**
Nanotechnology ________________________________________ changes in medicine.

7 I am not self-confident because I am afraid people will criticize [UK: criticise] me.
**STEMS**
My lack ________________________________________ my fear of criticism.

8 To be successful, you need to be able to sell your ideas.
**COMES**
Success ________________________________________ ability to sell your ideas.

Answer key:

| Exercise A | Exercise B | Exercise C |
|---|---|---|
| 1 A | 1 B | 3 problem lies in our |
| 2 B | 2 A | 4 suggestions were ruled out |
| 3 A | 3 D | 5 women account for about half |
| 4 A | 4 C | 6 will bring about drastic |
| 5 B | 5 E | 7 of self-confidence stems from |
| 6 B | 6 D (C is also possible) | 8 comes down to your/the |

# 32 CALL FOR

## 1 WHAT IT MEANS

**When you call for a particular course of action, you publicly ask for it to happen:**

▶ The protesters are calling for the prime minister's resignation.

= The protesters are demanding that the prime minister resign.

## 2 HOW IT WORKS

1 ***Call for*** **takes an object (i.e., what you call for). The object always goes at the end, whether it is a noun or a pronoun:**

☑ They are calling for her resignation.

☑ They are calling for it.

☒ They are ~~calling her resignation for~~.

☒ They are ~~calling it for~~.

2 ***Call for*** **can be used in the passive voice:**

☑ Her resignation is being called for.

## 3 HOW YOU USE IT IN REAL LIFE

***Call for*** **tends to attract words describing social and political activism. Notice the prepositions in bold, too:**

1 **Starting things:**

▶ A number of scientists are **calling for** the **creation of** the largest protected area on Earth for wildlife, in Antarctica.

▶ The 9/11 Commission **called for** further **investigation by** the U.S. Government **into** the Al Qaeda-Hezbollah relationship.

2 **Changing things:**

▶ New videos of fatal shootings by police officers have led to protests **calling for** police **reform**.

▶ The 2020 Republican platform **called for** a constitutional **amendment** to protect homeschooling.

▶ Ahead of World Pancreatic Cancer Day on November 17, experts worldwide are **calling for** increased **awareness of** the disease.

3 **Ending things:**

▶ Clashes took place as protesters gathered to **call for** a **boycott of** parliamentary elections.

▶ The state **called for** a **ban on** most abortions during the coronavirus pandemic, deeming them "non-essential" procedures.

▶ The Iraqi prime minister and parliament both **called for** the immediate **withdrawal of** foreign troops from Iraq.

▶ A **cease-fire** was **called for** by the UN Security Council on October 22 and went into effect shortly after that.

## 4 RELATED MEANINGS

1 ***Call for* also means to ask for something urgently:**

▶ If your car is submerged, don't panic. Go out of the window, climb onto the vehicle, and **call for help**.

▶ The police **called for backup**, and five squad cars appeared on the scene.

2 **When something calls for a particular quality or action, it requires it:**

▶ This is a situation that **calls for** the negotiating **talents** of highly skilled diplomats.

▶ Congratulations! This **calls for a party**, don't you think?

▶ Being a teacher **calls for** putt**ing** aside your personal needs so that you can meet your students'.

3 **Common expression –** ***desperate times call for desperate measures*****:**

▶ I know what I'm about to do seems crazy, but **desperate times call for desperate measures**. (= Difficult times require extreme actions.)

## 5 CONVERSATION TIP

**Imagine a friend has given you some good news, and you want to celebrate. Here's what you can say:**

**Congratulations! This calls for a celebration!**

# 33 STAND BY

## 1 WHAT IT MEANS

**1 When you stand by something you previously said, promised, or decided to do, you stay true to it:**

▶ I still stand by every single word I said.

= I haven't changed my mind about any of the things I said.

**2 After you finish this lesson, turn to page 246 for additional meanings of *stand by*.**

## 2 HOW IT WORKS

**This meaning of *stand by* takes an object (i.e., what or who you stand by). The object always goes at the end, whether it is a noun or a pronoun:**

☑ I stand by what I said.

☑ I stand by it.

☒ I ~~stand what I said by~~.

☒ I ~~stand it by~~.

## 3 HOW YOU USE IT IN REAL LIFE

**1 *Stand by + promise* and other related words:**

stand by a promise

▶ In last night's debate, the Republican nominee said he **stood by** his **promise** not to raise taxes.

▶ As I said earlier, the **decision** has been made, and I will **stand by** it no matter what happens tomorrow.

▶ In the wake of the Paris attacks last week, New York City will **stand by** its **pledge** to welcome Syrian refugees, the mayor said yesterday.

**2 *Stand by + statement* and other related words:**

▶ "The president **stands by** the **statement** made on May 14 and will not be making further comments," the press secretary added.

▶ The congressman continues to **stand by** his **comments**, despite objections from both sides of the aisle.

▶ A Harvard University scientist who said the mysterious flying object might be an alien spacecraft is **standing by** his **claim**.

▶ During the interview, I **stood by** my **assertion** that antidepressants are overprescribed.

3 ***Stand by*** **+ words describing what you believe in or believe will happen:**

▶ Maya Angelou was a passionate woman who always **stood by** her **principles** on her path to success.

▶ We all have to **stand by** our **words** and **convictions**, and my late grandmother was a good example of that.

▶ I know it seems crazy, but I **stand by** my **prediction** that one bitcoin will be worth $350,000 by 2024.

## 4 RELATED MEANING

**When you stand by someone, you remain loyal and continue to support them, especially in a difficult situation:**

▶ First of all, I'd like to thank all of my supporters, who have **stood by me** from day one.

▶ Hillary Clinton, years ahead of her presidential run, **stood by her husband** as impeachment proceedings began.

▶ I dedicate this book to my wife, Jill, who has lovingly **stood by my side** (= supported me) through the good, the bad, and the very bad.

## 5 CONVERSATION TIP

**Imagine you posted something controversial on social media. A friend thinks you should delete the post, but you disagree. Here's what you can say:**

**I really do think that (...), and I stand by my words.**

# 34 STAND FOR

## 1 WHAT IT MEANS

**1 When you stand for certain ideas, principles, or values, you support them, and they represent you:**

▶ The Olympic Flame stands for peace, unity, and friendship.

= The Olympic Flame represents peace, unity, and friendship.

**2 After you finish this lesson, turn to page 246 for an additional meaning of *stand for*.**

## 2 HOW IT WORKS

***Stand for* takes an object (i.e., what you stand for). The object always goes at the end, whether it is a noun or a pronoun:**

☑ The Olympic Flame stands for peace.

☑ The Olympic Flame stands for it.

☒ The Olympic Flame ~~stands peace for~~.

☒ The Olympic Flame ~~stands it for~~.

## 3 HOW YOU USE IT IN REAL LIFE

**1 *Stand for* often attracts the words *something*, *everything*, and *what*:**

▶ Have you ever had an experience that made you have second thoughts about religion and **everything** it **stands for**?

▶ I miss those days when we **stood for something** and believed that we could change the world.

▶ We will spend time with you to understand exactly **what** your brand **stands for** and then market it to the correct audience.

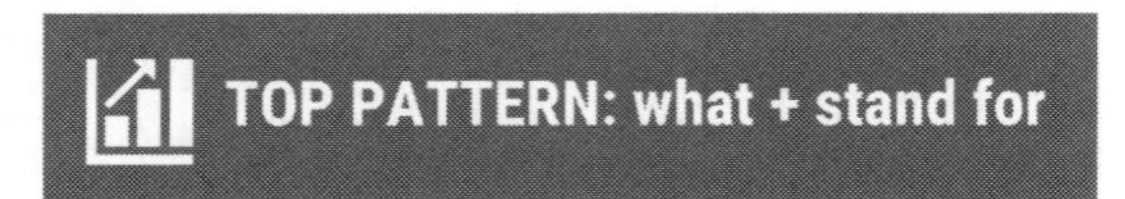

2 *Stand for* **also tends to attract words describing values and beliefs:**

▶ Memorial Day ceremonies remember all our fallen heroes, who **stood for freedom** and helped build this nation.

▶ What's going on with the U.S.? Aren't we supposed to be the country that **stands for human rights**?

▶ To me, veganism is more than a plant-based diet. It is an integral part of what **standing for animal rights** means.

▶ When one child is mistreated, it affects an entire society. This is why we must **stand for justice** now.

▶ Show you understand the company's mission. Find out the **values** it **stands for** and use this information in your interview.

▶ ***Stand For Truth*** is a daily digital newscast that focuses on data-driven reports for millennial viewers.

## 4 RELATED MEANING

**If a group of letters, numbers, or symbols stands for a word, it represents the short form of that word:**

▶ The **letters** Bcc **stand for** "blind carbon copy," and, as the name suggests, Bcc allows you to hide recipients in email messages.

▶ As you know, the **abbreviation** p2p **stands for** peer-to-peer, which, in our case, means client-to-client.

▶ I've heard the **acronym** OPEC a thousand times, but, for some reason, I keep forgetting what it **stands for**.

## 5 CONVERSATION TIP

**Imagine a friend asks why you voted for a certain candidate. Here's what you can say:**

**Well, I like (Simpson) and everything she stands for.**

# 35 STAND UP FOR

## 1 WHAT IT MEANS

***To stand up for* means to defend a person or an idea when they are under attack, making your opinion very clear:**

▶ I believe it's time we stood up for our rights.

= I believe we should start defending our rights.

## 2 HOW IT WORKS

***Stand up for* takes an object (i.e., what or who you stand up for). The object always goes at the end, whether it is a noun or a pronoun, so never separate the verb (*stand*) from the particles (*up, for*):**

☑ We should stand up for our rights.

☑ We should stand up for them.

☒ We should ~~stand up our rights for~~.

☒ We should ~~stand them up for~~.

## 3 HOW YOU USE IT IN REAL LIFE

1 ***Stand up for* + *myself, herself,* etc.:**

▶ Stop playing the victim and **stand up for yourself**. You should never let anyone take advantage of you!

▶ I remember how hard it was to **stand up for myself** when I first started my job. It took me a while to become more assertive.

▶ I have three daughters, and I've always taught them how to **stand up for themselves** against bullies.

2 ***Stand up for* + words describing values and beliefs:**

▶ There are very few people who will **stand up for** the **rights** of the LGBT community in the Middle East.

▶ Fifty years ago today, Dr. Martin Luther King Jr. **stood up for freedom** with his famous "I Have a Dream" speech.

▶ What we need right now is a Congress that **stands up for democracy**, rather than stands in its way.

▶ Impeaching the president doesn't come without risks, but it's ultimately about **standing up for** our **Constitution** and **the rule of law**.

▶ As the play unfolds, we learn about the power of voicing your opinions and **standing up for** your **beliefs**, no matter how old you are.

▶ I told my boss I disagreed with the new policies, and she fired me. I may have lost my job, but at least I **stood up for** my **principles**.

▶ Strong leaders **stand up for** their core **values** when faced with tough decisions.

## 4 MORE REAL-LIFE DATA

***Stand up for* is often preceded by words and expressions related to courage:**

▶ I applaud your **courage to stand up for** others.

▶ It takes a lot of **guts to stand up for** your convictions. (*Guts* is an informal way of saying *courage*.)

▶ One of the things I love about you is that you're **not afraid to stand up for** what you believe is right.

▶ My father was a guy who was **willing to stand up for** things that were not accepted by society, and he paid the price for it.

▶ I've always tried to surround myself with people who are **brave enough to stand up for** what they believe in.

## 5 CONVERSATION TIP

**Imagine you are giving a farewell speech, and you want to praise your colleague. Here's something you can say:**

**When faced with tough decisions, (Frank) always stood up for his values.**

# 36 STAND UP TO

## 1 WHAT IT MEANS

**When you stand up to a person, institution, or country, you refuse to be intimidated or treated unfairly by them:**

▶ If you don't stand up to your boss, she'll never respect you.

= If you let your boss treat you unfairly, she'll never respect you.

## 2 HOW IT WORKS

***Stand up to*** **takes an object (i.e., what or who you stand up to). The object always goes at the end, whether it is a noun or a pronoun, so never separate the verb (*stand*) from the particles (*up, to*):**

☑ You should stand up to your boss.

☑ You should stand up to her.

☒ You should ~~stand up your boss to~~.

☒ You should ~~stand her up to~~.

## 3 HOW YOU USE IT IN REAL LIFE

1 ***Stand up to*** **+ people who (you think) are more powerful than you:**

▶ The protesters said they were marching to **stand up to bullies** and support victims of sexual harassment.

▶ Carter is a tough **boss**, and he will eat you alive unless you learn how to be assertive and **stand up to** him.

▶ Carla is not afraid to **stand up to** senior **board members** if she thinks they're wrong about something.

2 ***Stand up to*** **+ countries and corporations:**

▶ "I will not wait until the last months of my presidency to **stand up to Russia**," the president said.

▶ If a country has nuclear weapons, it can **stand up to** more powerful **rivals** without outside support.

▶ Democrats, by **standing up to** powerful insurance **companies**, have traditionally cast themselves as champions of protecting poor patients.
▶ It is important to create an environment where small businesses have the power to **stand up to** bigger **businesses**.
▶ I'd like to take this opportunity to thank Senator Warren for her courage and leadership in **standing up to** big **banks**.

## 4 RELATED MEANING

stand up to inspection

***Stand up to*** **also means to still seem true after being examined carefully. Notice the underlined adjectives, which are also common:**
▶ The new system will be implemented only if we are sure that it is robust and **stands up to** <u>close</u> **inspection**.
▶ Chapter 4 of my upcoming book is called "Does Piaget's theory **stand up to** <u>rigorous</u> **examination**?"
▶ Some pseudoscientific theories are rejected not because they are controversial, but because they do not **stand up to** basic <u>scientific</u> **scrutiny**.

## 5 CONVERSATION TIP

**Imagine a friend who is being bullied by their boss asks your advice. Here's what you can say:**

**You've got to learn to stand up to (him)!**

# 37 WEIGH IN (ON)

## 1 WHAT IT MEANS

**When you weigh in on a plan, decision, or discussion, you offer your opinion about it:**

▶ At the meeting, top executives weighed in on a number of key economic issues.

= At the meeting, top executives gave their opinion about a lot of important economic issues.

## 2 HOW IT WORKS

1 ***Weigh in on*** **takes an object (i.e., what you weigh in on). The object always goes at the end, whether it is a noun or a pronoun, so never separate the verb (*weigh*) from the particles (*in, on*):**

☑ They weighed in on key issues.

☑ They weighed in on them.

☒ They ~~weighed in key issues on~~.

☒ They ~~weighed them in on~~.

2 ***Weigh in***, **without *on*, takes no object. In this case, it is often followed by *with*:**

☑ Are you in favor [UK: favour] of the new law? Please weigh in with your thoughts.

☑ The president has not weighed in with an opinion yet.

## 3 HOW YOU USE IT IN REAL LIFE

1 ***Weigh in on* + *issue*** **and other related words:**

weigh in on an issue

▶ Courts across the country continue to **weigh in on** the **issue** of social media and the spread of fake news.

▶ Bill Gates **weighed in on** the **subject** of higher taxes for the wealthy at various times throughout 2019.

▶ It'll be interesting to see how the economic downturn will affect air travel. Looking forward to you **weighing in on** the **topic** in our next interview.

▶ Students at public universities should be able to **weigh in on matters** of public concern without threats of reprisals.

2 *Weigh in on* + *controversy* **and other related words:**

▶ The press secretary was asked to **weigh in on** the **controversy** surrounding the president's words, but she declined to comment.

▶ In tonight's show, Dr. Lee **weighs in on** the **debate** about eggs and cholesterol. Stay tuned.

▶ Residents are invited to **weigh in on** the **discussion** by taking part in a survey.

▶ In the article, I **weighed in on** the **dispute** between the federal government and Apple over data on a suspected terrorist's phone.

3 *Weigh in on* + *plan* **and other related words:**

▶ Health officials have **weighed in on** the governor's **plan** to open Indiana schools this fall.

▶ Anthony Miller was one of the fifty-three citizens who spent more than three hours **weighing in on** the **proposal** at the meeting.

▶ In the survey, Covington residents were asked to **weigh in on** the **proposed** elimination of some bus routes in the city.

## 4 MORE REAL-LIFE DATA

***Weigh in on* often attracts phrases with *whether (or not)*. Notice the <u>underlined</u> structures:**

1 ***Whether* (*or not*) + <u>clause</u>:**

▶ The board members **weighed in on whether** <u>they want to keep</u> or suspend the campaign.

▶ In today's episode, two ophthalmologists **weigh in on whether or not** <u>your headaches are caused</u> by eye problems.

2 ***Whether* (*or not*) + *to* + <u>verb</u>:**

▶ Hundreds of people took part in the survey, **weighing in on whether to** <u>keep</u> the school's current name.

▶ Members of staff were asked to **weigh in on whether or not to** <u>ban</u> phones from classrooms.

## 5 CONVERSATION TIP

**Imagine you are reporting the results of a survey. Here's how you can explain what it tried to discover:**

**Respondents were asked to weigh in on whether (...).**

# CHECK YOUR PROGRESS 6

**A Write the phrasal verbs in the box next to their meanings.**

| call for | stand by | stand for | stand up to | stand up for | weigh in on |
|---|---|---|---|---|---|

1 Politicians aren't always willing to ______________ (offer their opinion) controversial issues.
2 The bill prompted protesters to ______________ (publicly ask for) a boycott on GM foods.
3 Before creating a logo, ask yourself: What does my company ______________ (represent)?
4 People want me to quit, but I will ______________ (stay true to) my promise to carry on.
5 My mother always taught me to ______________ (not be intimidated by) bullies.
6 Never be afraid to ______________ (defend) your beliefs in the face of opposition.

**B Look at the photos and complete the sentences with the right particles. The first one is done for you.**

| by | for (x2) | ~~up for~~ | up to |
|---|---|---|---|

These people are marching to stand (1) ___*up for*___ freedom of speech.

This man has decided to stand (2) ________ his decision to protest, even if he gets arrested.

The protesters are standing (3) ________ gun lobbyists and calling (4) _______ stricter laws.

The symbol on the sign stands (5) ________ "Black Lives Matter."

## C Choose the correct option.

1 The board members weighed in on [if / whether] or not to hold new elections.
2 My wife has always stood by my [front / side], through thick and thin.
3 I love the fact that you're willing [for / to] stand up for your convictions.
4 Does anyone know what "CBS" stands [for / to]?
5 You have made the right decision. Desperate [time / times] call for desperate measures.
6 The theory sounds interesting, but does it stand up [for / to] scrutiny?
7 You got promoted? This calls for [a / the] big celebration!

## D EXTRA CHALLENGE! Circle the correct options.

1 The new scandal has led to a massive wave of protests [called / calling] for the president's resignation.
2 This poem reminds me of my late grandfather and everything he [stood / has stood] for.
3 I think you're too soft on bullies. I wish you [stand / would stand] up for yourself.
4 If I'd known I'd end up losing my job, I wouldn't [stand / have stood] up to my boss like that. Too late now.
5 During my interview tomorrow, I'm looking forward to [weigh / weighing] in on the issue of social media and fake news.
6 During the campaign, the candidate promised to change immigration laws. When she won, she [stood / had stood] by her promise.

### Answer key:

Exercise A
1 weigh in on
2 call for
3 stand for
4 stand by
5 stand up to
6 stand up for

Exercise B
2 by
3 up to
4 for
5 for

Exercise C
1 whether
2 side
3 to
4 for
5 times
6 to
7 a

Exercise D
1 calling
2 stood
3 would stand
4 have stood
5 weighing
6 stood

# 38 BACK UP

## 1 WHAT IT MEANS

1 ***To back something up*** **means to provide supporting evidence that it is true:**

▶ There is no evidence to back up your claims.

= There is no evidence that what you are saying is true.

2 **You can also use *back up* when referring to people:**

▶ There is no evidence to back him up.

= There is no evidence that what he is saying is true.

3 **After you finish this lesson,** **turn to page 247** **for additional meanings of *back up*.**

## 2 HOW IT WORKS

1 ***Back up*** **takes an object (i.e., what or who you back up). If the object is a noun, it tends to go at the end:**

☑ You can't back up your claims. (more common)

☑ You can't back your claims up. (less common)

2 **If the object is a pronoun, it always goes in the middle:**

☑ You can't back them up. ☒ You can't ~~back up them~~.

3 ***Back up*** **+ *what* is also possible:**

☑ You need evidence to back up what you're saying.

4 ***Back up*** **is often used in the passive voice:**

☑ Your theory needs to be backed up by scientific evidence.

## 3 HOW YOU USE IT IN REAL LIFE

***Back up*** **usually attracts words related to opinion and <u>proof</u>:**

▶ You should make a logical, well-researched argument that uses hard <u>**data**</u> to **back up** your **claims**.

▶ You do make some valid points, but the <u>**evidence**</u> you used to **back up** your **argument** needs some clarification.

▶ If you have any links to <u>statistics</u> that **back up** your **assertion**, I would be interested in seeing those.

▶ The **theory** that men are more likely to be struck by lightning than women is **backed up** by several <u>studies</u>.

▶ You have no <u>facts</u> to **back up** your **statement**, and yet you have just decided to bring your negativity into this conversation.

▶ This <u>finding</u> **backs up** previous **research** that showed similar results in women.

## 4 RELATED MEANINGS

***To back up* also means to:**

**1 Support someone:**

▶ Some indie authors don't have a large print company to **back them up**, so they go into self-publishing.

▶ If the team members are encouraged to **back each other up**, then the project as a whole will benefit.

**2 Make a copy of information on a device:**

▶ If you've done nothing to make sure your most important **data** is* **backed up**, you are playing with fire.

▶ You can choose to have your **files backed up** daily, weekly, or monthly.

▶ The new software shouldn't pose a threat to Dropbox, which focuses on **backing up** your **photos**, not preparing them for sharing.

## 5 CONVERSATION TIP

**Imagine you are discussing something with a group of friends, most of whom disagree with you. You want someone to support you. Here's what you can say:**

**Come on, (Bill)! Back me up here.**

*In formal contexts, some people prefer to say *data are*.

# 39 BRING IN (1)

## 1 WHAT IT MEANS

**When you bring in someone from outside a team or company, you ask them to be involved in a job, discussion, etc.:**

▶ The company will bring in an expert to deal with the problem.

= The company will ask an expert for help so it can deal with the problem.

## 2 HOW IT WORKS

1 ***Bring in*** **takes an object. If the object (i.e., who you bring in) is a noun, it tends to go at the end:**

☑ The company will bring in experts. (more common)

☑ The company will bring experts in. (less common)

2 **If the object is a pronoun, it always goes in the middle:**

☑ The company will bring them in.

☒ The company will ~~bring in them~~.

3 **This meaning of *bring in* is often used in the passive voice:**

☑ Experts will be brought in.

## 3 HOW YOU USE IT IN REAL LIFE

1 ***Bring in*** **+ words indicating expertise:**

▶ How to **bring in** new **talent** is always a problem for a start-up.

▶ The company has **brought in** a group of international **experts** to test its systems and then write a detailed report.

▶ After the break, we'll **bring in** our **panel** to talk about the controversy surrounding the president's speech.

▶ And now, let's **bring in** CNN White House **correspondent**, Abby Phillip, for more.

▶ Having worked as a teacher for many years, I would caution schools against **bringing in consultants** with no knowledge of their context.

▶ The device was malfunctioning, and a **specialist** was **brought in** to determine the nature of the problem.

2 **Common expression – *bring in new blood*:**

▶ To turn the business around, we had to **bring in new blood**. (= attract people expected to provide fresh ideas and vitality)

3 ***Bring in* + words related to legal matters:**

▶ An **adviser** has been **brought in** to arbitrate the dispute between senior management and the union.

▶ "I'll give you half an hour to get ready, and then I'm **bringing in the jury**," Judge Cornelius said sternly.

▶ On Friday, the defense **brought in witnesses** who praised Doctor Murphy's character.

## 4 MORE REAL-LIFE DATA

**The following adjectives are relatively common after this meaning of *bring in:***

▶ This is an entirely new technology, and we'll need to **bring in outside** help if we want to implement it.

▶ Miriam has pushed hard to update the office by **bringing in new** technology.

▶ When running a company, we do ourselves a disservice by not **bringing in fresh** ideas and perspectives.

## 5 CONVERSATION TIP

**Imagine you are having a business meeting. Here's how you can give your opinion about a policy you disagree with:**

**How can we bring in new talent with so few benefits?**

# 40 COUNT ON (1)

## 1 WHAT IT MEANS

**1 When you count on someone, you rely on them to help or support you, especially in a difficult situation:**

▶ I'm counting on Matt to help me out.

= I'm depending on Matt's help.

**2 You can count on something, too:**

▶ I'm counting on Matt's support.

= I'm depending on Matt's support.

## 2 HOW IT WORKS

**1 *Count on* takes an object (i.e., what or who you count on). The object always goes at the end, whether it is a noun or a pronoun:**

☑ I'm counting on Matt. ☑ I'm counting on him.

☒ I'm ~~counting Matt on~~. ☒ I'm ~~counting him on~~.

**2 *Count on* is sometimes used in the passive voice, especially with *can* and *could*:**

☑ He is someone who can be counted on in any situation.

## 3 HOW YOU USE IT IN REAL LIFE

**You can use *count on* with a very wide range of nouns. The following word combinations are especially common:**

count on someone's help

**1 *Count on* + *support* and other related words:**

▶ There's no need to make lame excuses. No one is **counting on** your **help** anyway.

▶ In times of trouble, your spouse needs to know they can **count on** your **support** and **encouragement**.

▶ "Our Canadian friends can always **count on** our close **cooperation**," the president said.

2 *Count on* + **words describing institutions:**

▶ If we can't **count on** our own **government** to protect our civil rights, who will?

▶ It's such a shame that we can't **count on the media** for honest, unbiased news.

▶ I have been blessed with a loving **family** I can **count on.**

3 ***Count on* + *loyalty, generosity,* and other related words:**

▶ Many voters supported Macron reluctantly, simply to keep Le Pen out, so he knows that he can't **count on** their **loyalty**.

▶ Faculty, as well as students, could always **count on** Dr. Mayer's **generosity** as a mentor. She will be missed.

▶ This is classified information, so I **count on** your **discretion**.

▶ I have been in this business for over a decade, and you can **count on** my **honesty**.

▶ People who want social media apps to filter out poisonous content and fake news are implicitly **counting on** the **goodwill** and judgment of those doing the filtering.

## 4 MORE REAL-LIFE DATA

1 ***Count on* attracts the modal verbs *can* and *could* more than any other word:**

▶ If there is one thing you **can count on** after many years of marriage, it is the unconditional support of your spouse in times of tribulation.

▶ I grew up in a dysfunctional family, and there were very few people I **could count on**.

▶ Although their studio albums were often hit-and-miss affairs, the band **could** always **be counted on** for good live performances.

2 **The pattern *count on <u>someone</u> to <u>do something</u>* is very common:**

▶ Beyoncé has always known she can **count on** <u>her fans</u> **to** <u>be</u> there for her through it all.

▶ I was surprised when Mia said she was **counting on** <u>me</u> **to** <u>finish</u> her autobiography.

## 5 CONVERSATION TIP

**Imagine you want to reassure a friend who is in trouble. Here's what you can say:**

**Remember you can count on me, no matter what.**

# 41 GO ALONG WITH

## 1 WHAT IT MEANS

**1 When you go along with an idea, a decision, a rule, or a policy, you agree with it and/or actively support it:**

▶ That's a good idea. I'd be happy to go along with it.

= Your idea is good, and I support it.

**2 You can also go along with a person:**

▶ I can't believe you convinced me to go along with you.

= I can't believe you persuaded me to be part of what you decided to do.

**In both cases, notice the connection to the basic physical meaning of *go along*, which is to accompany someone somewhere.**

## 2 HOW IT WORKS

***Go along with* takes an object (i.e., what or who you go along with). The object always goes at the end, whether it is a noun or a pronoun, so never separate the verb (*go*) from the particles (*along, with*):**

☑ I'd be happy to go along with your idea.

☑ I'd be happy to go along with it.

☒ I'd be happy to ~~go along your idea with~~.

☒ I'd be happy to ~~go it along with~~.

## 3 HOW YOU USE IT IN REAL LIFE

go along with an idea

**1 *Go along with* + *idea* and other related words:**

▶ I didn't think my parents would **go along with** such a crazy **idea**, but, to my surprise, they both said yes!

▶ After some initial hesitation, it looks as if the mayor may be **going along** with the **plan**.

▶ I was a bit skeptical [UK: sceptical] at first, and just kind of **went along with** it, but, in the end, it was the right **decision**.

2 *Go along with* + **words related to rules and policies:**

▶ "**Going along with** the Democrats' tax **increase** was a huge mistake," an unidentified source said.

▶ Europe is not likely to **go along with** the **sanctions** imposed by the United Sates government.

▶ Barbra was surprisingly cooperative and said she would **go along with** the **agreement** on all counts.

▶ The ministers seemed happy to **go along with** the president's political **agenda**.

3 *Go along with* + *whatever* **(+ noun):**

▶ I have mixed feelings about the new tax plan, but I suppose we'll just have to **go along with whatever** the majority decides.

▶ I trust you completely, and I will **go along with whatever plan** you come up with.

4 **Common expression –** ***go along with the crowd*****:**

▶ He keeps lying to himself in order to **go along with the crowd** (= do or believe in what other people expect him to) and be liked.

## 4 MORE REAL-LIFE DATA

*Go along with* **is often preceded by words and phrases expressing (un)willingness:**

▶ The House seems **willing to go along with** the tax cuts that the president wants.

▶ I couldn't be bothered to vote, so I **was prepared to go along with** whatever the majority decided.

▶ Goldstein was killed when he **refused to go along with** the scheme, an inside source said.

▶ Dr. Morris eventually accepted the idea and **reluctantly went along with** it.

## 5 CONVERSATION TIP

**Imagine you and a friend are planning a surprise birthday party. You have nothing original to suggest. Here's what you can say:**

**I'd be happy to go along with whatever you decide.**

# 42 REACH OUT (TO)

## 1 WHAT IT MEANS

**When you reach out to someone or a group of people, you show that you are interested in them and/or want to help them:**

▶ Politicians need to find new ways of reaching out to young people.

= Politicians need to find new ways of showing young people that they want to listen to them and/or help them.

**Notice the connection to the basic physical meaning of *reach out*, which is to stretch your arm in order to touch or hold someone or something.**

## 2 HOW IT WORKS

**1 *Reach out to* takes an object (i.e., what or who you reach out to). The object always goes at the end, whether it is a noun or a pronoun, so never separate the verb (*reach*) from the particles (*out, to*):**

☑ Politicians need to reach out to young people.

☑ Politicians need to reach out to them.

☒ Politicians need to ~~reach out young people to~~.

☒ Politicians need to ~~reach them out to~~.

**2 *Reach out*, without *to*, takes no object:**

☑ They need to reach out and bring young people in.

## 3 HOW YOU USE IT IN REAL LIFE

**1 *Reach out to* can be followed by any word referring to a person (e.g., *reach out to my mother, reach out to Tim*). It tends to attract words indicating groups of people:**

▶ The health department is **reaching out to** the local **community** to encourage vaccination.

▶ While new technology allows campaigns multiple ways to **reach out to voters**, TV commercials have by far the widest reach.

▶ If the Republican Party wants to win the next election, it's important to **reach out to women** in their 20s.

▶ Many Catholic schools boast success stories about **reaching out to** promising **students** from disadvantaged backgrounds.

▶ The president-elect has not yet put forward a platform that **reaches out to minority groups.**

▶ In an effort to **reach out to** their younger **fans**, the band started offering live sessions on Instagram.

2 ***Reach out* often attracts the verb *help*:**

▶ Even in times of social distancing and self-isolation, we can **reach out to help** others in our communities.

## 4 RELATED MEANINGS

***Reach out (to)* also means to initiate contact with someone in order to:**

1 **Ask for help:**

▶ When you're feeling depressed, it's OK to spend some time in solitude, but allow yourself to **reach out to others** who love you.

▶ After watching the last episode of *Game of Thrones*, I **reached out to friends** who had watched it so we could commiserate.

2 **Increase your network of friends, acquaintances, business partners, etc. This meaning is more common in American English:**

▶ I lost myself in my job for a few years, so I'm trying to **reach out and meet** some new people.

▶ To expand your network, make an effort to connect with absolutely everyone who **reaches out to you** via LinkedIn.

▶ Some of us are reluctant to **reach out to people** to explore untapped job opportunities.

## 5 CONVERSATION TIP

**Imagine a business partner leaves a message on your phone. Here's how you can say you will be in touch soon:**

**Thanks for reaching out. I'll get back to you (tomorrow).**

# 43 TURN TO

## 1 WHAT IT MEANS

**1 When you turn to something, you use it as a way of dealing with a problem or difficult situation:**

▶ Some people turn to drugs to fill the void in their lives.

= Some people use drugs so they don't feel empty inside.

**2 When you turn to someone for help, you try to get it from them:**

▶ She turned to her parents for financial support.

= She asked her parents to help her financially.

**3 After you finish this lesson, turn to page 247 for additional meanings of *turn to*.**

## 2 HOW IT WORKS

***Turn to* takes an object (i.e., what or who you turn to). The object always goes at the end, whether it is a noun or a pronoun:**

☑ She turned to her parents.

☑ She turned to them.

☒ She ~~turned her parents to~~.

☒ She ~~turned them to~~.

## 3 HOW YOU USE IT IN REAL LIFE

**1 *Turn to* + words describing coping mechanisms:**

▶ I was really stressed out, so I **turned to music** to feel better.

▶ While schools are under lockdown, teens often feel isolated and **turn to social media** for entertainment.

▶ A lot of people **turned to religion** after September 11.

**2 *Turn to* + words describing illegal and/or dangerous activities:**

▶ People sometimes **turn to drugs** to get away from a life that offers them no hope.

▶ I was shattered by the breakup and **turned to alcohol** to cope.

▶ The book is about a 22-year-old aspiring singer who **turned to** high-priced **prostitution** to get to the top.

▶ As the economy struggled, and the president lost confidence in winning elections fairly, he **turned to violence** and **repression**.

▶ He is by no means a bad citizen who **turned to crime**; he is a good citizen who was driven to despair.

## 4 MORE REAL-LIFE DATA

**1 *Turn to somebody or something* tends to be followed by words and phrases expressing purpose. Notice the patterns after these words:**

▶ After Simon lost his mother, he **turned to** his aunt **for** emotional <u>support</u>. (*for* + <u>noun</u>)

▶ These developers have been left with little choice but to **turn to** crowdfunding **in order to** <u>complete</u> their prototypes. (*in order to* + <u>verb</u>)

▶ With the advent of the coronavirus, more people than ever have **turned to** gardening **as a way to** <u>enjoy</u> time outdoors. (*as a way to* + <u>verb</u>)

▶ The researcher has noticed a spike in people **turning to** Internet porn **as a means of** <u>escaping</u> tough financial situations. (*as a means of* + *-<u>ing</u>* <u>verb</u> – formal)

**2 Notice the use of *increasingly* + *turn to* when you describe trends:**

▶ German car buyers have hundreds of choices, and, **increasingly**, they are **turning to** imports to supply their needs.

▶ The savviest political reporters are **increasingly turning to** Twitter to promote their scoops or unveil the latest polls.

## 5 CONVERSATION TIP

**Imagine you are at a business meeting. Here's how you can explain why sales have dropped:**

**As you know, more and more people are turning to illegal downloads.**

# CHECK YOUR PROGRESS 7

**A Tim has just started college, and he is having trouble keeping up with his schoolwork. Complete his friends' advice with the correct verb. Refer back to phrasal verbs 38–43, if necessary.**

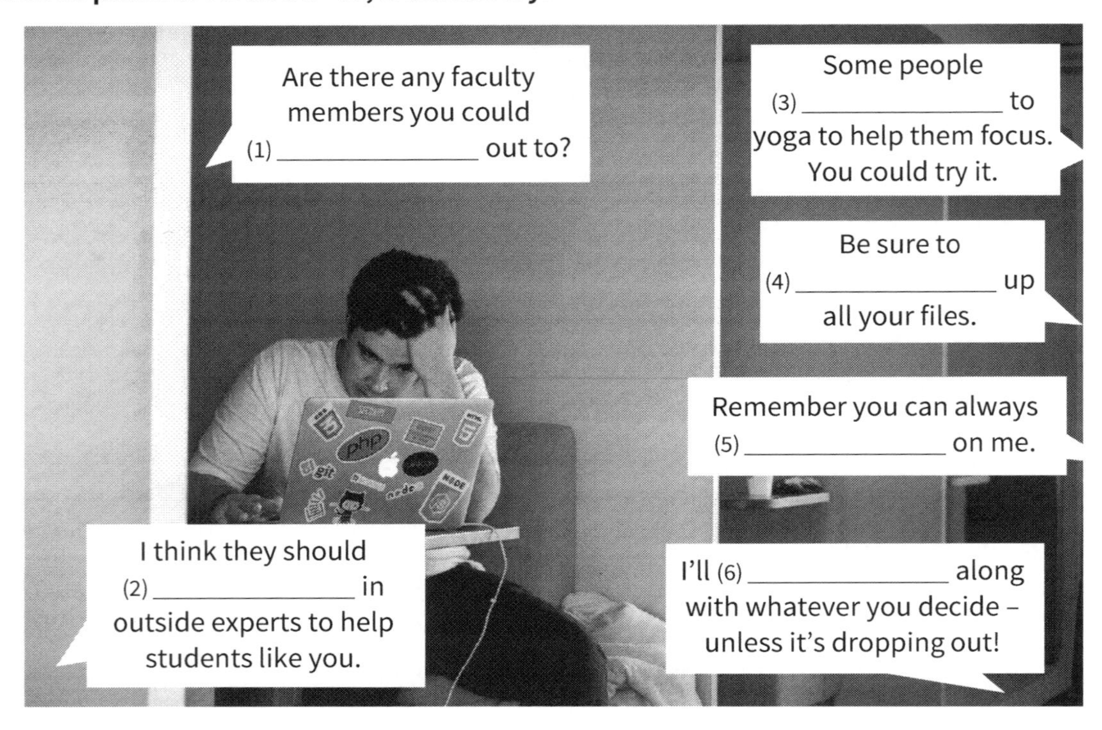

Are there any faculty members you could (1) ______________ out to?
I think they should (2) ______________ in outside experts to help students like you.
Some people (3) ______________ to yoga to help them focus. You could try it.
Be sure to (4) ______________ up all your files.
Remember you can always (5) ______________ on me.
I'll (6) ______________ along with whatever you decide – unless it's dropping out!


**B Rewrite the sentences below using the pronouns *it* and *them*. Make certain the pronouns are in the correct position. The first one is done for you.**

1 I'm happy to go along with your idea.
I'm happy to *go along with it*.

2 Do you have any evidence to back up your theory?
Do you have any evidence to ______________________________?

3 We need to bring in outside experts.
We need to ______________________________.

4 It's good to know I can count on my friends.
It's good to know I can ______________________________.

5 When I'm stressed out, I usually turn to music.
When I'm stressed out, I usually ______________________________.

6 To win an election, you need to reach out to young voters.
To win an election, you need to ______________________________.

**C In each sentence, cross out the [word] that does not make sense.**

1 After the divorce, Louis turned to [drugs / religion / meditation / stress / his friends] to help him cope.
2 As part of the campaign, she is reaching out to [minority groups / college-educated voters / the community / young people / opinion polls] to win the election.
3 Greg is the kind of person who usually goes along with [the crowd / his wife's decisions / whatever his wife decides / loyalty / the government's political agenda].
4 It's reassuring to know that I can count on [your help / her support / Sue's loyalty / his dishonesty / the local government].
5 This company needs to bring in [new blood / fresh ideas / more waste / a team of experts / outside talent] if it wants to survive.
6 When you write an essay, it's important to back up [your claims / what you say / your Word document / your spelling / your opinions].

**D EXTRA CHALLENGE! Choose the correct options.**

1 Her arguments ___ up by solid evidence.
A was backed B were backed C were backing D was backing

2 This company is not keeping up with the times. It's time ___ in new blood.
A we brought B to brought C we bringing D to bringing

3 Some people ___ to alcohol to help them cope with life's problems.
A turn B turns C are turned D has turned

4 Bruce is someone who can ___ on in any situation.
A count B counted C be count D be counted

5 If I'd known what a stupid idea this would turn out to be, I ___ along with it.
A won't go B don't go C wouldn't go D wouldn't have gone

6 People suffering from depression rarely feel like ___ out to others.
A reach B reached C reaching D to reach

Answer key:

| Exercise A | Exercise B | Exercise C | Exercise D |
|---|---|---|---|
| 1 reach | 2 back it up | 1 stress | 1 B |
| 2 bring | 3 bring them in | 2 opinion polls | 2 A |
| 3 turn | 4 count on them | 3 loyalty | 3 A |
| 4 back | 5 turn to it | 4 his dishonesty | 4 D |
| 5 count | 6 reach out to them | 5 more waste | 5 D |
| 6 go | | 6 your spelling | 6 C |

# 44 BRING OUT

## 1 WHAT IT MEANS

1 ***To bring out*** **a particular quality means to make it easier to see, taste, notice, etc.:**

▶ I'm sure this rug will bring out the beauty of the room.

= The room is beautiful, and I'm sure this rug will make it more obvious.

## 2 HOW IT WORKS

1 ***Bring out*** **takes an object (i.e., what you bring out). If the object is a noun, it usually goes at the end:**

☑ It will bring out the beauty of the room.

2 **If the object is a pronoun, it always goes in the middle:**

☑ It will bring it out.

☒ It will ~~bring out it~~.

## 3 HOW YOU USE IT IN REAL LIFE

1 *Bring out + the best/worst in*:

▶ Great leadership involves **bringing out the best in** your followers. (= helping them be the best they can be)

▶ Sometimes the anonymity of the Internet **brings out the worst in** people.

▶ I was in an abusive relationship for ten years, and, looking back, it's clear that we **brought out the worst in** each other.

▶ John and Gary are the perfect couple. They complement each other well and **bring out the best in** each other.

2 *Bring out* + **phrases with** *side*:

▶ You **bring out a side of** me that no one else has ever seen.

▶ The teaching assistant has an optimistic, friendly attitude that **brings out the finer side of** people.

▶ There's an old saying that alcohol tends to **bring out** someone's **real side**.

3 *Bring out* + *inner* **and** *hidden* + <u>noun</u>:

▶ Over the years, I've found that one of the benefits of working alone is that it **brings out** your **hidden** <u>talents</u>.

▶ On the next page, you'll find five more tips to **bring out** the **inner** <u>optimist</u> in you.

4 *Bring out* + **what you can perceive through the senses:**

▶ Here's a little tip for you: Adding a little black pepper helps **bring out** the underlying **flavor** [UK: flavour] of the meat.

▶ The photos look great because I added a sharpness filter and did a little extra work to **bring out** the **detail** in the picture.

▶ I would suggest wearing yellow at the ceremony. I think it will help **bring out** the **color** [UK: colour] of your eyes.

▶ Once a week, you should apply a conditioning mask to **bring out** the **beauty** of your skin.

## 4 RELATED MEANING

**When you bring out the truth or facts, you reveal them:**

▶ I consider myself very talented at **bringing out the truth** of what people actually believe in their heart of hearts.

▶ This study **brings out** very interesting **facts** that will definitely help businesses worldwide.

## 5 CONVERSATION TIP

**Imagine you are recommending someone to a leadership position. Here's what you can say:**

> **(Mia) has an uncanny ability to bring out the best in the people she works with.**

# 45 COME OUT (1)

## 1 WHAT IT MEANS

**When information comes out, it becomes known to people, especially after it has been kept hidden:**

▶ I'm sure the truth will come out eventually.

= I'm sure people will discover the truth sooner or later.

**Notice the connection to one of the basic physical meanings of *come out*, which is to appear in the sky. (e.g., *The sun came out.*)**

## 2 HOW IT WORKS

***Come out* takes no object. You simply say that something comes out:**

☑ The truth will come out.

☒ The truth ~~will come it out~~.

☒ ~~It will come out the truth~~.

## 3 HOW YOU USE IT IN REAL LIFE

1 ***Come out* tends to attract words describing hidden information:**

▶ Sooner or later, the **truth** will **come out** because it always does, no matter how hard we try to hide it.

▶ Angela's marriage was shaken to the core when her long-held **secret came out**: She'd had an affair with her husband's boss.

▶ How can we ask people not to panic as new **facts come out**, and it hits them that the situation is worse than they imagined?

▶ The general consensus is that the **leaks coming out** of government agencies are deeply troubling.

▶ This a summary of all the **revelations** that have **come out** so far from Bob Woodward's explosive book.

2 **Common expression – *come out into the open*:**

▶ Please be discreet. If the whole thing **comes out into the open** (= is revealed), I could lose my job and my wife.

## 4 RELATED MEANINGS

**When something comes out, it is released to the public:**

1 **Lists and rankings:**

▶ The Oscar **nominations came out** early this morning, and there weren't many surprises.

▶ The ABC News poll is similar to the Monmouth University **poll** that **came out** earlier this week.

2 **Official information:**

▶ An hour or so after the official **statement came out**, the mayor herself contradicted it in front of reporters at Nationals Park.

▶ The NBA is currently in talks with a major animation studio, and a big **announcement** is expected to **come out** later this week.

3 **Entertainment:**

▶ The **movie** [UK: film] doesn't even **come out** until November, but there is already a lot of buzz about the trailer.

▶ Guns N' Roses' groundbreaking **album**, *Appetite For Destruction,* **came out** 25 years ago this past Saturday.

▶ I thoroughly enjoyed the first part of this **book**, and I will definitely be interested in reading the next part when the **sequel comes out**.

## 5 CONVERSATION TIP

**Imagine you are asking a friend to be discreet about a secret. Here's what you can say:**

**This is between us, OK? If the truth comes out, I'm in trouble.**

# 46 GET ACROSS (TO)

## 1 WHAT IT MEANS

**When you get an idea across, you manage to make other people understand it:**

▶ He was so nervous he couldn't get his ideas across.

= He was nervous, so he had trouble making himself understood.

## 2 HOW IT WORKS

**1 *Get across* usually takes an object (i.e., what you get across). If the object is a noun, it tends to go in the middle:**

☑ He couldn't get his ideas across. (more common)

☑ He couldn't get across his ideas. (less common)

**2 If the object is a pronoun, it always goes in the middle:**

☑ He couldn't get them across.

☒ He couldn't ~~get across them~~.

**3 Use *to* if you want to mention the listener or reader:**

☑ He couldn't get his ideas across to the audience.

## 3 HOW YOU USE IT IN REAL LIFE

trying to get his ideas across

**1 *Get across* tends to attract words related to communicating messages:**

▶ When you write your draft, it's OK to cross out words and sentences so you can try different ways to **get** your **ideas across** to the reader.

▶ Writers sometimes shock their audiences to **get** their **point across**, but there are more effective strategies.

▶ If you create a new logo, keep in mind that some designs are better than others in terms of **getting** the **message across**.

▶ Her grammar was rusty, but she was fluent and **got** her **meaning across** well enough.

▶ **Getting** the **concept across** to the market was a primary challenge facing the new advertising company.

2 **Notice the use of pronouns to refer to something that was said before:**

▶ Everyone knows that studying math is important, but **getting that across** to children and teens can be complicated.

▶ B.B. King didn't just play the blues. He was the man who **got it across** to a mainstream audience.

▶ Customers like to feel valued by companies, and there is something about print marketing that **gets this across** really well.

## 4 MORE REAL-LIFE DATA

1 ***Get across*** **is sometimes followed by (noun +) a** ***that*** **clause:**

▶ At the meeting, the most important thing to **get across** is **that** the company is actually doing an amazing job.

▶ If you've done something wrong, offer an apology that **gets across the idea that** you're really sorry, and that you won't do it again.

2 ***Get across*** **can sometimes be followed by** ***what***, ***how***, **etc.:**

▶ Sometimes I can't quite **get across what** I want to say in words, so I try to express myself through my art.

▶ A picture is worth a thousand words, but this photo can't **get across how** amazing these freshly-baked baguettes really smell.

▶ An effective business plan should try to **get across why** you think your idea is a great opportunity.

## 5 CONVERSATION TIP

**Imagine you are discussing relationship problems with a close friend. Here's something you can say:**

**(I'm not a child anymore), but I can't seem to get it across to (my parents).**

# 47 LAY OUT

## 1 WHAT IT MEANS

1 **When you lay out ideas, plans, or principles, you describe or explain them clearly:**

▶ The document lays out the plans in plain English.

= The document explains what the plan is all about using simple English.

2 **After you finish this lesson, turn to page 247 for additional meanings of *lay out*.**

## 2 HOW IT WORKS

1 ***Lay out* takes an object (i.e., what you lay out). If the object is a noun, it tends to go at the end:**

☑ The document lays out the plans clearly. (more common)

☑ The document lays the plans out clearly. (less common)

2 **If the object is a pronoun, it always goes in the middle:**

☑ The document lays them out clearly.

☒ The document ~~lays out them~~ clearly.

3 ***Lay out* is often used in the passive voice:**

☑ The plans are laid out clearly in the document.

## 3 HOW YOU USE IT IN REAL LIFE

1 ***Lay out* + words related to facts, arguments, etc.:**

▶ If you've been harassed, first you should approach your manager, **lay out** the **facts**, and ask for help.

▶ In 1967, neuroscientist Eric Lenneberg **laid out** his **argument** for a "critical period" in second language acquisition.

▶ The **evidence laid out** in this report provides compelling reasons for the agency to formally pursue the matter.

▶ Congress has **laid out** the **rules** of the game, and we will have no choice but to play by these rules.

▶ By the late 1920s, physicists had **laid out** the mathematical **framework** for a new theory of quantum mechanics.
▶ The president has made it clear that the **principles** she **laid out** are non-negotiable.
▶ Manhattan prosecutors began **laying out** their **case** against Thomas Gilbert Jr. this week, presenting new details about the crime.

2 ***Lay out*** **+ words describing future scenarios:**
▶ Tom listened to Julia's ambitious **plans** as she **laid** them **out**.
▶ The president will address the nation tomorrow to **lay out** his new **strategy** for Afghanistan.
▶ Maybe Hillary lost because America didn't buy into the **vision** she'd **laid out**.
▶ In the study, the scientists **laid out** a **scenario** in which HIV patients could be given an injection every couple of months.
▶ The first section of the book **lays out** concrete **steps** for designing successful performance management systems.

## 4 MORE REAL-LIFE DATA

***Lay out*** **is often followed by phrases with** ***detail*****:**
▶ The article **laid out in detail** how a major earthquake could hit San Francisco within the next 50 years.
▶ This issue of Der Spiegel **lays out in some detail** the mechanics of Greece's exit from the euro.
▶ The book **lays out in great detail** an investment strategy that the author has found to be a success.

## 5 CONVERSATION TIP

**Imagine you are conducting a meeting. At one point, you hand out a document with further details. Here's what you can say:**

> **This document lays out (the strategy) in more detail.**

# 48 MAKE OUT

## 1 WHAT IT MEANS

**1 When you make something out, you manage with difficulty to see, hear, or understand it:**

▶ I heard some voices, but I couldn't make out the words.

= I heard some voices, but I couldn't understand what they were saying.

**2 *Make out* can refer to people, too:**

▶ I saw a shadow of a man, but I couldn't make out his face.

= I saw a shadow of a man, but I couldn't see his face clearly.

**3 After you finish this lesson, turn to page 248 for additional meanings of *make out*.**

## 2 HOW IT WORKS

**1 *Make out* takes an object (i.e., what you make out). If the object is a noun, it tends to go at the end:**

☑ I couldn't make out the words. (more common)

☑ I couldn't make the words out. (less common)

**2 If the object is a pronoun, it always goes in the middle:**

☑ I couldn't make them out.

☒ I couldn't ~~make out them~~.

**3 *Make out* can be followed by a *wh-* word, usually *what* and *who*:**

☑ I couldn't make out what they were saying.

## 3 HOW YOU USE IT IN REAL LIFE

**In the following examples, notice the frequent use of words describing ability:**

**1 *Make out* + things or people you are trying to see:**

▶ Wynona searched the hooded figures in the dim light, trying to **make out** their **faces** in the fading light.

▶ Jennifer could only **make out** Tom's **silhouette**, as he stood next to the window, bathed in sunlight.

▶ As I squinted through the lens of my camera, I could **make out** the **shape** of a large dark fish, perhaps six feet in length, almost shark-like.

▶ Yawning, I rubbed my eyes and tried to **make out** the **outline** of the closet across from my bed. "Am I going blind?" I thought.

▶ I saw a car speeding away, but I couldn't **make out who** was inside because I was blinded by the headlights.

**2 *Make out* + speech you are trying to hear or understand:**

▶ I heard the couple next door yelling at each other, but it was hard to **make out** the **words**.

▶ We couldn't see the people behind those lights, but we could **make out** their **voices**.

▶ We heard shouting outside, but we couldn't **make out what** was being **said**.

## 4 MORE REAL-LIFE DATA

***Make out* tends to attract words and expressions that mean *manage with difficulty*:**

▶ It was dark, but he **could vaguely make out** some of the shadows around him.

▶ Melinda had left her glasses at home, so she **could barely make out** the letters on the license [UK: licence] plate.

▶ It was so foggy we **could hardly make out** the Statue of Liberty from a distance.

▶ Lucy squinted, **straining her eyes to make out** the blurred yellow shape near the tree.

▶ On this album, Young's voice is auto-tuned and modulated in so many ways that **it is hard to make out** the lyrics.

## 5 CONVERSATION TIP

**Imagine you are taking a speaking exam. You are asked to describe some photographs, but the images are not very clear. Here's what you can say:**

**I can't make out exactly what this object is.**

# 49 SPELL OUT

## 1 WHAT IT MEANS

**When you spell something out, you explain it in a clear way:**

▶ The contract should spell out all the details of your agreement.

= The contract should clearly explain all the details of your agreement.

## 2 HOW IT WORKS

**1 *Spell out* takes an object (i.e., what you spell out). If the object is a noun, it usually goes at the end:**

☑ The contract should spell out the details.

**2 If the object is a pronoun, it always goes in the middle:**

☑ The contract should spell them out.

☒ The contract should ~~spell out them~~.

**3 *Spell out* can be followed by a *wh-* word (i.e., *what, why, how,* etc.):**

☑ The contract should spell out what is expected of you.

**4 *Spell out* can be used in the passive voice:**

☑ All the details should be spelled out.

## 3 HOW YOU USE IT IN REAL LIFE

**1 *Spell out* tends to attract words related to agreements, rules, and regulations. Notice the prepositions in bold, too:**

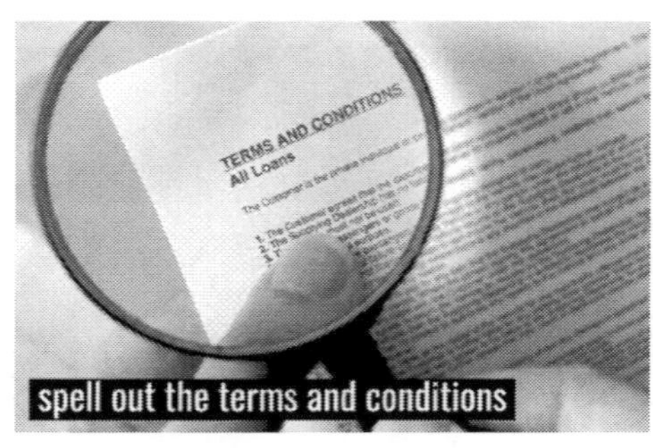

spell out the terms and conditions

▶ The written offer should **spell out** the **terms of** the job you're about to start, as well as your **obligations to** the company.

▶ The key to a productive bring-your-own-device workplace is to create policies that **spell out** the **conditions under** which employees can use their devices.

▶ We work under a written agreement that clearly **spells out** our **rights** and our **responsibilities as** employees.

▶ The documents released on Tuesday did not **spell out details of** the president's visit, other than the fact that it lasted almost five hours.

▶ California's plan for cutting greenhouse gas emissions **spelled out** over 30 new **rules for** refineries and factories.

**2 *Wh-* words are very common, too, especially *what* and *how*. Notice the use of the underlined adverbs, which *spell out* often attracts:**

▶ Some students prefer test rubrics that **spell out** exactly **how** they will be assessed, and teachers should take that into account.

▶ The department has a 12-page document that clearly **spells out what** officers should do in domestic violence situations.

▶ The site requires users to create a PIN for "another layer of security," without explicitly **spelling out why** this is necessary.

## 4 MORE REAL-LIFE DATA

***Spell out* often attracts phrases with *detail*:**

▶ Some people say that there are certain things that you shouldn't **spell out in detail** to a potential client before the deal is closed.

▶ The author's analysis is **spelled out in some detail**, and it makes the simplicity of her ideas even more obvious.

▶ When you delegate, try to avoid **spelling** things **out in great detail**. Otherwise, you'll be telling your employee how you yourself would do the job.

▶ This is a very depressing article to read on a Sunday morning because it **spells out in complete detail** the reality of the wars in the Middle East.

## 5 CONVERSATION TIP

**Imagine you are arguing with your spouse, who doesn't understand something obvious to you. Here's what you can say:**

**Do I have to spell it out for you?**

# CHECK YOUR PROGRESS 8

**A Read the mini-dialogues and choose the correct options.**

1 A: How's it going between you and Tom?
B: I think I'm in love. We [bring out / lay out] the best in each other.

2 A: I love this song.
B: It's from Jessie Ware's new album. It [came out / laid out] last week.

3 A: How do you like the new teacher?
B: Hmm. He talks too much, and it takes him hours to [get his point across / make his point out].

4 A: This is a long document!
B: Yes, it [lays out / makes out] in detail the procedures to be followed.

5 A: What were the neighbors [UK: neighbours] yelling about?
B: I don't know! I couldn't [make out / spell out] what they were saying.

6 A: Now that you've read the contract, do you think I should sign it?
B: I'm not sure. Shouldn't it [make out / spell out] the terms of the job more clearly?

7 A: I can't believe what they're saying about me on Twitter. It's all a pack of lies!
B: Don't let it get you down. Sooner or later, the truth will [come out / lay out].

8 A: So, what do you think? Should I wear white or yellow tonight?
B: I'd go for yellow. It [brings out / gets across] the green in your eyes.

**B Rewrite the sentences below using the pronouns *it* and *them*. Make certain the pronouns are in the correct position. The first one is done for you.**

1 It's good to know I can count on my friends.
It's good to know I can *count on them*.

2 Adding a bit of lemon to the recipe helps bring out the flavor [UK: flavour].
Adding a bit of lemon to the recipe helps ______.

3 When I speak in public, I have trouble getting my message across.
When I speak in public, I have trouble ______.

4 The report should lay out all the facts.
The report should ______.

5 It was dark, so I could hardly make out Ann's silhouette.
It was dark, so I could hardly ______.

6 The article clearly spells out all relevant details.
The article clearly ______.

**C EXTRA CHALLENGE! Rewrite the sentences without changing the meaning. Use the bold words to create phrasal verbs. The first two are done for you.**

1 Do you have any evidence proving that what you are saying is true?
**BACK**
Do you have any evidence *to back up your* claims?

2 The protesters are demanding that the mayor resign immediately.
**CALLING**
The protesters are *calling for the mayor's immediate* resignation.

3 My boss causes me to show my worst qualities.
**BRINGS**
My boss ________________________________ me.

4 Taylor's new album is expected to be released in June.
**COME**
Taylor's new album is ________________________________ until June.

5 Good writers can convey their ideas relatively effortlessly.
**GET**
Good writers can ________________________________ much effort.

6 The document should explain what you are responsible for.
**SPELL**
The document should ________________________________ responsibilities.

7 The principles I have described cannot be negotiated.
**LAID**
The principles ________________________________ non-negotiable.

8 I enjoyed the song, but I found it hard to understand what the singer was saying.
**MAKE**
I enjoyed the song, but I had trouble ________________________________ lyrics.

Answer key:

Exercise A
1 bring out
2 came out
3 get his point across
4 lays out
5 make out
6 spell out
7 come out
8 brings out

Exercise B
2 bring it out
3 getting it across
4 lay them out
5 make it out
6 spells them out

Exercise C
3 brings out the worst in
4 not expected to come out/expected not to come out
5 get their ideas across/get across their ideas without
6 spell out (all/all of) your
7 (that) I have laid out are
8 making out the

# 50 COME OUT (2)

## 1 WHAT IT MEANS

**1 To come out in a certain way at the end of a process or an event means to be a in particular state or position as a result of it:**

▶ It was a tough divorce, but he came out all right.

= It was a hard divorce, but, in the end, he was OK.

**2 After you finish this lesson,** **turn to page 248** **for additional meanings of *come out*.**

## 2 HOW IT WORKS

**1 *Come out* takes no object. You simply say that something comes out in a certain way:**

☑ He came out all right.

☒ He ~~came it out all right~~.

**2 You can say *come out of something*, too:**

☑ He came out of the divorce all right.

## 3 HOW YOU USE IT IN REAL LIFE

**1 *How* and *way* + *come out*:**

▶ A company's ability to reinvent itself during a major crisis can predict **how** it will **come out** of it.

▶ "The recording was a very interesting process, and I'm delighted with **the way** it's **come out**," the singer added.

**2 *Come out* + words related to overcoming obstacles and winning:**

▶ I just read an article called "Amazon vs. Walmart: The next decade will decide which **comes out on top**."

▶ In early 2007, the Nokia N95 was still outselling the iPhone, but before the year was over, the Apple phone **came out ahead**.

▶ If you persevere long enough, you will **come out victorious**. It's the struggle that builds your endurance, so don't lose faith.

▶ My sister and I were bullied all through high school [UK: secondary school], but, guess what, we survived and **came out stronger**.

▶ Let's not fool ourselves: There are very few media companies **coming out** of the economic crisis **unscathed**.

3 **Common expression – *come out swinging* (informal):**

▶ When the band reunited in the late '70s, it **came out swinging** (= rose above adversity and started something new in a strong way) and quickly ended up back on the Billboard charts.

## 4 RELATED MEANINGS

1 **When you come out, you openly declare your sexual orientation, gender identity, or something else about yourself that you used to keep hidden:**

▶ To this day, Joe still wonders why it took him so long to **come out (as** bisexual) **to** his family and friends.

▶ I am lucky to live in a very progressive city, where **coming out as** an atheist is not exactly shocking.

2 **To come out also means to publicly agree or disagree with something:**

▶ Brazil's President Jair Bolsonaro **came out in support of** the protest that defended military intervention.

▶ As many as seven lawmakers have **come out in favor of** [UK: favour] moving ahead with impeachment proceedings.

▶ Several business groups are **coming out against** the new bill.

## 5 CONVERSATION TIP

**Imagine you are telling a friend about a difficult phase you and your family lived through. Here's what you can say:**

**We went through a rough patch, but we came out stronger.**

# 51 END UP

## 1 WHAT IT MEANS

***To end up*** **means to reach a place, state, or situation that was not originally planned or expected:**

▶ If you keep on doing that, you'll end up in serious trouble.
= If you continue to do that, in the end, you'll get into serious trouble.

## 2 HOW IT WORKS

1 ***End up*** **takes no object, but it is usually followed by words or phrases that mean** ***in a certain way, state, or place*****. Never separate the verb (*****end*****) from the particle (*****up*****):**

☑ You'll end up in trouble.
☒ You'll ~~end in trouble up~~.

2 **If you use a verb after** ***end up*****, put it in the** ***-ing*** **form:**

☑ You'll end up getting into trouble.

3 **You can use different prepositions after** ***end up*****:**

☑ End up **with** a hangover, end up **like** your father, end up **as** president, end up **in** Paris

## 3 HOW YOU USE IT IN REAL LIFE

1 ***End up*** **tends to attract verbs more often than nouns and adjectives. Here are the most common ones:**

▶ No matter what Gaga says or does, she always **ends up getting** lots of attention.
▶ Whenever I fly, I **end up having** panic attacks, even if people try to calm my nerves.
▶ I thought the news was fake, but it **ended up being** true.

2 ***End up*** **+ words and phrases related to trouble:**

▶ A lot of people who had potentially damaging inside information **ended up dead** under mysterious circumstances.

- Borrowing money we don't have is a sure way to **end up** (going) **bankrupt**.
- If it weren't for my parents' generosity, I'm pretty sure I would have **ended up homeless**.
- There's a chance that the governor will **end up in jail** if the truth comes out.
- If someone had told me last year I would **end up in this mess** because of gambling, I wouldn't have believed them.

3 *End up* + **negative emotions:**

- When you always compare what you get to what you expected, you usually **end up** (feeling) **disappointed**.
- Try to fill your mind with positivity, or you'll just **end up** (getting) **frustrated** all the time.

4 *End up* + **health issues:**

- Mom says I'll **end up getting sick** if I go out in the cold.
- She was hurt quite badly and **ended up in the hospital** [UK: in hospital].
- The young boy **ended up in a coma** and nearly died because the doctor had misdiagnosed him.

5 *End up* + **phrases related to discarding things:**

- By recycling, you'll reduce the amount of waste that **ends up in landfills**.
- If you don't make your subject line interesting, your email will **end up in the trash**.

## 4 MORE REAL-LIFE DATA

**Notice the pattern *end up with someone (not) doing something*:**

- Haven't we all been in situations where someone else's poor planning **ends up with** them blam**ing** us for whatever went wrong?
- My boss and I had a big argument that **ended up with** me not gett**ing** promoted.

## 5 CONVERSATION TIP

**Imagine you are urging a close friend who is under a lot of stress to work less. Here's what you can say:**

**Listen, if you don't slow down, you'll end up having a heart attack.**

# 52 LIVE UP TO

## 1 WHAT IT MEANS

**When something or someone lives up to a particular expectation or promise, the thing or person is as good as what was expected or promised:**

▶ The play didn't live up to my expectations at all.

= The play wasn't as good as I expected it to be.

## 2 HOW IT WORKS

***Live up to*** **takes an object (i.e., what you live up to). The object always goes at the end, whether it is a noun or a pronoun, so never separate the verb (*live*) from the particles (*up, to*):**

☑ It didn't live up to my expectations.

☑ It didn't live up to them.

☒ It ~~didn't live up my expectations to~~.

☒ It ~~didn't live them up to~~.

## 3 HOW YOU USE IT IN REAL LIFE

**These are some of the most common word combinations with *live up to*:**

▶ Sadly, this country has taken a long time to **live up to** the **promise** of equality. (= turn the promise into reality)

▶ *The Avengers* is good – not "epic." And it doesn't come close to **living up to the hype**. (= being as good as people said it would be)

▶ The Animal Planet network featured an African parrot that certainly **lives up to** its **name** – Einstein.

▶ Good managers should try to ensure that their employees **live up to** their **potential**. There's so much talent that goes to waste these days.

▶ Canadians really do **live up to** their **reputation** for being friendly and helpful, so if you get into trouble, just ask for help.

▶ Good management is a matter of setting **standards** and encouraging your employees to **live up to** them.

▶ Too often we fail to **live up to** our **ideals**; we become too concerned about material things and seek only our own glory.

▶ It is all too easy for us to create unrealistic **expectations** that a romantic partner can never **live up to**.

## 4 MORE REAL-LIFE DATA

***Live up to*** **often attracts (phrases with) the verbs** ***fail, try, and hope*****, with** ***fail*** **being the most frequent:**

▶ We should not be surprised when comedians **fail to live up to** the impossibly high standards we set.

▶ I won't judge you for **failing to live up to** my private moral code.

▶ Education is another area in which the government has **failed miserably** in its effort to **live up to** its responsibilities.

▶ Jenkins eventually came to the realization [UK: realisation] that **trying to live up to** his grandfather's name was an exercise in futility.

▶ Everyone who knew Mary Ann loved her and **tried hard to live up to** her great example. She will be sadly missed.

▶ I've spent a lot of money on this iMac. I **hope it lives up** to the hype.

## 5 CONVERSATION TIP

**Imagine you are taking over from a very popular manager. When you introduce yourself to the team, here's what you can say:**

**(Diana) set the bar very high, and I hope I can live up to it.**

# 53 PAY OFF

## 1 WHAT IT MEANS

**1 When something you have invested time, money, or energy in pays off, the result is good:**

▶ Your hard work will pay off when you take the exam.

= You worked hard, so you will probably pass the exam.

**2 After you finish this lesson, turn to page 249 for additional meanings of *pay off*.**

## 2 HOW IT WORKS

**This particular meaning of *pay off* takes no object. You simply say that something pays off:**

☑ Your hard work will pay off.

☒ Your hard work will ~~pay it off~~.

☒ Your hard work will ~~be paid off~~.

## 3 HOW YOU USE IT IN REAL LIFE

**1 *Hard work* and other related words + *pay off*:**

▶ Working in a situation where **hard work** does not **pay off** tends to reduce ambition and, some people say, work ethic.

▶ It's still too early to say whether their marketing **efforts** are **paying off**, so I think we should wait and see.

▶ Albert knew that his **dedication** had **paid off** when he was offered a position with the agency after completing his internship.

**2 *Patience* and other related words + *pay off*:**

▶ If you keep the lines of communication open with your kids, your **patience** will **pay off** in the long run.

▶ Some couples believe that their **persistence** will eventually **pay off**, and that IVF will succeed despite the odds.

▶ **Perseverance** will always **pay off** for those who are willing to risk failure to make their dreams come true.

3 *Risk* **and other related words +** *pay off*:

▶ Listen to this critic: "The author's calculated **risk pays off** in an original and compelling story. Highly recommended."

▶ The start-up took a gamble by turning to crowdfunding to help it launch the product, and it's a **gamble** that's **paid off**.

▶ It will probably take a few more years for the **investment** to **pay off**, but I'm sure it will do so eventually.

▶ After a few rocky years, Apple's **strategy** of focusing on user experience started to **pay off**, and the rest is history.

▶ It was a risky **move**, and whether it will **pay off** remains to be seen.

## 4 MORE REAL-LIFE DATA

***Pay off*** **often attracts adverbs that mean** ***in the end*****:**

▶ It looks as if Microsoft's partnership with IBM is **finally paying off**.

▶ Mathew's hard work **eventually paid off**, and today he and his wife are living practically debt-free.

▶ Ideology aside, most pundits seem to agree that the Iraq War **ultimately didn't pay off** politically.

## 5 CONVERSATION TIP

**Imagine you are congratulating a friend who worked hard to get into one of the country's top universities. Here's what you can say:**

> **I'm so happy that your dedication has paid off in such a big way.**

# 54 TURN INTO

## 1 WHAT IT MEANS

***To turn into*** **means to change into something different:**

▶ Did you know that this sofa can turn into a bed?

= Did you know that this sofa can become a bed?

## 2 HOW IT WORKS

**1 *Turn into* can take one or two objects. If you use only one object, it always goes at the end, whether it is a noun or a pronoun:**

☑ The sofa turns into a bed.

☑ The sofa turns into it.

☒ The sofa ~~turns a bed into~~.

☒ The sofa ~~turns it into~~.

**2 If you use two objects, one always goes in the middle, and the other one always goes at the end:**

☑ You can turn the sofa (object 1) into a bed (object 2).

☑ You can turn it (object 1) into one (object 2).

**3 With two objects, you can use the passive voice, too:**

☑ The sofa can be turned into a bed.

## 3 HOW YOU USE IT IN REAL LIFE

**1 *Turn into* + phrases with *something*:**

▶ There are signs that can tell you if what you and your friend have is **turning into something else** – like love.

▶ Most critics agree that the second season has **turned into something** very different from the first one. (*something* + adjective)

▶ Sometimes a simple case of lower back pain can **turn into something** a lot more serious. (*something* + comparative)

2 ***Turn into* + words related to problems:**

▶ Has the American dream **turned into** a **nightmare**?

▶ What should have been a nice evening **turned into** a complete **mess**.

▶ I can't believe the way the press has **turned** this story **into** such a **media circus**.

▶ Their trip started off well, but it quickly **turned into** a **battle** of epic proportions.

▶ In a few years, my husband's hobby **turned into** an **obsession**, and that obsession turned into a mental **illness**.

3 ***Turn into* + scary creatures:**

▶ I still remember how my sister would pretend to **turn into** a **monster** and chase me all around the house.

▶ The scene where the geologist **turns into** an impossible-to-kill **zombie** was a low point in the trailer.

4 ***Turn into* + books, movies** [UK: films]**, etc.:**

▶ I heard a rumor [UK: rumour] that the musical *Wicked* is being **turned into** a **movie**.

▶ Lots of popular movies have been **turned into musicals** this year.

## 4 MORE REAL-LIFE DATA

***Turn into* often attracts the following time adverbs:**

▶ The tropical wave that developed on October 21 **quickly turned into** a storm and then a Category 1 hurricane.

▶ You think you're doing well, but then one problem **suddenly turns into** three, and the whole thing falls apart.

▶ No matter how hard you try not to, **eventually**, you **turn into** your parents. It just happens!

## 5 CONVERSATION TIP

**Imagine you have bought the car of your dreams, but it is giving you nothing but trouble. Here's what you can say:**

**I guess my dream has turned into a nightmare!**

# 55 TURN OUT

## 1 WHAT IT MEANS

**1 When something turns out a certain way, it develops in that way or is found to have that particular quality, often surprisingly:**

▶ Despite my worries, everything turned out well.

= Even though I was worried, everything was OK in the end.

**2 You can also use it to talk about people:**

▶ The woman who lives across the street turned out to be a distant cousin!

= I discovered that the woman who lives across the street is actually a distant cousin of mine, which came as a surprise.

**3 After you finish this lesson, turn to page 249 for additional meanings of *turn out*.**

## 2 HOW IT WORKS

**1 *Turn out* takes no object, and it is usually followed by an adjective (e.g., *good*) or an adverb (e.g., *well*). Never separate the verb (*turn*) from the particle (*out*):**

☑ Everything turned out well.

☒ Everything ~~turned well out~~.

**2 You can use a verb in the infinitive form after *turn out*, usually *be* and, less commonly, *have*:**

☑ She turned out to be a distant cousin.

**3 You can use a *that* clause after *turn out*:**

☑ It turns/turned out that she was a distant cousin.

## 3 HOW YOU USE IT IN REAL LIFE

**1 You can use *turn out* + verb and *turn out* + *that* in a lot of different ways:**

▶ Dua Lipa's sophomore album, against all odds, **turned out to be** a huge success.

▶ In some English-speaking countries, a "lemon" is a (usually new) vehicle that **turns out to have** several manufacturing defects.

▶ I was convinced I was right, but, guess what, **it turned out that** I was wrong.

2 ***Turn out to be* often attracts *true*, *false*, and other related words:**

▶ This is all so silly that it might actually **turn out to be true.**

▶ Sometimes opinions **turn out to be correct**; other times, they **turn out to be** completely **false**.

▶ The governor's claims **turned out to be unfounded**.

▶ History books are filled with "experts" making bold predictions, but some have **turned out to be** more **accurate** than others.

3 ***Turn out* + words that answer the question *how good/well*?**

▶ Most of the time I experiment with cooking, it **turns out OK**. Occasionally, it **turns out badly**.

▶ My mother smoked during my pregnancy. I **turned out fine**, but that doesn't justify what she did.

▶ **How** did things **turn out**? **Well**, I hope.

4 **Common expression – *as it turns out*:**

▶ They initially said the repairs would cost around $10,000, but, **as it turns out** (= in the end), the final bill will be half that amount.

## 4 MORE REAL-LIFE DATA

**Notice how the words in bold express how the speaker/writer felt about the way something turned out:**

▶ I was rushed to the hospital [UK: to hospital] for what I thought was appendicitis. **Thankfully, it turned out that** it was just severe stomach cramps.

▶ Unfortunately, or **fortunately as it turned out**, we missed the plane and didn't make it to the wedding after all.

▶ I was reluctant to hire my cousin, but, **luckily, it turned out that** he was, for the most part, OK.

## 5 CONVERSATION TIP

**Imagine you are telling a friend about someone who betrayed you. Here's what you can say:**

**What a backstabber (Bill) turned out to be!**

# CHECK YOUR PROGRESS 9

**A Complete the quotes with the most logical phrasal verb, using the words in the box.**

| come | end | live | pay | turn (x 2) | into | off | out (x 2) | up | up to |
|---|---|---|---|---|---|---|---|---|---|

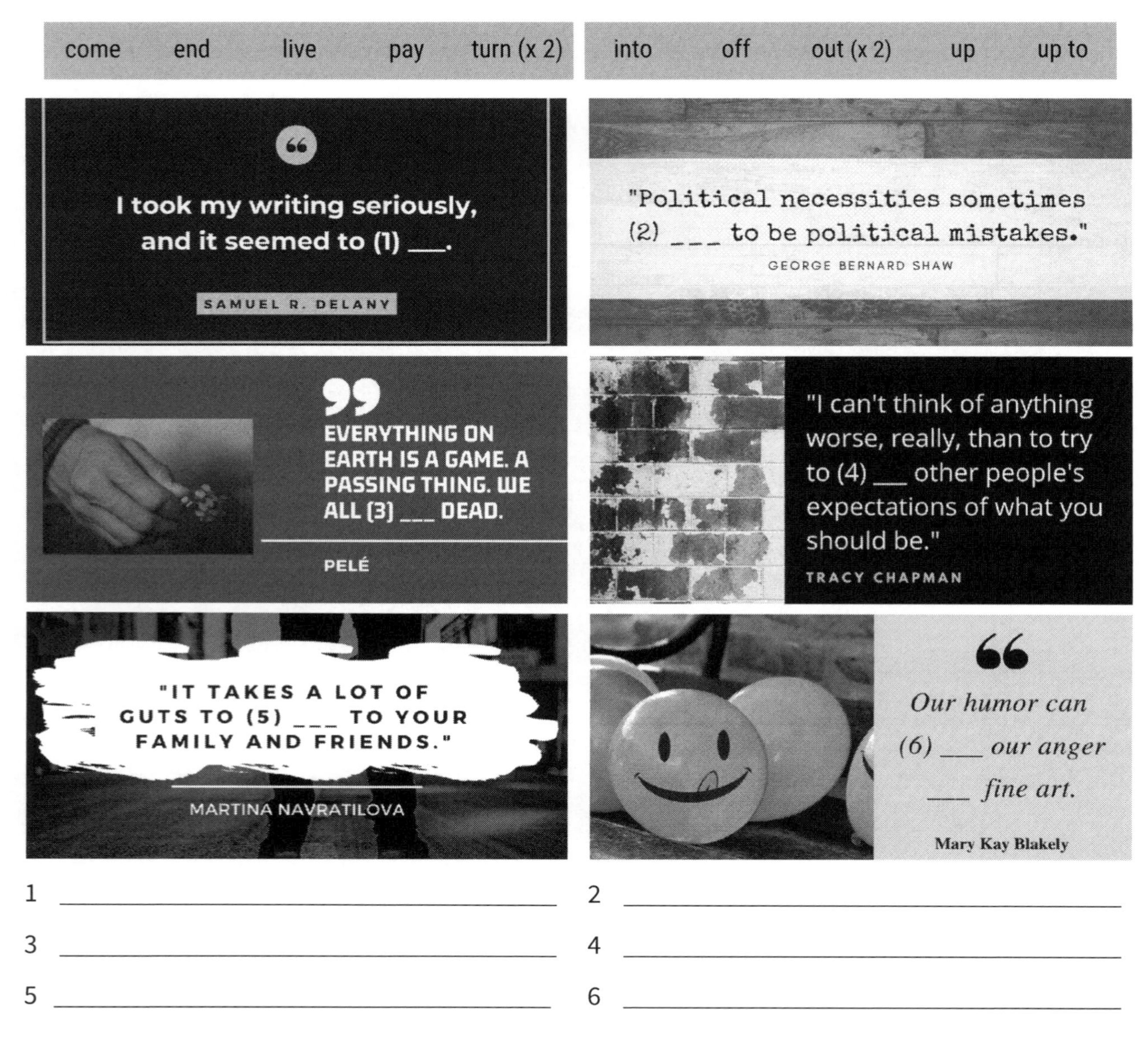

I took my writing seriously, and it seemed to (1) ___.
SAMUEL R. DELANY
"Political necessities sometimes (2) ___ to be political mistakes."
GEORGE BERNARD SHAW
EVERYTHING ON EARTH IS A GAME. A PASSING THING. WE ALL (3) ___ DEAD.
PELÉ
"I can't think of anything worse, really, than to try to (4) ___ other people's expectations of what you should be."
TRACY CHAPMAN
"IT TAKES A LOT OF GUTS TO (5) ___ TO YOUR FAMILY AND FRIENDS."
MARTINA NAVRATILOVA
Our humor can (6) ___ our anger ___ fine art.
Mary Kay Blakely


1 ____________________ 2 ____________________

3 ____________________ 4 ____________________

5 ____________________ 6 ____________________

**B Cross out the option that is illogical, unnatural, or ungrammatical.**

1 I didn't expect him to come out [against the proposal / as gay / atheist / victorious].
2 Tom keeps saying I will end up [in jail / get arrested / in the hospital / with a broken heart].
3 I failed to live up to my father's [example / ideals / high standards / money].
4 In the end, [my efforts / her strategy / the debt / their hard work] paid off.
5 A simple tweet turned into [a mess / a nightmare / complicated / something serious].
6 It turned out [badly / a few problems / that I was wrong / to be accurate].

**C EXTRA CHALLENGE! Read the mini-dialogues and choose the correct options.**

1 A: I think Smith should drop out of the race. Just look at the polls. He doesn't stand a chance!
B: I know! But he's convinced he [comes / will come] out on top next month.

2 A: Quick question: How can I prevent my emails from [end / ending] up in the spam folder?
B: Well, there's no magic formula, but emails that you reply to are rarely flagged as spam.

3 A: So, you're getting the new iPad?
B: Yeah. I hope it [lived / lives] up to the hype. I mean, a thousand dollars is a lot of money!

4 A: Martin looks amazing, doesn't he?
B: He really does. All those hours at the gym must have [paid / to pay] off.

5 A: This place has changed so much! Whatever happened to the park near the bus station?
B: It was [turned / turning] into a shopping mall [UK: shopping centre].

6 A: How did the interview go?
B: I thought I'd blown it, but, as it [turns / will turn] out, I got the job!

7 A: I'll never forgive myself for marrying Joseph. What was I thinking?
B: Well, sometimes good people [end / ends] up in bad relationships.

8 A: Your parents are amazing. I mean, they're so open-minded.
B: I know! Otherwise, I don't think I would [come / have come] out to them last year.

Answer key:

| Exercise A | Exercise B | Exercise C |
|---|---|---|
| 1 pay off | 1 atheist | 1 will come |
| 2 turn out | 2 get arrested | 2 ending |
| 3 end up | 3 money | 3 lives |
| 4 live up to | 4 the debt | 4 paid |
| 5 come out | 5 complicated | 5 turned |
| 6 turn/into | 6 a few problems | 6 turns |
| | | 7 end |
| | | 8 have come |

# 56 ALLOW FOR

## 1 WHAT IT MEANS

**When you allow for something, you take it into consideration when making plans, judgments, calculations, etc.:**

▶ Einstein's theory allows for the possibility of time travel.
= Einstein's theory considers time travel a real possibility and makes room for it.
▶ If you allow for inflation, I'm actually making less money now than I was five years ago.
= Considering the inflation of the past five years, I am earning less in relative terms.

## 2 HOW IT WORKS

***Allow for* takes an object (i.e., what you allow for). The object always goes at the end, whether it is a noun or a pronoun:**

☑ The theory allows for that possibility.
☑ The theory allows for it.
☒ The theory ~~allows that possibility for~~.
☒ The theory ~~allows it for~~.

## 3 HOW YOU USE IT IN REAL LIFE

**1 *Allow for* + words and phrases describing possibility:**

▶ The answer key at the back of the book must be comprehensive enough to **allow for** all **possible** responses to each question.

▶ Simply put, skepticism [UK: scepticism] is about always **allowing for the possibility that** you're wrong.

▶ Any passenger with an important reason to be somewhere should **allow for the possibility of** extreme delays, especially weather-related.

▶ The proposal **allowed for the possibility of** allocat**ing** emergency funds to cover hospital costs for the uninsured during the cholera outbreak.

▶ Leave for the airport early enough to **allow for potential** parking delays and long luggage check-ins.

▶ When planning a budget, always **allow for future** risks.

2 ***Allow for* + words and phrases describing change and variety. Notice the prepositions in bold, too:**

▶ Our cancellation policy has been made more flexible to **allow for** last-minute **changes in** your schedule.

▶ Keep in mind that every class is different, so following your lesson plan while **allowing for** some **variation** here and there is the way to go.

▶ When you buy new glasses, they may have to be adjusted to **allow for** small **differences in** the height of your ears.

▶ The present study is exploratory, **allowing for a range of** outcomes.

▶ The flexible furniture system **allows for a variety of** table arrangements to accommodate our customers' needs.

## 4 RELATED MEANINGS

***Allow for* also means to create the necessary conditions for something (to happen). The nouns and adjectives in bold are very common:**

1 ***Allow for* + noun:**

▶ Surgical robotics **allows for** the **use** of (= enables us to use) new instrumentation in our field.

▶ Our developmental period is longer than those of other animals, but this characteristic **allows for** the **development** of larger brains and speech, for example.

▶ The team of scientists will evaluate alternative research designs to **allow for** more **flexibility**.

2 ***Allow for* + adjective:**

▶ A flexible screen could **allow for** entirely **new** smartphone models.

▶ In the 1960s, the administration of New York City's public-school system was revamped to **allow for greater** community control.

▶ The open-endedness of the story **allows for multiple** interpretations.

## 5 CONVERSATION TIP

**Imagine a friend from a different city is worried about making it to the airport in time. Here's what you can say:**

**You should leave (an hour) early to allow for traffic.**

# 57 COUNT ON (2)

## 1 WHAT IT MEANS

**When you count on something, you expect to have it or accomplish it:**

▶ Robertson is counting on a victory in Ohio.

= Robertson expects to win in Ohio.

## 2 HOW IT WORKS

**1 *Count on* takes an object (i.e., what you count on). The object always goes at the end, whether it is a noun or a pronoun:**

☑ He's counting on a victory.

☑ He's counting on it.

☒ He's ~~counting a victory on~~.

☒ He's ~~counting it on~~.

**2 If you use a verb after *count on*, put it in the *-ing* form:**

☑ He's counting on winning in Ohio.

## 3 HOW YOU USE IT IN REAL LIFE

**1 You can use a wide range of nouns after *count on*. Here are some common words and phrases:**

▶ I couldn't afford to lose my job because my family was **counting on** the **money** I send home every single month.

▶ In a recent interview, the senator said he is not **counting on votes** from independents.

▶ Some gyms have a business model that **counts on the fact that** many people pay to join a gym and then stop going.

**2 Here are some common verbs that *count on* often attracts:**

▶ The biggest problem with mobile-payment apps is that you can't **count on being** able to use them.

▶ If you crash your car and try to sell it in the future, you can **count on getting** less money for it.

▶ When you talk to rescuers, they will tell you that, at this point, they're not **counting on finding** anyone alive.

▶ Marc had lost his phone and wasn't really **counting on** ever **having** it back, but someone found it and tracked him down.

▶ If you quit your day job to set up your own business, you can't really **count on making** the same amount of money you do now.

**3 Common expressions with *count on it*:**

▶ So, you think an MBA will help you find a good job? Well, **don't count on it**. (= You shouldn't necessarily expect that to happen.)

▶ Jennifer might show up later tonight, but, knowing her, **I wouldn't count on it**. (= That might not happen.)

▶ Do I think we're getting a bonus at the end of the month? Well, we've had a pretty good year, so **I'm counting on it**. (= I'm expecting that to happen.)

## 4 MORE REAL-LIFE DATA

**The pattern *count on <u>someone or something</u> <u>do</u>ing something* is very common:**

▶ Martin is a local who's been fishing in this area for years, so you can **count on** <u>him</u> <u>know</u>**ing** the best spots around. (= You can expect him to know the best spots.)

▶ If you're an indie author, you can't always **count on** <u>readers</u> find**ing** and <u>buy</u>**ing** your book in a big bookstore [UK: bookshop].

▶ Her three previous books were amazing, so I'm **counting on** <u>the next one</u> <u>be</u>**ing** just as good, if not better.

## 5 CONVERSATION TIP

**Imagine a friend is expecting some good news. You think this person is being too optimistic. Here's what you can say:**

**I wouldn't count on it if I were you.**

# 58 LIE AHEAD

## 1 WHAT IT MEANS

**When you say that something lies ahead, you think it will happen in the future:**

▶ How will we cope with the difficulties that lie ahead?

= How will we be able to deal with the difficulties that the future will bring?

## 2 HOW IT WORKS

1 ***Lie ahead*** **takes no object. You simply say that something lies ahead:**

☑ Many difficulties lie ahead.

☒ Many difficulties ~~lie them ahead~~.

2 **With this meaning,** ***lie*** **is an irregular verb. The example below is in the past:**

☑ She was able to cope with the difficulties that lay ahead.

☒ She was able to cope with the difficulties that ~~lied ahead~~.

## 3 HOW YOU USE IT IN REAL LIFE

**You can use a relatively wide range of nouns before** ***lie ahead,*** **but it tends to attract words describing future prospects:**

1 **Words expressing pessimism +** ***lie ahead*****:**

▶ "Can you give me a sense of what you think are the biggest **problems lying ahead**?" the reporter asked.

▶ The report suggests that **tough times** still **lie ahead** for the industry, with losses expected to double next year.

▶ With all these potential **dangers lying ahead**, it is essential to do as much as we can to bolster the resiliency of our economy.

▶ Despite all the **challenges** that still **lie ahead** of us, I see a thousand different reasons to be hopeful.

▶ If you had the opportunity to look into a crystal ball and see what health **risks lay ahead** for you, what would you do?

2 **Words expressing optimism +** ***lie ahead*****:**

▶ In last night's State of the Union Address, the president reminded us that the nation's **best days lie ahead**.

▶ If these figures are anything to go by, both surveys reveal a cautious optimism that brighter **opportunities lie ahead**.

▶ To give you a glimpse of all the **possibilities** that **lie ahead**, we've created a short video showing what the future of urban mobility might look like.

▶ No one knows what the future might hold, but I'd like to think that **good times lie ahead**.

▶ The article I'm writing is called "Nanotechnology in cancer detection and treatment: a **bright future** lies ahead."

## 4 MORE REAL-LIFE DATA

***Lie ahead*** **often attracts the words** ***what*** **(+ noun) and** ***whatever*** **(+ noun):**

▶ The book is a fascinating, eye-opening, and often shocking look at **what lies ahead** for Germany and the world at large.

▶ No matter **what future lies ahead** of you, remember to make it *your* future.

▶ These are tough times, but we need to save our strength for **whatever lies ahead**.

▶ "**Whatever challenges lie ahead**, we will settle for nothing less than getting this country back on track," said the president.

## 5 CONVERSATION TIP

**Imagine the team you manage is feeling demotivated. Here's what you can say to boost people's morale:**

**There are big challenges lying ahead, but, together, we will meet them.**

# 59 MOVE ON (TO)

## 1 WHAT IT MEANS

**1 When you move on, you finish what you started so you can to go on to a different place, subject, activity, etc.:**

▶ I like my job, but I feel it's time to move on (to a better one).

= I like my job, but I feel I should quit and look for a new one.

**2 You can use *move on* when referring to people, too, especially in romantic relationships:**

▶ Don is a great guy, but I feel it's time to move on (to someone new).

= Don is a great guy, but I feel I should leave him and find someone new.

## 2 HOW IT WORKS

**1 *Move on*, without *to*, takes no object (i.e., what or who you move on to). You simply say that someone moves on:**

☑ It's time to move on.

☒ It's time to ~~move on my life~~.

**2 *Move on to* is followed by an object. The object always goes at end, whether it is a noun or a pronoun, so never separate the verb (*move*) from the particles (*on, to*):**

☑ It's time to move on to something new.

☒ It's time to ~~move on something new to~~.

☑ It's time to move on to it.

☒ It's time to ~~move it on to~~.

## 3 HOW YOU USE IT IN REAL LIFE

**1 *Move on to* + *the next* + noun:**

▶ Before we **move on to the next step**, is there anything you'd like to add?

▶ This is how the game works: You get two shots. The winner **moves on to the next round**, and the loser is out.

▶ It looks as if Dolores and William have **moved on to the next phase** of their relationship.

▶ The thing about Apple is that it never just casually **moves on to the next thing**. It doesn't release new products without a clear strategy.
▶ We have limited time, so let's **move on to the next topic**.
▶ Damian has **moved on to the next chapter** in his life.

2 ***Move on to + another, other* + noun:**
▶ Congress needs to get past this issue and **move on to other** more important **matters**.
▶ Before we wrap things up, I'd like to **move on to another** important **issue**.

3 ***Move on to + something, someone/somebody + else*:**
▶ I'm thinking about **moving on to something else** – maybe teaching.
▶ If your wife can't get your attention, she might **move on to someone else** who will cherish her.

4 **Common expressions:**
▶ A breakup is tough, but, at some point, you have to **move on with your life** and get over it.
▶ "It's time for our country to **move on to bigger and better things**," the president said.
▶ Many scientists working for the government have **moved on to greener pastures** (= found better opportunities) in the private sector.

## 4 MORE REAL-LIFE DATA

***Move on* often attracts words and expressions related to time:**
▶ **Before** we can **move on**, we need to admit that we're part of the problem.
▶ After an uneventful start, the democratic debate **quickly moved on to** national security concerns.
▶ This is a city of renters, which attracts people who don't establish roots. They live here for a while and **eventually move on**.

## 5 CONVERSATION TIP

**Imagine you are holding a meeting. You want to make sure that everyone is heard. Here's what you can say:**

**Before we move on to the next item on the agenda, does anyone have anything else to say?**

# 60 SET OUT (TO)

## 1 WHAT IT MEANS

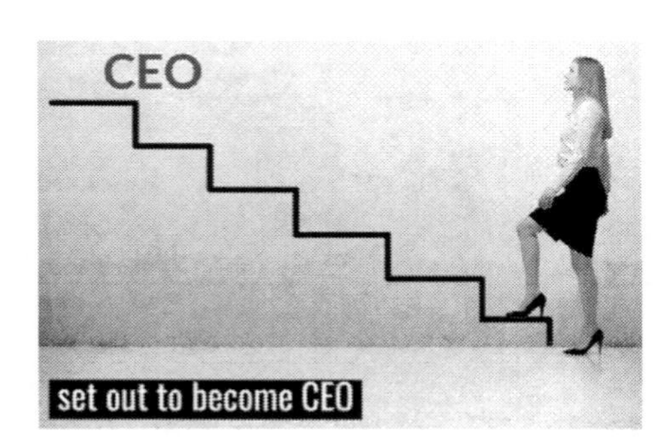

set out to become CEO

***To set out*** **means to start doing something or making plans to do something with a particular goal:**

▶ When Sue joined the company, she set out to become CEO.

= Sue's goal was to become CEO of the company, so, when she joined the company, she started working to make it happen.

## 2 HOW IT WORKS

**This meaning of *set out* takes no object. You simply say that someone sets out to do something:**

☑ She set out to become CEO.

☒ She ~~set it out~~ to become CEO.

☒ She ~~is set out~~ to become CEO.

## 3 HOW YOU USE IT IN REAL LIFE

**You can use *set out* with a wide range of verbs, especially those related to achievements and discoveries:**

1 ***Set out to*** **+ verbs related to achievements:**

▶ This president hasn't accomplished half of what he'd **set out to accomplish**.

▶ If the company **set out to create** a device that can serve both as a phone and a tablet, it's certainly achieved that with the new model.

▶ Here's my first question: In what ways is the book you wrote different from the book you **set out to write**?

▶ After much deliberation, the company **set out to build** a detachable cover that could be used as a keyboard.

2 ***Set out to* + verbs related to discoveries:**

▶ When Beale-Ellis discovered one of the students in her class had Asperger's, she **set out to discover** more about the condition.

▶ To help parents and students, *Money* magazine has once again **set out to find** great schools that are truly worth the investment.

▶ In this episode, Gregg Wallace **sets out to solve** a long-standing mystery: What happened to his great-grandfather?

## 4 MORE REAL-LIFE DATA

1 ***Set out to* is often used to describe the aim of a scientific study or an academic paper:**

▶ In the present study, we **set out to examine** the nature and the extent of semantic deficits in bilingual children.

▶ The researchers **set out to determine** whether an antiviral medication used to treat influenza could also be effective for COVID-19.

▶ This paper **sets out to establish** some of the key differences between ethics and morality in pre-Socratic Greece.

2 **When *set out* is followed by *on*, it means to try to achieve a particular goal:**

▶ When Tom lost his wife, he **set out on a journey** to figure out what he wanted to do with his life.

▶ With a background in graphic design, I **set out on a mission** to find a simple and inexpensive way to create our site.

▶ The plot centers [UK: centres] around a woman who **sets out on a path** of death and destruction to satisfy her craving.

## 5 CONVERSATION TIP

**Imagine you are presenting a project at a science fair. Here's how you can introduce it:**

**I set out to create a device that could (help people with dyslexia).**

# CHECK YOUR PROGRESS 10

**A Complete the horoscope excerpts with a verb and a particle.**

| allow | count | lie | move | set |
|---|---|---|---|---|

| ahead | for | on (x 2) | out |
|---|---|---|---|

| | |
|---|---|
| ARIES | Mars will stay in your sign throughout the month, bringing lots of courage and luck. With hard work and a little discipline, you'll be able to achieve virtually anything that you (1) ________________ to do. |
| LEO | The full moon on September 14 will bring lots of insight and inspiration. If you're struggling with a difficult problem, you can (2) ________________ finding an answer when you least expect it, thanks to this positive lunar force. |
| LIBRA | Mercury will be in full swing on September 12, which should help clear up some misunderstandings that have been bothering you lately. Rejoice, dear Libra, as this will give you renewed energy to (3) ________________ to a new chapter in your life. |
| CANCER | The past month has been tough, but the good news is that the sun finally enters your sign later this week. This will give you the strength to deal with all the challenges that (4) ________________ so you can face life's problems with a renewed sense of optimism. |
| PISCES | Saturn goes direct on September 22. This means that it's time to get serious about future goals and what you're going to do to reach them. But remember to be flexible and (5) ________________ last-minute changes to your plans. |

**B Complete the sentences with a suitable word.**

1 The book is about a businesswoman who quits her job and sets out __________ a mission of self-discovery as she travels the world.

2 Can I give you some advice? Stop wondering what might have been. It's time to move on __________ your life.

3 It's important to develop students' critical thinking skills so they can be prepared for __________ lies ahead.

4 Sarah said she'd pay you back by the end of the month, but I wouldn't count on __________. She's let me down before.

5 Our new multiple-choice test software allows for a range __________ possible question types and can include pictures.

6 My therapist said I should try to let go of the past so I can move on to bigger __________ better things.

7 Don't count on __________ able to access the Internet on campus during your presentation.

**C EXTRA CHALLENGE! Choose the correct options.**

1 ___ Ellen became CEO, she hasn't accomplished half of what she had set out to accomplish.

A Since

B When

2 Teenagers are fickle consumers, and once the novelty ___ off, they quickly move on to the next thing.

A wear

B has worn

3 ___ all the problems lying ahead, I'm sure that things will turn out all right in the end.

A Despite

B Although

4 I ___ my wallet and wasn't counting on ever getting it back, but someone found it and returned it to me.

A had lost

B have lost

5 Last week, Hill County declared a state of emergency, ___ allows for the possibility of state and federal funds.

A what

B which

Answer key:

| Exercise A | Exercise B | Exercise C |
|---|---|---|
| 1 set out | 1 on | 1 A |
| 2 count on | 2 with | 2 B |
| 3 move on | 3 what/whatever | 3 A |
| 4 lie ahead | 4 it | 4 A |
| 5 allow for | 5 of | 5 B |
| | 6 and | |
| | 7 being | |

# 61 BRING IN (2)

## 1 WHAT IT MEANS

***Bring in* means to make a certain amount of money or produce a certain amount of profit:**

▶ Her freelance work brings in about $30,000 a year.

= As a freelancer, she earns about $30,000 a year.

## 2 HOW IT WORKS

**1 *Bring in* takes an object (i.e., what you bring in). If the object is a noun, it usually goes at the end:**

☑ She brings in $30,000 a year.

**2 If the object is a pronoun (rare in this case), it always goes in the middle:**

☑ She brings it in.

☒ She ~~brings in it.~~

## 3 HOW YOU USE IT IN REAL LIFE

**1 This meaning of *bring in* tends to attract words related to money. In some of the sentences, notice the underlined adjectives, which are relatively common:**

▶ We know from the governor's tax filings in 2018 that he **brought in** $60,000 **dollars** more than he spent.

▶ The new product lines are expected to **bring in** an additional $150 **million** this year, which no one could have anticipated.

▶ The new antidiabetic drug has **brought** in **billions** of dollars for its manufacturer, but it is reported to cause a number of life-threatening side effects.

▶ If you're looking for some ideas to **bring in** a little extra **cash** at the end of the month, I have some tips for you.

▶ Developing a good eCommerce website that **brings in revenue** involves knowing what your buyers want and how they think.

▶ I wasted a lot of time writing this novel, time that I could have spent **bringing in** actual **income** to keep this roof over my head.

▶ While it is true that some people can go broke advertising online, there are also lots of ways to **bring in** <u>huge</u> **profits** with cheap online ads.

2 **Common expression – *bring in the (big) money*:**

▶ In this day and age, it is touring, not streaming, that **brings in the big money** (= enables you to make a lot of money) if you're a musician.

## 4 RELATED MEANINGS

***Bring in* also means to attract people to a business, media outlet, or event:**

bring in viewers

▶ I'm in the process of re-uploading my YouTube videos in HD so I can **bring in** more and more **viewers**.

▶ In the interview, instead of saying "I **brought in** new **clients** and increased revenue," say exactly how much you increased the revenue by.

▶ We're lucky enough to live in a small town, so an ad in the local paper **brings in customers** like crazy.

▶ The battle to **bring in** new TV **audiences** and retain them is becoming harder and harder to fight.

▶ Last night's football game **brought in** higher-than-average **ratings** for FOX and NBC.

▶ In the late 1990s, Elton John and Billy Joel appeared together in a series of "Face to Face" tours that **brought in** huge **crowds**.

## 5 CONVERSATION TIP

**Imagine you want to move to a different city but worry about the cost of living. Here's what you can ask a close friend who lives there:**

> **"I bring in about $(6,000) net each month. Is that enough for (San Diego)?**

# 62 CUT BACK ON

## 1 WHAT IT MEANS

**When you cut back on something such as the amount of money you spend or the amount of food you eat, you reduce it:**

▶ We're doing our best to cut back on non-essential spending.

= We are trying hard to spend less on things we don't really need.

## 2 HOW IT WORKS

***Cut back on*** **takes an object (i.e., what you cut back on). The object always goes at end, whether it is a noun or a pronoun, so never separate the verb (*****cut*****) from the particles (*****back, on*****):**

☑ We're trying to cut back on spending.

☑ We're trying to cut back on it.

☒ We're trying to ~~cut back spending on~~.

☒ We're trying to ~~cut it back on~~.

## 3 HOW YOU USE IT IN REAL LIFE

cut back on expenses

1 ***Cut back on*** **+ words describing how money is spent:**

▶ Women and those under 33 were most likely to **cut back on expenses**, the survey revealed.

▶ With this economy, we might have to **cut back on** some of the **services** that we're currently providing.

▶ Is it true that the governor is planning to **cut back on** entitlement **programs** [UK: programmes]?

▶ With the global economy in shambles, major studios have been **cutting back on spending**, which is why the sequel was put on hold.

▶ Knowing how much you are spending, and on which items, can help you find ways to **cut back on non-essentials** and save for a rainy day.

2 *Cut back on* + **words related to health and fitness:**

▶ Approximately 30% of millennials say they're **cutting back on alcohol**, *Business Insider* reports.

▶ When people **cut back on fat**, they often switch to foods full of carbs, which can be just as harmful.

▶ To **cut back on sugar** and **calories**, I use Splenda rather than sugar.

3 *Cut back on* + *use* **(noun):**

▶ Minnesota officials have urged residents to **cut back on** their water **use**.

▶ If everyone **cuts back on the use of** plastic bags, we can reduce the number given out by almost 70 million a year.

4 *Cut back on* + *amount* **and** *number*:

▶ Facebook has **cut back on the amount of** news in its algorithm. (*amount of* + uncountable nouns)

▶ Cable networks have been **cutting back on the number of** commercials they run per hour. (*number of* + countable nouns)

## 4 MORE REAL-LIFE DATA

***Cut back on* often attracts expressions describing necessity:**

▶ We **need to cut back on** advertising expenses. What are our options?

▶ Many people lost their jobs and **had to cut back on** basics like food and clothing.

▶ Recent heart trouble has **forced** him **to cut back on** his work schedule.

▶ The recession has left families with **no choice but to cut back on** essentials.

## 5 CONVERSATION TIP

**Imagine you have lost some weight, and a friend asks if you are on a diet. Here's what you can say:**

**It's not really a diet, but I've been trying to cut back on (carbs).**

# 63 MAKE UP (1)

## 1 WHAT IT MEANS

***Make up* has several different meanings. One of the most common is to constitute:**

▶ In this company, women make up nearly half of the workforce.

= In this company, almost half of the workers are women.

## 2 HOW IT WORKS

**1 *Make up* takes an object. The object (usually a word expressing quantity) always goes at the end:**

☑ Women make up half of the workforce.

☒ Women ~~make half of the workforce up~~.

**2 Add *of* to use *make up* in the passive voice:**

☑ Half of the workforce is made up of women.

## 3 HOW YOU USE IT IN REAL LIFE

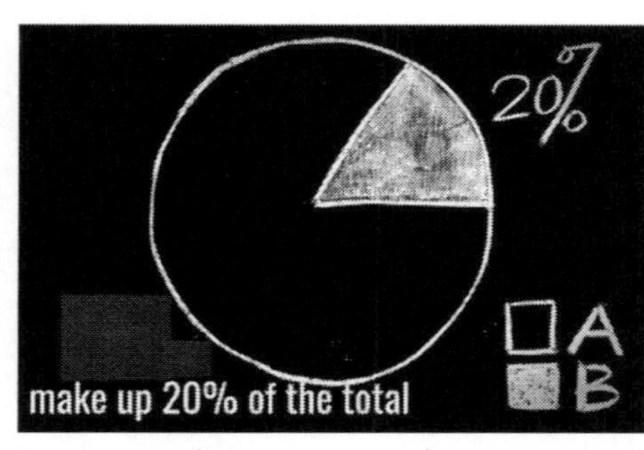


***Make up* usually attracts words and phrases expressing quantity. In some of the sentences, notice the underlined adjectives, which are also common:**

▶ Hispanics, mostly of Mexican origin, **make up** about 20 **percent of** the state's population.

▶ Police officers **make up** only **a** small **fraction of** the nation's estimated 20 million government employees.

▶ According to a study commissioned by the United Nations, African children will **make up half of** the world's poor by 2030.

▶ Women **make up the majority of** the U.S. population, but, in many respects, we're still treated like second-class citizens.

▶ It should be abundantly clear by now that extremists **make up a** tiny **portion of** the world's 1.3 billion Muslims.

▶ Homeless people **make up a** significant **proportion of** participants in the Occupy Movement in cities across the United States.

▶ The Kunming lake covers an area of over 200 hectares, **making up three-quarters of** the whole garden.

▶ Our print ad revenue, which is shrinking day by day, still **makes up the bulk of** the overall revenue.

▶ African American and Hispanic voters **make up a** larger **percentage of** the electorate in Illinois than they do nationally.

▶ The business has been around for about a year and already **makes up a** big **chunk of** my income.

## 4 MORE REAL-LIFE DATA

***Make up*** **often attracts the adverbs in bold below. Notice that** ***mostly*** **and** ***entirely*** **usually appear in passive sentences:**

▶ Rural areas **make up nearly** 97% of the total U.S. land.

▶ Over the past decade, African Americans have **made up approximately** 40 percent of HIV diagnoses.

▶ A lot will be revealed right after the polls close because early voters **make up roughly** two-thirds of the state's voters.

▶ Her heartfelt performance before a crowd **made up mostly of** baby boomers served as a fitting finale to the two-week festival.

▶ The documentary is **made up entirely of** rare BBC archive interviews and performances.

## 5 CONVERSATION TIP

**Imagine you are giving a business presentation. Here's how you can describe your target customers:**

**(Senior citizens) make up about (half) of our customer base.**

# 64 NARROW DOWN

## 1 WHAT IT MEANS

***To narrow down* means to reduce the number of possibilities or choices:**

▶ We've decided to narrow down the initial list to three candidates.

= We have deleted some names from the initial list, and now there are only three candidates left.

## 2 HOW IT WORKS

**1 *Narrow down* takes an object (i.e., what you narrow down). If the object is a noun, it can go at the end or in the middle:**

☑ We've narrowed down the list.

☑ We've narrowed the list down.

**2 If the object is a pronoun, it always goes in the middle:**

☑ We've narrowed it down. ☒ We've ~~narrowed down it~~.

**3 *Narrow down* can be used in the passive voice. In this case, it is often followed by *to*:**

☑ The list was narrowed down to three names.

## 3 HOW YOU USE IT IN REAL LIFE

**1 *Narrow it down to* is the most common phrase with the verb *narrow down*. *To* is often followed by a number:**

▶ With so many islands to choose from in the Caribbean, it's hard to **narrow it down to** just **two**.

▶ I've tried lots of methods and have **narrowed it down to** the **two** I find most effective.

**2 *Narrow down* + words indicating choice:**

▶ If you have a preferred airline, it will be easier to **narrow down** your **choices** for the best flight option.

▶ It is critical that you take the time to **narrow down** the **options** before actually assessing each one.

▶ After **narrowing down** my **selection** to 20 photos, I printed them out.

3 *Narrow down* + **adjectives and nouns indicating possibility:**

▶ Your doctor will help you **narrow down** the **possible** causes of your erectile dysfunction so that you choose the right treatment.

▶ The cause of the incident has been **narrowed down to** several **possibilities**.

▶ I haven't started my dissertation yet. I'm currently in the process of **narrowing down potential** topics.

▶ With a project feasibility study, you can **narrow down** the **scope** of the business problem under consideration.

4 *Narrow down* + **words related to online searches:**

▶ While using the app, you can **narrow down** your **search** based on your current location.

▶ Once your search is complete, you can **narrow down** your **results** by city or area.

## 4 MORE REAL-LIFE DATA

***Narrow down*** **often attracts the verb** ***help*****:**

▶ We have divided our list into different categories, which should **help you** quickly **narrow down** your search.

▶ Over 1,000 French vineyards are open to the public, but our experts have **helped narrow down** the list to three top choices.

## 5 CONVERSATION TIP

**Imagine a friend asks you about your all-time favorite** [UK: favourite] **song. Here's what you can say:**

**I think if I had to narrow it down to just one song, it'd be ("Imagine").**

# 65 SET ASIDE

## 1 WHAT IT MEANS

**When you set something aside, you save it and keep it available for a particular purpose:**

▶ Every month, I try to set aside some money for emergencies.

= Every month, I try to save some money in case there is an emergency.

## 2 HOW IT WORKS

1 ***Set aside*** **takes an object (i.e., what you set aside). If the object is a noun, it tends to go at the end:**

☑ I try to set aside some money. (more common)

☑ I try to set some money aside. (less common)

2 **If the object is a pronoun, it always goes in the middle:**

☑ I try to set it aside.

☒ I try to ~~set aside it~~.

3 ***Set aside*** **can be used in the passive voice:**

☑ How much money was set aside for emergencies?

## 3 HOW YOU USE IT IN REAL LIFE

1 ***Set aside*** **+** ***money*** **and other related words:**

set aside some money

▶ Some finance experts suggest that vacation [UK: holiday] **money** should be **set aside** in a separate savings account.

▶ The U.S. has **set aside** over 10 billion **dollars** to rebuild the country's infrastructure.

▶ What is the best way to **set aside funds** for future college tuition costs?

▶ We strongly recommend **setting aside resources** to meet your spending needs for at least six months, just in case you have unexpected expenses.

2 ***Set aside** + **time*** **and other related words:**

▶ I work two jobs, so when someone suggests I **set aside** some **time** for myself, I always wonder exactly how I'm supposed to do that.

▶ The school I work for **sets aside** 90 **minutes** each week for teachers to talk about best practices and professional development.

▶ Two **days** were **set aside** for the meeting, and every participant was given a generous time slot to present their findings.

3 ***Set aside** + **space*** **and other related words:**

▶ The report recommends the university **set aside** enough **space** to accommodate at least 30 research groups.

▶ The state legislature has **set aside** nearly 700,000 **acres** of **land** that are required to be kept wild forever.

▶ National reserves are **areas set aside** for conservation purposes.

## 4 RELATED MEANING

***Set aside*** **also means not to be influenced by something (often a different point of view) because other things are more important:**

▶ I suppose it would be in our mutual interest to **set aside** our **differences** (= forget about our disagreements), don't you think?

▶ In a meeting like this, how do we **set aside** our **biases** and **assumptions** (= suspend judgment) to make sure we're listening to all sides with an open mind?

## 5 CONVERSATION TIP

**Imagine you are encouraging a friend to start saving money. Here's what you can say:**

> **Have you considered setting aside some money each month for (emergencies)?**

# 66 TAKE UP (1)

## 1 WHAT IT MEANS

**To take up a certain amount of space or time means to fill it completely:**

▶ These files take up far too much disk space.

= These files are too large, and they use more disk space than desirable.

## 2 HOW IT WORKS

1 ***Take up* takes an object (i.e., the space/time someone or something takes up). If the object is a noun, it usually goes at the end:**

☑ They take up too much space.

2 **If the object is a pronoun (rare with this meaning of *take up*), it always goes in the middle:**

☑ They take it up.

☒ They ~~take up it~~.

3 ***Take up* can be used in the passive voice:**

☑ Too much disk space is taken up by temporary files.

## 3 HOW YOU USE IT IN REAL LIFE

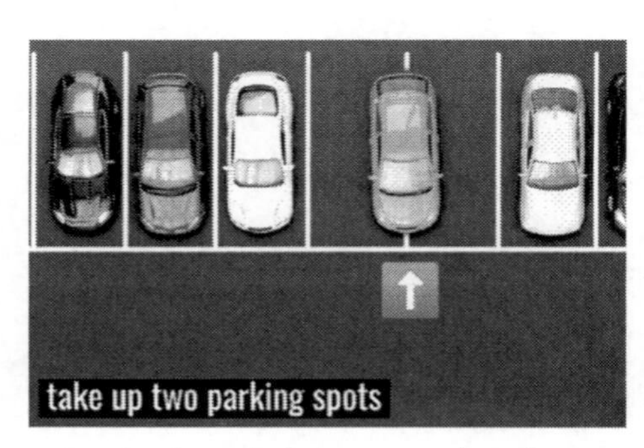


***Take up* tends to attract words related to space (literal or figurative) and time:**

▶ Sue's car is always parked across the street from her house, **taking up** two parking **spots**.

▶ E-books are the way to go. They don't **take up** any **room** in a warehouse and don't cost anything to ship.

▶ The strange thing about this detective story is that the actual crime **takes up** only a few **pages** of the book.

▶ Climate change **took up** a large **portion** of the president's speech today.

▶ Social media addiction **takes up hours** of our time, as we mindlessly stroll through our feeds day after day.

▶ Junk food **takes up** a large **chunk** of most people's monthly budget, so eating healthily is one of the easiest ways to cut costs.
▶ This year, women candidates will **take up** 77 **slots** on the legislative ballot, an all-time record we should be proud of.
▶ Question: Why is Google Chrome **taking up** so much **memory** in a MacBook Pro running on Monterey? Big Sur seemed to be more memory-efficient.
▶ The good thing about Dropbox is that your files don't **take up** disk **space** on your phone until you download them.

## 4 MORE REAL-LIFE DATA

***Take up* is often used with the adjectives in bold below:**
▶ The house was so big it **took up** the **entire** block, with its main entrance located on one of the corners.
▶ Our bedroom is so small that a queen-size bed practically **takes up** the **whole** room.
▶ Food mixers are really bulky and heavy, and they **take up precious** counter space.
▶ Law enforcement agencies have reported that false alarms from security alarm systems are **taking up valuable** police time.

## 5 CONVERSATION TIP

**Imagine you need to speak to someone who is very busy. Here's what you can say:**

**I know how busy you are, so I don't want to take up too much of your time.**

# CHECK YOUR PROGRESS 11

**A Complete the sentences with a verb. The phrasal verb should mean the same as the word in parentheses. Refer back to phrasal verbs 61–66, if necessary.**

1 King-size beds ______________ up (= fill) a lot of space.
2 I know I should ______________ aside (= save) some money every month.
3 Click here to ______________ down (= reduce the scope of) your search.
4 Women ______________ up (= constitute) nearly half of the population.
5 You should try to ______________ back on (= reduce) spending.
6 The new vaccine is expected to ______________ in (= make) huge profits.

**B Read the three possible ways to continue each sentence. Fill in the blanks with the words in the box.**

| bulk | cash | customers | expenses | fraction | sugar |
|---|---|---|---|---|---|

| | |
|---|---|
| What's the best way to bring in | • some extra (1) ______________ to pay the bills?<br>• younger viewers to my channel?<br>• new (2) ______________ and keep the existing ones? |
| Print books currently make up | • the (3) ______________ of our revenue.<br>• a significant chunk of our catalog [UK: catalogue].<br>• a small (4) ______________ of our sales. |
| I'm doing my best to cut back on | • excess (5) ______________ in my diet.<br>• the amount of time I spend online.<br>• my monthly (6) ______________. |

| biases | causes | chunk | funds | selection | space |
|---|---|---|---|---|---|

| | |
|---|---|
| A specialist will help you narrow down | • your initial (7) ______________ of stocks.<br>• your choices to two or three.<br>• the possible (8) ______________ of the pain. |
| People tell me I should set aside | • (9) ______________ for my kids' college tuition.<br>• some time for myself.<br>• my (10) ______________ and keep an open mind. |
| These documents take up | • too much disk (11) ______________.<br>• the whole shelf.<br>• a big (12) ______________ of my hard drive. |

**C Some of the sentences below have an extra word that is grammatically wrong. Cross it out.**

1 He brings it in about $40,000 a year.
2 The company will have no choice but to cut it back on a few services.
3 More than half of the faculty is made up of female teachers.
4 The list was narrowed it down to just a few items.
5 Three days were set aside for meetings and workshops.
6 As kids get older, much of their free time is taken it up with homework.
7 We only had an afternoon available, so we set it aside to discuss the most pressing issues.

**D EXTRA CHALLENGE! Choose the correct options.**

1 My freelance work [bring / brings] in about $25,000 a year.
2 Taylor Swift's tours usually [bring / brings] in huge crowds.
3 When people [cut / cuts] back on carbs, they often feel weak.
4 A sprinkler system [cut / cuts] back on the use of water by watering plants more effectively.
5 Thousands of sea turtles can be saved if everyone [cut / cuts] back on the use of plastic bags.
6 The initial list of candidates [have / has] been narrowed down to two names.
7 The cause of the train crash [were / was] narrowed down to three main possibilities.
8 The United States [have / has] set aside billions of dollars for infrastructure projects.
9 These files [take / takes] up far too much disk space.
10 Homework correction often [take / takes] up valuable class time.
11 In the mining industry, men [make / makes] up roughly 85% of the workforce.
12 The documentary about the impact of social media on our lives [are / is] made up mostly of interviews.

Answer key:

Exercise A
1 take
2 set
3 narrow
4 make
5 cut
6 bring

Exercise B
1 cash
2 customers
3 bulk
4 fraction
5 sugar
6 expenses
7 selection
8 causes
9 funds
10 biases
11 space
12 chunk

Exercise C
Sentences 1, 2, 4, and 6 have an extra word: *it*.

Exercise D
1 brings
2 bring
3 cut
4 cuts
5 cuts
6 has
7 was
8 has
9 take
10 takes
11 make
12 is

# 67 BACK OUT (OF)

## 1 WHAT IT MEANS

**When you back out of something you had agreed to do, you change your mind and refuse to do it:**

▶ I can't believe they backed out of the deal at the last minute.

= I'm surprised they initially agreed to the deal and then suddenly said no.

## 2 HOW IT WORKS

1 ***Back out of* takes an object (i.e., what you back out of). The object always goes at the end, whether it is a noun or a pronoun, so never separate the verb (*back*) from the particles (*out, of*):**

☑ They backed out of the deal.

☑ They backed out of it.

☒ They ~~backed out the deal of~~.

☒ They ~~backed it out of~~.

2 **If the sentence provides enough context, you can use *back out* without an object:**

☑ It was a good deal, but they backed out.

## 3 HOW YOU USE IT IN REAL LIFE

1 ***Back out of* + phrases with *deal*:**

▶ The contract has a clause that might give you a chance to **back out of** the **deal** if you're having second thoughts.

▶ It is crucial to contact a lawyer before attempting to **back out of** a **real estate deal**, or the process may become even more complicated.

▶ Actress Pamela Anderson Lee was sued for **backing out of** a **movie deal** because of her reluctance to do sex scenes.

▶ No one in their right mind would say no to a six-figure **book deal**, so I have no idea why he decided to **back out**.

2 *Back out of* + **other words describing formal arrangements:**

▶ The purchase agreement lists all the conditions under which the buyer or seller can legally **back out of** the **agreement**.

▶ A week before the opening night, the leading actor **backed out of** the **contract**, and the understudy had to take over.

▶ It's important to have a backup plan in case your supplier can't deliver on time or simply **backs out of** the **project**.

▶ After **backing out of** the **race**, candidate Bernie Sanders decided to endorse Joe Biden for the presidency.

▶ Our negotiation ended well, and though I thought he might **back out of** his **commitments** entirely, he just made a few reasonable demands.

## 4 RELATED MEANING

**When a vehicle backs out (of a place), it is made to go backwards. Notice the phrases with *into*:**

▶ A woman **backed out of** a **parking lot** right into my wife's car and cracked the back bumper. Thank goodness we're fully insured.

▶ The bus **backed out** into the lane, and Kelly watched the terminal slowly disappear.

▶ She **backed (the car) out of** the **garage** into the street.

## 5 CONVERSATION TIP

**Imagine you signed a lease to rent a house, but now you are having second thoughts. Here's what you can ask your lawyer:**

**Can they sue me if I back out of the deal?**

# 68 SETTLE FOR

## 1 WHAT IT MEANS

**When you settle for something, you accept it even though it is not the best option or exactly what you wanted:**

▶ With this economy, I'll have to settle for a low-paying job.

= The economy is bad, so I have no choice but to take a job that doesn't pay well.

## 2 HOW IT WORKS

1 ***Settle for*** **takes an object (i.e., what you settle for). The object always goes at the end, whether it is a noun or a pronoun:**

☑ I'll settle for a low-paying job.

☑ I'll settle for it.

☒ I'll ~~settle a low-paying job for~~.

☒ I'll ~~settle it for~~.

2 **If you use a verb after *settle for,* put it in the *-ing* form:**

☑ I'll settle for having a low-paying job.

## 3 HOW YOU USE IT IN REAL LIFE

**You can use *settle for* with a lot of different words. The following word combinations are especially common:**

1 ***Settle for*** **+ phrases with *less*:**

▶ Sometimes I wonder if, as the years go by, I'm learning to **settle for less.**

▶ I refuse to **settle for less than** the life I know I'm supposed to have.

▶ More and more job seekers won't **settle for anything less than** manager status.

2 *Settle for* **+ phrases with** ***second*****:**

▶ "Michele Obama was a remarkable first lady, who never **settled for second place**," the senator said.

▶ A new study has found that seven out of ten people feel they **settled for second best** when it comes to their partner.

▶ I wanted to study law, but my grades weren't good enough, so I **settled for** my **second choice**: dramatic arts.

3 ***Settle for* + *inferior* and other related words:**

▶ Don't **settle for** an **inferior** product. Test our award-winning security door systems today.

▶ Consumers shouldn't have to **settle for lesser** quality for the sake of price.

▶ Brenda has **settled for mere** existence, wasting years in a loveless marriage.

## 4 MORE REAL-LIFE DATA

1 ***Settle for* often attracts words and phrases expressing willingness and necessity:**

▶ I need a cup of coffee so badly **I'll** even **settle for** decaf!

▶ The 128GB model is out of stock, so I guess **I'll have to settle for** the one with 64GB.

▶ **I'm not willing to settle for** such a mediocre life just yet.

▶ I wanted a cat, but my husband is allergic to cats, so I **had to settle for** a houseplant.

2 ***Settle for* is often used to describe legal negotiations:**

▶ The company agreed to **settle for** approximately $1 **million**, with no admission of liability.

▶ The sexual harassment case was dismissed after both parties **settled for an undisclosed sum**.

3 ***Settle for* is also used to describe sports scores:**

▶ Portugal is not **settling for a tie** with the U.S., says coach Paulo Bento: "Either we win or we pack our suitcases."

▶ Clear favorites [UK: favourites] before the event, the Dutch had to **settle for silver**. (= a silver medal)

## 5 CONVERSATION TIP

**Imagine a friend has recently gone through a divorce and might rush into another bad relationship. Here's what you can say:**

**Don't settle for anything less than what you deserve.**

# 69 TAKE ON

## 1 WHAT IT MEANS

**1 When you take on responsibility, especially if it is something challenging, you accept it:**

▶ I try not to take on more responsibility than I can handle.

= I try not to agree to do more than I can deal with.

**2 After you finish this lesson, turn to page 249 for additional meanings of *take on*.**

## 2 HOW IT WORKS

**1 *Take on* takes an object (i.e., what you take on). If the object is a noun, it usually goes at the end:**

☑ I took on too much responsibility.

**2 If the object is a pronoun, it always goes in the middle:**

☑ I took it on.

☒ I ~~took on it~~.

## 3 HOW YOU USE IT IN REAL LIFE

**1 *Take on* tends to attract words describing what needs to be done:**

▶ If you **take on responsibility** for something that somebody else should be doing, you shift the expectation from them to you.

▶ Before **taking on** a **task**, check that the results will be worth the time you put in.

▶ This is a **challenge** that the president must **take on** as it has a significant impact on our democracy.

▶ I have stopped **taking on projects** that are outside the realm of what I really want to do.

▶ *Skyfall* writer John Logan is expected to **take on** screenwriting **duties** for the next two 007 movies [UK: films].

2 **The following word combinations are common, too:**

▶ More Americans feel confident about **taking on debt** (= borrowing money) in 2020, even as delinquencies rise, a new study reveals.

▶ We need a leader who is ready and willing to **take on** the **role** of nation builder.

## 4 RELATED MEANING

***Take on*** **also means to develop or acquire a particular character:**

▶ Vegetation started to take hold, and eventually the whole region **took on** the **appearance** it has today.

▶ Book promotion has **taken on** greater **importance** for authors and publishers alike as the shift to digital continues.

▶ With change being a constant in our lives, higher education **takes on** greater **significance** in preparing students to meet new challenges.

▶ As the virus began spreading across the state's capital, paid sick leave **took on** new **urgency.**

▶ Certain brands are so strong that their names **take on** a **meaning** of their own. Case in point: People say Jet Ski, which is a brand, rather than "personal watercraft."

▶ The Chinese believe that people born in a particular year **take on** the **characteristics** of the animal associated with that year.

▶ Liquids **take on** the **shape** of whatever container they are in because they contain particles that can slide past each other.

## 5 CONVERSATION TIP

**Imagine you want to help a friend who is working too hard and can't say no at work. Here's what you can say:**

**I think you're taking on more than you can handle.**

# 70 TAKE UP (2)

## 1 WHAT IT MEANS

**1 When you take up something such as a challenge, a question, or a problem, you accept it and/or try to deal with it:**

▶ I've decided I'm going to take up the challenge.

= I've decided to say yes to the challenge and try to deal with it.

**2 After you finish this lesson,** **turn to page 249** **for additional meanings of *take up*.**

## 2 HOW IT WORKS

**1 This meaning of *take up* also takes an object (i.e., what you take up). If the object is a noun, it usually goes at the end:**

☑ I'm going to take up the challenge.

**2 If the object is a pronoun, it always goes in the middle:**

☑ I'm going to take it up.

☒ I'm going to ~~take up it~~.

## 3 HOW YOU USE IT IN REAL LIFE

***Take up* tends to attract the words in bold below:**

▶ Which president said, "I am not the first president to **take up** this **cause**, but I am determined to be the last"?

▶ This morning, abortion opponents praised the Supreme Court for finally agreeing to **take up** the **issue**.

▶ I can't help but think that world leaders are failing to **take up** the **challenge** of global warming.

▶ Senator Rand Paul formally objected to **taking up** the new **legislation** unless the Senate considered his amendment to it.

▶ Both lawyers had dealt with cases similar to mine and said they were willing to **take up** my **case**.

▶ Mia's research **takes up** the **question** of religious identity and the intersection of religion and politics in Spain.

## 4 RELATED MEANING

***Take up*** **also means to become interested in a new activity and spend some time doing it. If you use a verb after *take up*, put it in the *-ing* form:**

▶ When you're feeling depressed, don't seek comfort in the shopping mall [UK: shopping centre]. **Taking up** a **hobby** is a better alternative.

▶ When Tiger Woods became popular, there was an explosion in the number of Americans who **took up golf**.

▶ There's absolutely no evidence that young people are **taking up smoking** as a result of advertising.

▶ In India, recent clinical studies have shown that men and women who **take up yoga** report vast improvements in their sex lives.

▶ I decided to **take up painting** while in quarantine, and it took me a while to get the hang of it, but now I'm hooked!

▶ One of the new **habits** I've **taken up** this year is an evening walk with my wife every single day.

## 5 CONVERSATION TIP

**Imagine a friend is having trouble concentrating at work. You think yoga might help. Here's what you can say:**

**My concentration has improved a lot since I took up yoga. You should try it!**

# 71 TURN DOWN

## 1 WHAT IT MEANS

**1 When you turn something down, you refuse to accept or agree to it:**

▶ I decided to turn down the job offer.

= Someone offered me a job, but I decided not to accept it.

**2 After you finish this lesson, turn to page 250 for additional meanings of *turn down*.**

## 2 HOW IT WORKS

**1 *Turn down* takes an object (i.e., what you turn down). If the object is a noun, it tends to go at the end:**

☑ I turned down the offer. (more common)

☑ I turned the offer down. (less common)

**2 If the object is a pronoun, it always goes in the middle:**

☑ I turned it down.

☒ I ~~turned down it~~.

**3 *Turn down* is often used in the passive voice. In passive sentences, *get* is more informal than *be*:**

☑ My application was/got turned down.

## 3 HOW YOU USE IT IN REAL LIFE

***Turn down* tends to attract words related to offers and requests. In most of the sentences, notice the prepositions in bold and the word *to*:**

▶ You say you've been feeling lonely, so stop **turning down invitations from** friends **to** do things. Just enjoy life!

▶ After two years out of work, I knew she wasn't going to **turn down** the **offer of** a temporary position at IBM.

▶ I don't particularly care for oysters, but I certainly wasn't going to **turn down** an **offer to** share food with a celebrity.

▶ Our **request for** an interview was **turned down**, and they didn't even explain why.

turn down an application

▶ Apparently, our **application for** a business loan was turned down because our credit score is too low.

▶ David Bowie, then based in New York, repeatedly **turned down requests to** perform or appear in public.

▶ I'm surprised the president said no. Few politicians would **turn down** an **opportunity to** air their views on late night TV.

▶ Remember you don't have to settle for second best. You have the power to **turn down** any **job** you don't want.

▶ My sister graduated in 2003 and, to dad's despair, she **turned down** a Rhodes **scholarship** so she could serve in Iraq.

## 4 RELATED MEANING

***To turn someone down*** **means to say no to a person's offer or request:**

▶ I still can't understand why the bank **turned** me **down** for a **loan** (= refused to lend me any money).

▶ Acceptance into the course was very competitive, with approximately four applicants **turned down** for each accepted.

▶ The report looked at over five million **mortgage applications** and found that, shockingly, African Americans were **turned down** twice as much as whites.

## 5 CONVERSATION TIP

**Imagine a close friend declined a great job offer. You are shocked to hear the news. Here's what you can say:**

> **What do you mean you turned it down? You're kidding, right?**

# CHECK YOUR PROGRESS 12

**A Read the speech balloons. Then match questions 1–6 to the people's names.**

1 Who took up a hobby? ______________
2 Who backed out of a deal? ______________
3 Who turned down a job offer? ______________
4 Who settled for second best? ______________
5 Who took up a cause? ______________
6 Who took on too much responsibility? ______________

I appreciate your considering me for the position, but now is not the best time to leave my current job.

Raul

I never thought I'd enjoy painting so much, but now I can't get enough of it. What a great way to pass the time!

Vivian

I can't believe I agreed to work on three projects at the same time. It was really stressful and took a toll on my health.

Judy

I wanted the new iMac, but it was out of my price range, so I bought a used MacBook. It's not bad, really.

Jimena

Listen, I don't think I'm going to be able to afford this car after all. Sorry I wasted your time! I hope you find a new buyer.

Hanna

I created a Facebook page urging people to adopt – not buy – dogs and cats. It's hard work, but it's worth it.

Barry

**B Rewrite the sentences below using the pronouns *it* and *them*. Make certain the pronouns are in the correct position. The first one is done for you.**

1 I'm happy to go along with your suggestion.
I'm happy to *go along with it*.
2 I can't believe you backed out of the project!
I can't believe you ______________________________!
3 In the end, I had to settle for my second choice.
In the end, I had to ______________________________.
4 I've decided to take up the challenge.
I've decided to ______________________________.
5 I keep turning down requests to speak in public.
I keep ______________________________.
6 Are you willing to take on the role of mediator?
Are you willing to ______________________________?

**C EXTRA CHALLENGE! Match the first part of each sentence to the correct way to continue it a–c. There is one extra choice in each group.**

1 It was a great opportunity! You
2 It'll be a great opportunity! You

a [ ] shouldn't have turned it down.
b [ ] shouldn't turn it down.
c [ ] shouldn't have been turning it down.

3 Garry thanked me
4 Peter begged me

a [ ] about taking up his case.
b [ ] for taking up his case.
c [ ] to take up his case.

5 If I knew more about the task, I
6 If I'd known more about the task, I

a [ ] will definitely take it on.
b [ ] might take it on, but I'm a bit in the dark.
c [ ] might have taken it on. Too late now.

7 I think you'll regret
8 I swear I won't let you

a [ ] to settle for less than you deserve.
b [ ] settle for less than you deserve.
c [ ] settling for less than you deserve.

9 I'll make him an offer he can't refuse. I
10 I can't believe he said no in the end. I

a [ ] hope he doesn't back out of the deal.
b [ ] wish he didn't back out of the deal.
c [ ] wish he hadn't backed out of the deal.

Answer key:

| Exercise A | Exercise B | Exercise C | |
|---|---|---|---|
| 1 Vivian | 2 backed out of it | 1 A | 7 C |
| 2 Hanna | 3 settle for it | 2 B | 8 B |
| 3 Raul | 4 take it up | 3 B | 9 A |
| 4 Jimena | 5 turning them down | 4 C | 10 C |
| 5 Barry | 6 take it on | 5 B | |
| 6 Judy | | 6 C | |

# 72 COME ABOUT

## 1 WHAT IT MEANS

**When something comes about, it happens or starts to happen, especially in a way that is not planned:**

▶ Could you tell me how the problem came about?

= Could you tell me how the problem started?

## 2 HOW IT WORKS

***Come about* takes no object. You simply say that something comes about:**

☑ How did the problem come about?

☒ How did the problem ~~come it about~~?

☒ How ~~came about the problem~~?

## 3 HOW YOU USE IT IN REAL LIFE

**1 Words describing developments + *come about*:**

▶ It's important for all of us to understand the essential facts on how the **situation** in North Korea **came about**.

▶ A non-violent, long-lasting **revolution** can **come about** through education.

▶ After the break, we will look at how such an economic **transformation** might **come about**, along with the challenges involved.

▶ We had no choice but to adapt to the **changes** that were **coming about** as a result of the economic downturn.

▶ A lot of people expect that some kind of miracle will occur, and that **change** will **come about** very quickly.

**2 Words describing new ideas + *come about*:**

▶ The whole **idea** for this post **came about** after a conversation I had with a friend this morning.

▶ The **concept** of human rights **came about** only after many long and troublesome wars.
▶ Our aim in the present chapter is to provide the background on how this **discovery came about** and to link it to recent studies.

## 4 MORE REAL-LIFE DATA

**1 *How* is the most frequent *wh-* word used with *come about*. The nouns in bold are common, too:**

▶ Science has not proven everything there is to know, so no human can truly explain **how life came about**.
▶ Is it possible to explain **how the universe came about** without bringing God into it?
▶ Brazilian pop star Anita explained to Billboard magazine **how** the **collaboration** with Madonna **came about**.
▶ This is a huge **project**. **How** exactly did it **come about**?

**2 *Come about* is often followed by words and expressions explaining why something happened:**

▶ The shift to greener products has largely **come about because of** intensive lobbying from environmental groups.
▶ America's most meaningful changes **came about through** public debate, compromise, and consensus.
▶ This impressive victory **came about as a result of** the team's considerable work ethic.

## 5 CONVERSATION TIP

**Imagine you are interviewing an app developer for a school project. Here's something you can ask:**

**How exactly did the idea for the app come about?**

# 73 COME ACROSS (1)

## 1 WHAT IT MEANS

***To come across*** **means to meet, find, or discover something or someone by chance:**

▶ If you come across an unknown word, first, try to figure out what it means.

= If you find a word you don't know, first, try to guess what it means.

## 2 HOW IT WORKS

***Come across*** **takes an object (i.e., what or who you come across). The object always goes at the end, whether it is a noun or a pronoun:**

☑ I came across an unknown word.

☑ I came across it.

☒ I ~~came an unknown word across~~.

☒ I ~~came it across~~.

## 3 HOW YOU USE IT IN REAL LIFE

**You can use *come across* with a very wide range of words. It often attracts nouns related to communication, especially in writing:**

▶ My jaw dropped when I **came across** this really interesting **article** on the genetic similarities between humans and chimpanzees.

▶ I **came across** your **site** while doing research on neurological diseases, and I have to say I love your content.

▶ I'm so glad to have **come across** your **post**. You have essentially put my thoughts into words. Thank you!

▶ I've been looking for smart inspirational **quotes**, but, so far, I haven't **come across** a single one that I like.

▶ I recently lost a baby, and I **came across** this **poem** on your blog today. I just want to say thank you, from the bottom of my heart.

▶ While dreaming of a fresh start, Donna **comes across** an **ad** that seems too good to be true. As it turns out, it really was too good to be true.

- I can't even begin to explain how excited I get when I **come across** a new **recipe**, and I have all the ingredients at home.
- Recently, I've **come across references** to homeschoolers not getting credit for courses, which caught me by surprise.
- The other day, while searching the web, I **came across** a YouTube **video** of New Yorkers airing their views on euthanasia.

## 4 MORE REAL-LIFE DATA

***Come across* is often used in sentences containing more than one past idea. Notice the underlined verb tenses:**

- I **came across** an interesting German **word** when I <u>was doing</u> my homework: "backpfeifengesicht" – a face that deserves to be slapped! (past continuous – ongoing action)
- The book <u>had been</u> out of print for decades when I **came across** a **copy** on eBay. (past perfect – earlier action)
- When Gloria **came across** a **stranger** lying half-naked on the couch, she <u>let out</u> a loud scream. (simple past – second action in a sequence)

## 5 CONVERSATION TIP

**Imagine you were surfing the web and found an article you think a friend might be interested in. Here's what you can say:**

**I came across this article, and I thought you might find it useful.**

# 74 COME ALONG

## 1 WHAT IT MEANS

**1 When something comes along, it appears and becomes available:**

▶ I haven't made up my mind. I'm still waiting for the right opportunity to come along.

= I haven't decided yet. I'm still waiting for the right opportunity to appear.

**2 People can come along, too:**

▶ I'm still waiting for the perfect partner to come along.

= I'm still waiting for the perfect partner to come into my life.

**3 After you finish this lesson, turn to page 250 for additional meanings of *come along*.**

## 2 HOW IT WORKS

***Come along* takes no object. You simply say that something comes along:**

☑ The right opportunity will come along.

☒ The right opportunity will ~~come it along~~.

☒ ~~It will come along the right opportunity~~.

## 3 HOW YOU USE IT IN REAL LIFE

**You can use *come along* with a lot of different nouns, but the following uses are especially common. Also, notice the underlined time words and expressions, which *come along* often attracts:**

**1 Words describing opportunities + *come along*:**

▶ I'd take the job if I were you. This is an **opportunity** that doesn't come along every day.

▶ The book is about two teenagers who find themselves running out of options until the **chance** of a lifetime **comes along,** and they audition for *American Idol*.

**2 *Someone, something,* etc. + *come along*:**

▶ I've never had a girlfriend, but I'm still hopeful that one day **someone** will **come along** and make me happy.

▶ Book critics can be pretty cruel. You spend years writing what you think is the perfect story, and then **somebody comes along** and gives it one star.

▶ I've been out of work for what feels like an eternity, but I'm optimistic that **something** will eventually **come along**.

**3 Major innovations and inventions +** ***come along*****:**

▶ I've always wondered what hashtags were used for before **Twitter came along**.

▶ When 'talking **movies' came along** in the late 1920's, Charles Chaplin kept making silent films for a number of years.

▶ By the time **CDs came along** in the late 1980s, LP sales had been falling steadily for a decade.

**4 Influential people +** ***come along*****:**

▶ Computers were big boring blue boxes until **Steve Jobs came along** and turned the industry upside down.

▶ Rock was never the same after **the Beatles came along** and started a cultural revolution.

## 4 MORE REAL-LIFE DATA

***Come along*** **tends to attract the verb** ***wait*** **and the pattern** ***wait for someone or something to come along:***

▶ The moment the baby was born, we both realized [UK: realised] just how long we'd been **waiting for** her **to come along** and fill the void in our lives.

▶ Once I read a quote that said, "Don't sit around and **wait for** the perfect opportunity **to come along** – find something and make it an opportunity."

▶ "Read this book if you are in love, out of love, or **waiting for** it **to come along**," the review said.

## 5 CONVERSATION TIP

**Imagine you want to persuade a friend to accept a job offer. Here's what you can say:**

**An opportunity like this might never come along again.**

# 75 COME UP

## 1 WHAT IT MEANS

**1 When something comes up, it happens unexpectedly:**

▶ Something came up, and I can't make it to the party tonight.

= I had a problem I wasn't expecting, so I can't go to the party tonight.

**2 *Come up* also means about to happen soon. In this case, it is usually used in the *-ing* form:**

▶ I have a deadline coming up, so I need to learn how to get my priorities straight.

= I have some work to finish soon, so I need to learn how to focus on the most important tasks first.

**3 After you finish this lesson, turn to page 250 for additional meanings of *come up*.**

## 2 HOW IT WORKS

***Come up* takes no object. You simply say that something comes up:**

☑ The deadline is coming up.

☒ The deadline is ~~coming it up.~~

☒ ~~It is coming up the deadline~~.

## 3 HOW YOU USE IT IN REAL LIFE

**1 Words indicating unexpected problems + *come up*:**

▶ I'm sorry, but **something** has **come up**. Do you think we could reschedule for tomorrow at the same time?

▶ We were such a great team, right? Whenever an **issue came up**, everyone worked together to solve it.

▶ The **problem came up** when I installed the update. How can I fix it?

2 **Words describing big events +** ***come up*****:**

▶ Do you have a wedding **anniversary coming up**? If so, you should definitely consider celebrating in style.

▶ My **birthday** is **coming up**, but all I want is to be invisible or hide out somewhere for one day so no one finds me!

▶ Since the **holidays** are **coming up**, and the kids will be out of school next week, we'll be heading to the mountains.

▶ With the **election coming up**, this week I thought I'd share a few highlights of past elections I've covered as a reporter since 2010.

3 ***Come up*** **is typically used in TV and radio announcements:**

▶ **Coming up** in our **next half-hour of** *CBS This Morning*, a shopping trip you definitely won't want to miss.

▶ **Coming up after the break**: Iran's Supreme Leader ruled out talks with the U.S. amid the row over Saudi Arabia.

## 4 RELATED MEANING

***Come up*** **also means to be mentioned or discussed:**

▶ Your **name came up** at our executive team meeting this morning, and I'd like to discuss the possibility of doing some business together. Please call me.

▶ During last night's presidential debate, the **topic** of Israel **came up** repeatedly.

▶ Bob and Shirley never talked about having children, and it wasn't until after they were married that the **subject** finally **came up**.

## 5 CONVERSATION TIP

**Imagine a friend invited you to dinner, but you feel like staying home, so you make an excuse. Here's what you can say:**

**Sorry, but something came up. Can I take a raincheck?**

# 76 POP UP

## 1 WHAT IT MEANS

**When something pops up, it appears in a place or situation, usually unexpectedly. *Pop up* is an informal phrasal verb, often used to talk about technology:**

▶ Click here, and a list with your recent files will pop up.
= Click here, and a list with your recent files will appear on the screen.

## 2 HOW IT WORKS

***Pop up* takes no object. You simply say that something or someone pops up:**

☑ A list will pop up.
☒ A list will ~~pop it up~~.
☒ ~~It will pop up a list~~.

## 3 HOW YOU USE IT IN REAL LIFE

message popping up

***Pop up* can be followed by a lot of different words. The following word combinations are especially common:**

▶ Ian took a deep breath as the error **message popped up** again. "What am I doing wrong?" he wondered.

▶ Whenever I try to log in, a **window pops up** asking for my username, and then it disappears before I click "send."

▶ The software is free to try, but every two minutes or so, an **ad** will **pop up** in the corner of the screen.

▶ While a lot of U.S. retail stores are fast disappearing, dollar **stores**, where you can buy things for a dollar or less, are **popping up** in a lot of cities.

▶ There's probably something wrong with my phone. Shouldn't a **notification pop up** as soon as I get a text message?

▶ A **phrase** that **pops up** a lot in investigative journalism is *follow the money*.

▶ If you smile whenever her **name pops up** on your phone, you might be falling in love.

**TOP COLLOCATION: name + pop up**

## 4 MORE REAL-LIFE DATA

**1 *Pop up* tends to attract the verb *keep*:**

▶ I'm tired of those surveys that **keep popping up** in the media telling us how little Americans know about foreign cultures.

▶ I'm not really into Miley Cyrus, so I have no idea why she **keeps popping up** on my Spotify suggestions.

▶ I couldn't stop watching the show because, even as old mysteries were solved, new questions **kept popping up**, and I wanted to know the answers.

**2 *Pop up* often attracts words and expressions with *-where*:**

▶ Have you noticed that every time you learn a new word, it suddenly starts **popping up everywhere**?

▶ Joe's Frozen Custard, the best food truck in the Bay Area, will **pop up somewhere** new next month. Follow us on Instagram for more details.

▶ As a journal reviewer, I usually check a manuscript under review by copying the abstract and pasting it into Google to see if it **pops up elsewhere**.

▶ In this video, you will learn how to deal with negative thoughts that seem to **pop up out of nowhere**. (= unexpectedly)

## 5 CONVERSATION TIP

**Imagine you are talking about technology pet peeves with a friend. Here's something you can say:**

**I can't stand those ads that pop up out of nowhere.**

# 77 RUN INTO

## 1 WHAT IT MEANS

**1 When you run into an unpleasant situation, you unexpectedly begin to experience it:**

▶ The company ran into financial difficulties last year.

= Last year, the company had financial problems it wasn't expecting.

**2 After you finish this lesson, turn to page 251 for additional meanings of *run into*.**

## 2 HOW IT WORKS

***Run into* takes an object (i.e., what you run into). The object always goes at the end, whether it is a noun or a pronoun:**

☑ The company ran into difficulties.

☑ They company ran into them.

☒ The company ~~ran difficulties into~~.

☒ The company ~~ran them into~~.

## 3 HOW YOU USE IT IN REAL LIFE

1 ***Run into* + words describing problems and obstacles:**

▶ I am trying to get my photos off my phone and onto my laptop, but I'm **running into** all kinds of **issues**.

▶ The $100 million project was abandoned mid-construction last month when the developer **ran into** financial **difficulties**.

▶ My phone is getting really hot for no reason. Is there anybody **running into** the same **situation**?

▶ Even when we are doing our best, we will **run into obstacles** that can bring frustration and disappointment.

- Don’t give up! Whenever you **run into** a **roadblock**, stop and think of ways to get around, over, or through the block.
- Whether you're an experienced or a novice teacher, you’re bound to **run into challenges** when teaching teens.
- When the police showed up, they **ran into** a big **problem**: The suspect didn’t speak English, and they couldn't find a translator.
- If you **run into trouble**, please call the Tech line at 291-TECH (8524), option 2, for help.

2 *Run into* + **words describing differences of opinion:**

- Plans for the development of a 700-home residential development in West Gainesville **ran into** strong **opposition** from local residents.
- Many of the president’s budget proposals are likely to **run into** stiff **resistance** from lawmakers on Capitol Hill.

## 4 RELATED MEANING

**When you run into someone, you meet them by chance:**

- I never quite know what to say when I **run into** an old **friend** (= meet an old friend unexpectedly) I haven’t seen in a while.
- Nina and Jacob work in the same part of town, so they **run into each other** at least once or twice a month.

## 5 CONVERSATION TIP

**Imagine you met an old friend by chance. You share the news with your spouse. Here’s what you can say:**

**You’ll never guess who I just ran into at the supermarket!**

# CHECK YOUR PROGRESS 13

**A Put the words in the correct order to form sentences. Check your answers before you do exercise B.**

1 might / opportunity / this / come / like / never / along

An ______________________________________________ again.

2 best-selling / for / idea / about / my / came / book

The ______________________________________________ quickly.

3 across / while / your / doing / came / some / site

I ______________________________________________ schoolwork.

4 problems / they / should / come / with / as soon as / deal

You ______________________________________________ up.

5 up / popped / and / message / computer / error / the

An ______________________________________________ crashed.

6 into / of / difficulties / because / the / ran / company

The ______________________________________________ pandemic.

**B Match each sentence 1–6 above to the most logical way to continue it.**

[ ] a. I think I might have to reinstall Windows.
[ ] b. You'd be a fool not to take it!
[ ] c. It was the actual writing that took forever.
[ ] d. It's a miracle it didn't go out of business.
[ ] e. Congratulations on the excellent content you provide.
[ ] f. Otherwise, they might snowball into something bigger.

**C Choose the correct options.**

1 Which inventions came about [as / with] a result of the scientific revolution?
2 [How / Why] did the idea for this song come about? Is it true that it came to you in a dream?
3 The album [had / has] been out of print for years when I came across a copy on eBay.
4 You should stop waiting for the perfect job [to / will] come along. Maybe it never will!
5 [By / On] the time Spotify came along, music downloads had been falling steadily for years.
6 Coming up [after / with] the break: an exclusive interview with Ed Sheeran you won't want to miss.
7 Don't you just hate those ads that [keep / stay] popping up when you're online?
8 The mayor's plan ran into strong opposition [against / from] the population.

**D EXTRA CHALLENGE! Complete the text with the phrasal verbs in the box. Use the correct form and tense. The first one is done for you.**

| | | | | |
|---|---|---|---|---|
| gaps 1–4: | ~~come about~~ | come across | figure out | pop up |
| gaps 5–8: | come along | end up | run into | turn out |

## ACCIDENTAL DISCOVERIES

It is often thought that most groundbreaking inventions and discoveries usually require a lot of research. But sometimes great ideas (1) *come about* unexpectedly, and the so-called eureka moments just seem to (2) ______________ out of nowhere, as a result of serendipity or chance! There are cases of scientists who (3) ______________ how to solve complicated problems by dropping something on the floor, forgetting to wash their hands, or (4) ______________ something while searching for something else. Here are two well-known examples:

Penicillin: When Scottish biologist Alexander Fleming returned to work after a short vacation, he found a strange fungus in a culture that he had left in his lab. As it (5) ______________, the fungus had killed off most of the bacteria in the culture! This is how penicillin (6) ______________, and the invention changed modern medicine forever.

Post-it notes: In 1968, a man called Dr. Spencer Silver was trying to develop a strong adhesive backing. But he (7) ______________ all kinds of issues and, to his disappointment, (8) ______________ creating a much weaker adhesive. Six years later, Dr. Silver's discovery resurfaced and became the post-it note that we know today.

Answer key:

Exercise A
1 opportunity like this might never come along
2 idea for my best-selling book came about
3 came across your site while doing some
4 should deal with problems as soon as they come
5 error message popped up and the computer
6 company ran into difficulties because of the

Exercise B
a 5
b 1
c 2
d 6
e 3
f 4

Exercise C
1 as
2 How
3 had
4 to
5 By
6 after
7 keep
8 from

Exercise D
2 pop up
3 figured out
4 coming across
5 turns/turned out
6 came along
7 ran into
8 ended up

# 78 BRING UP

## 1 WHAT IT MEANS

**1 When you bring something up, you mention it or start to talk about it:**

▶ I never bring up politics around my family.

= I never start a discussion on politics when I'm with my family.

**2 After you finish this lesson, turn to page 251 for additional meanings of *bring up*.**

## 2 HOW IT WORKS

**1 *Bring up* takes an object (i.e., what you bring up). If the object is a noun, it tends to go at the end:**

☑ I never bring up politics. (more common)

☑ I never bring politics up. (less common)

**2 If the object is a pronoun, it always goes in the middle:**

☑ I never bring it up. ☒ I never ~~bring up it~~.

**3 *Bring up* can be followed by a *wh-* word (i.e., *what, how,* etc.):**

☑ I try not to bring up what I consider to be sensitive topics.

☑ In a casual conversation, it's usually impolite to bring up how much money one makes.

**4 *Bring up* can be used in the passive voice:**

☑ The issue wasn't brought up at the meeting.

bring up an issue

## 3 HOW YOU USE IT IN REAL LIFE

**You can use *bring up* with virtually any word or phrase (*bring up his name, bring up religion, bring up what happened last fall*), but the following word combinations are especially common:**

▶ Sometimes I find myself thinking about **issues** that you have **brought up** as I go about my day.

- I have a question: Do I wait for him to **bring up** the **subject**, or should I be the one to initiate the discussion?
- In Thursday's column, Dr. Anderson **brought up** the **topic** of bullying, and it generated quite a response.
- Throughout the book, the author **brings up** the **question** of solitude, without going beyond a very superficial analysis.
- I'd never thought about some of the **points** you **brought up**. Thank you for opening my eyes.

## 4 MORE REAL-LIFE DATA

**Notice the use of *wh-* words after *issue* and *question*:**

- So far nobody has **brought up the issue of how** this technology is impacting our kids' health.
- The article also **brings up the issue of why** aging [UK: ageing] is singled out as a contributor to high health-care costs, as opposed to obesity.
- Your point **brings up the question of what** incentives can and should be used to retain senior managers.
- The video caused an uproar and **brought up the question of whether** those in the public eye have the right to privacy.
- The case has raised a lot of controversy, with lawyers across the country **bringing up the issue of whether or not** the sentence was fair.

## 5 CONVERSATION TIP

**Imagine you are holding a meeting to make an important decision. You want to give people a chance to say what they think. Here's what you can say:**

**If you have any questions or concerns, now is the time to bring them up.**

# 79 COME ACROSS (2)

## 1 WHAT IT MEANS

**When someone comes across in a certain way, they make that impression on other people:**

▶ He comes across really well on TV.

= He creates a really positive image of himself when he appears on TV.

## 2 HOW IT WORKS

**1 *Come across* takes no object, and we never separate the verb (*come*) from the particle (*across*):**

☑ He comes across well.

☒ He ~~comes well across~~.

**2 Use *as* if *come across* is followed by an adjective, a phrase with an adjective, or a phrase with *someone*:**

☑ He comes across as smart.

☑ He comes across as a smart person.

☑ He comes across as someone who knows his stuff.

**3 If you use a verb after *come across* (usually *be*), put it in the *-ing* form:**

☑ He comes across as being smart.

## 3 HOW YOU USE IT IN REAL LIFE

**1 *Come across* often attracts the words *way and how*:**

▶ I can't stand the thought of **coming across** the **way** I do. Please help me show people that I actually care.

▶ We don't always know **how** we are **coming across** on stage until we have actually performed and received feedback.

**2 You can use *come across as* with a very wide range of words. It often attracts adjectives and nouns describing people's attitudes:**

▶ In his interviews and tweets, he **comes across as** a **confident** man, sometimes verging on **arrogant**.

▶ If you **come across as humble** and **genuine**, I'm sure that people will naturally gravitate towards you.

▶ Despite her reputation, Sue **comes across as** a **sensitive** and **likeable** manager, incredibly **concerned** about those around her.

▶ The secret lies in staying true to what you believe in, without **coming across as rude** or **as a know-it-all**.

▶ Laura uses social media well, but she **comes across as** a bit **inauthentic**. Why can't she show people who she really is?

▶ While your point is valid, you **came across as** very **condescending**.

## 4 RELATED MEANING

**When an idea, emotion, or personality trait comes across, it is expressed in the way it was intended to. Notice the use of the adverbs in bold:**

▶ I think I **came across well** in the interview, and they said they would contact me soon. Fingers crossed!

▶ What a great presentation! The point you tried to make **came across clearly**, and the audience loved you.

## 5 CONVERSATION TIP

**Imagine a friend is badmouthing someone you hardly know. You don't like to gossip. Here's something you can say:**

**Well, we only spoke once, but he came across as (a charming and friendly guy).**

# 80 GIVE AWAY

## 1 WHAT IT MEANS

**1 When you give away information that should be kept secret, you reveal it to other people, intentionally or otherwise:**

▶ She was fired for giving away company secrets.

= She lost her job because she shared confidential business information.

**2 A person can be the object of *give away*, too:**

▶ I tried to smile, but my tears gave me away.

= I tried to smile, but my tears revealed that I wasn't happy.

**3 After you finish this lesson, turn to page 251 for additional meanings of *give away*.**

## 2 HOW IT WORKS

**1 *Give away* takes an object (i.e., what or who you give away). If the object is a noun, it usually goes at the end:**

☑ She gave away company secrets. (more common)

☑ She gave company secrets away. (less common)

**2 If the object is a pronoun, it always goes in the middle:**

☑ She gave them away.

☒ She ~~gave away them~~.

## 3 HOW YOU USE IT IN REAL LIFE

**1 *Give away* + *information* and other related words:**

▶ It was a weird date. The guy asked me about my personal life without ever **giving away** too much **information** about his own.

▶ The group is planning something big, I'm sure, but they have not **given away** any important **details** yet.

▶ Ronald, listen, I hope you didn't feel I was **giving away** a **secret** when I said you're going to be 85 next week.

2 *Give away* + **words related to works of fiction:**

▶ The trailer is way too long, and it **gives away** the **plot**.

▶ I won't **give away** the **ending** of the book, but, let me warn you, it's definitely not a happy one.

▶ Warning: This article contains pictures that may **give away** some **spoilers** from the eighth season of the show.

3 *Give away* + *myself, yourself*, **etc.:**

▶ If you scratch your face when you tell a lie, you'll **give yourself away**!

▶ Ellen was trying to lie low, but, with that Instagram post, she might have just **given herself away**.

4 *Give away* + **words with** *thing*:

▶ The press secretary was pushed for more definitive answers, but, not surprisingly, he **gave nothing away** at the press conference.

▶ Your wedding dress looks absolutely stunning. I don't want to **give anything away**, but I'm sure you'll love what you see.

## 4 RELATED MEANING

***Give away*** **is often used to describe what our body language reveals:**

▶ I said absolutely nothing so my voice wouldn't **give me away**.

▶ Martha tried to keep a straight face so she wouldn't **give herself away**.

▶ He raised his head and stared at me. I had no idea whether he was happy or sad. His face **gave nothing away**.

## 5 CONVERSATION TIP

**Imagine you think you accidentally revealed something. You check with a friend who was there. Here's what you can say:**

**I gave myself away, didn't I?**

# 81 MAKE UP (2)

## 1 WHAT IT MEANS

**1 When you make up an excuse, a story, etc., you invent it, sometimes in order to deceive someone:**

▶ You don't have to tell her the real reason why you're late. Just make up an excuse!
= When you tell her why you're late, invent an excuse that you think she will believe.

**2 After you finish this lesson, turn to page 252 for an additional meaning of *make up*.**

## 2 HOW IT WORKS

**1 *Make up* takes an object (i.e., what you make up). If the object is a noun, it tends to go at the end:**

☑ I made up an excuse. (more common)
☑ I made an excuse up. (less common)

**2 If the object is a pronoun, it always goes in the middle:**

☑ I made it up.
☒ I ~~made up it.~~

**3 The words *things* and *stuff* tend to go in the middle:**

☑ She's making things up. (more common)
☑ She's making up things. (less common)

**4 *Make up* can be used in the passive voice:**

☑ This story was probably made up.

## 3 HOW YOU USE IT IN REAL LIFE

***Make up* is often used with the words in bold below:**

▶ Why do you think I'm lying? If I was going to **make up** a **story**, I'm sure I could have come up with something much better than that.

- Those **numbers** are 100% false. Somebody must have **made** them **up** out of thin air.
- As I grew up, I compensated for a lonely childhood by **making up stories** in my head. Now, as a writer, I make a living off them.
- I have no idea how to play this game, so I guess we'll just have to **make up** our own **rules** as we go along.
- As long as you're my student, don't ever **make up an excuse** for turning in [UK: handing in] work late. I'd much rather you were honest about it.
- Please don't just **make stuff up**. If everybody **makes up lies**, then people won't listen to each other anymore.
- Inconsistency is typical of fabrication: When **making things up**, people often find it hard to stick with the same story.

## 4 MORE REAL-LIFE DATA

***Make up*** **often attracts adjectives that mean** ***not real*****:**

- No one in their right mind would **make up** a **fake** lottery ticket to get attention, as this man obviously has.
- For years, the local police simply **made up imaginary** informants to justify searches and seizures.
- If you've lost interest, be honest. Don't **make up** a **lame** excuse as to why you haven't returned his calls.
- We all know how that candidate **makes up bogus** stories in order to push his agenda by playing on people's feelings.

## 5 CONVERSATION TIP

**Imagine a close friend is telling you a story. You think your friend might be exaggerating a little. Here's what you can say:**

**Oh, come on! Stop making stuff up!**

# 82 PICK UP ON

## 1 WHAT IT MEANS

**When you pick up on something that was not communicated directly, you notice and become aware of it:**

▶ The teacher obviously didn't pick up on the students' lack of interest in the subject.

= The teacher obviously didn't notice that the students were not interested in the subject.

## 2 HOW IT WORKS

***Pick up on*** **takes an object (i.e., what you pick up on). The object always goes at the end, whether it is a noun or a pronoun, so never separate the verb (*pick*) from the particles (*up, on*):**

☑ He didn't pick up on the students' lack of interest.

☒ He didn't ~~pick up the students' lack of interest on~~.

☑ He didn't pick up on it.

☒ He didn't ~~pick it up on~~.

## 3 HOW YOU USE IT IN REAL LIFE

1 *Pick up on + things* and *something*:

▶ Our instinct is always able to **pick up on things** that are below the conscious level, so we should learn to trust our intuition.

▶ In our last session, my therapist **picked up on something** that I wasn't remotely aware of since no one had ever pointed it out to me before.

2 *Pick up on + the fact that*:

▶ Even though your children may not know about the impending divorce, they will likely **pick up on the fact that** something is wrong.

3 *Pick up on + nuances* **and other related words:**

▶ When I came home, Boris **picked up on** my **mood** immediately, so he sat right next to me.

▶ With the new speakers, I **picked up on nuances** I had never heard before in songs.

▶ If you feel confident and grateful, people around you will **pick up on** that **vibe**.

- ▶ Children with Asperger's have a hard time **picking up on** social **cues** and making friends.
- ▶ Babies can understand what their mothers are saying by **picking up on** the **tone** of their voices.
- ▶ People born under Pisces tend to **pick up on subtleties** in the environment that others ignore.
- ▶ As a couples therapist, over the years, I've **picked up on** a number of **patterns** that point to what makes a successful relationship.
- ▶ Most cases of acquired hearing loss are gradual, and many people don't **pick up on** the **signs** until it is too late.

**In the examples under item 3, you can usually omit** ***on.*** **(e.g.,** ***pick up nuances*** **=** ***pick up on nuances*****)**

## 4 RELATED MEANINGS

**1 When you pick up on something that was previously mentioned, you return to it and turn your attention to it:**

- ▶ Jill **picked up on** a **point** that Susan had made earlier about GM foods.
- ▶ Let me just **pick up on what** you said at the beginning of the show.
- ▶ Several news agencies around the world have **picked up on** the president's **comments**.

**2 You can use** ***pick up*** **(without** ***on*****) to talk about noticing smells, sounds, and electronic signals:**

- ▶ The dogs must have **picked up** her **scent,** so they started barking.
- ▶ As I watched the video again, I realized [UK: realised] that my mic had **picked up** the **sound** of my cooling fan.
- ▶ If a radio transmitter sends out a **signal**, you need a receiver that can **pick** it **up**.

## 5 CONVERSATION TIP

**Imagine you are at a meeting, and a colleague made a point you would like to return to. Here's what you can say:**

**Can I just pick up on something (Ann) said earlier?**

# 83 POINT OUT

## 1 WHAT IT MEANS

**When you point something out, especially something you think is important, you mention it:**

▶ The teacher pointed out some mistakes in my paper.

= The teacher told me there were some mistakes in my paper.

## 2 HOW IT WORKS

**1 *Point out* takes an object (i.e., what you point out). If the object is a noun, it usually goes at the end:**

☑ He pointed out some mistakes. (more common)

☑ He pointed some mistakes out. (less common)

**2 If the object is a pronoun, it always goes in the middle:**

☑ He pointed them out.

☒ He ~~pointed out them~~.

**3 Use *to* if you want to mention the person:**

☑ He pointed out some mistakes to me.

☒ He ~~pointed me out some mistakes~~.

**4 You can use a *that* clause and a *wh-* word after *point out*:**

☑ He pointed out that there was a mistake.

☑ He pointed out what was wrong.

☑ He pointed out why the theory was wrong.

**5 *Point out* is often used in the passive voice:**

☑ A few problems were pointed out.

## 3 HOW YOU USE IT IN REAL LIFE

**When *point out* is followed by a noun, it tends to attract words related to errors:**

▶ The critic was quick to **point out** the theoretical **shortcomings** of the book.

▶ It's always going to upset people if you **point out** their **faults**.

▶ This week's report by the committee **points out** glaring **inconsistencies**.

point out flaws in others

▶ People who like to **point out flaws** in others are usually trying to cover up the flaws in themselves.

▶ The **error** was **pointed out** to us privately, but our reputation might have been damaged if we had not corrected it quickly.

▶ Who better than a burglar to **point out weaknesses** in your home security system?

## 4 MORE REAL-LIFE DATA

1 **Notice the use of *as* to mention the <u>person</u> who pointed something out:**

▶ The president's posts are filled with lies, **as** <u>several commentators</u> **have pointed out** time and time again.

▶ **As** <u>Smith</u> **points out** in his 2019 article, there are two major traditions in the field of social psychology.

2 **Notice the use of *point out* in expressions meaning "I'd like to say that ...":**

▶ This discussion has been very interesting. However, **I would like to point out that** I disagree with some of the statements made.

▶ Even though there are similarities in their profile, **it is worth pointing out** a few differences.

▶ While these results are not encouraging, **it should be pointed out that** cloth masks did demonstrate some COVID-19 protection.

## 5 CONVERSATION TIP

**Imagine a colleague spots a mistake in a project you are working on. Here's how you can thank this person:**

**You're right! What was I thinking? Thanks for pointing it out!**

# 84 TALK INTO/OUT OF

## 1 WHAT IT MEANS

**1 When you talk someone into (doing) something, you persuade them to do it:**

▶ My mother managed to talk me into getting married.

= My mother convinced me to get married.

**2 When you talk someone out of (doing) something, you persuade them not to do it:**

▶ I tried to talk Sue out of buying a new phone.

= I tried to convince Sue not to buy a new phone.

## 2 HOW IT WORKS

**1 The verbs *talk into/out of* take two objects. The first one (i.e., who you are trying to persuade/dissuade) always goes in the middle:**

☑ I talked Sue into keeping her phone.

☒ I ~~talked into Sue~~ keeping her phone.

☑ I talked her out of buying a new phone.

☒ I ~~talked out of her~~ buying a new phone.

**2 The second object can be a noun, a pronoun (usually *it*), or, most commonly, an *-ing* verb. It always goes at the end:**

☑ She talked me into marriage.

☑ She talked me into it.

☑ She talked me out of getting married.

**3 *Talk into/out of* can be used in the passive voice:**

☑ She was talked into getting married.

☑ She was talked out of it.

## 3 HOW YOU USE IT IN REAL LIFE

**1 *Talk into/out of* can be followed by a very wide range of verbs. These are some of the most frequent ones:**

▶ I'm not going, and no one is going to **talk me into going**. Period.

trying to talk her into doing something

▶ Stick to your decision! Don't be **talked into doing** something you don't want to do.

▶ Who hasn't been **talked into buying** expensive makeup only to have it sitting in the drawer for months, unworn?

▶ Someone **talked me into taking** out a loan that I can't pay back, and now I just don't know what to do. Help!

▶ If you've recently ended an abusive relationship, you should be prepared for your partner to try to **talk you into getting** back together.

2 **You often use *talk into/out of* + *it* to refer to something that was said previously:**

▶ So, you need an investor? Well, with your good looks and effortless charm, I'm sure you can **talk** anyone **into it**. (*it* = investing in your business)

▶ When I told my friends I was going from brown to blond, they tried to **talk** me **out of it**. (*it* = changing my hair)

## 4 MORE REAL-LIFE DATA

1 **The verb *try* is often used before *talk into/out of*:**

▶ Be wary of telemarketers who make cold calls and **try to talk** you **into** switching to their company.

▶ Mom [UK: mum] was still **trying to talk** me **out of** it when I finally hung up the phone.

2 **Reflexive pronouns (i.e., *myself, yourself*, etc.) are relatively common after *talk into/out of*:**

▶ I kept trying to **talk myself into** accepting the offer, but for whatever reason, it just didn't seem right.

▶ Research has shown that the strategy of **talking yourself out of** eating can be effective for weight loss.

## 5 CONVERSATION TIP

**Imagine you let a friend convince you to do something that you later regretted. Here's what you can say:**

**I shouldn't have let you talk me into it!**

# CHECK YOUR PROGRESS 14

**A What is the most logical way to continue each sentence? Choose the correct option.**

1 Mike brought up the subject because
A he really wanted to talk about it.
B he didn't want to talk about it.

2 Ann talked me out of reading that book, so
A I'm going to order it from Amazon.
B I'm going to pick another title.

3 Bernie gave away classified information, and
A that's why his boss congratulated him.
B that's why his boss was mad at him.

4 Pierre made up the numbers, and
A people soon realized [UK: realised] they were accurate.
B people soon realized they were false.

5 The teacher picked up on the students' mood, so she
A carried on with the lesson as usual.
B stopped and asked them what was wrong.

6 My editor pointed out a few spelling mistakes, but
A I don't know why he chose to ignore them.
B I haven't had time to fix them yet.

**B Rewrite sentences 1–6 above using *it* or *them*. Make certain the pronouns are in the correct position. The first one is done for you.**

1 Mike *brought it up*.
2 Ann ________________________________________
3 Bernie ________________________________________
4 Pierre ________________________________________
5 The teacher ____________________________________
6 My editor _____________________________________

**C Each box has three logical ways to continue the sentences on the left. Match boxes A–F to sentences 1–6. The first one is done for you.**

1 At the meeting, they brought up [ *B* ].
2 Can't you tell that he made up [ ]?
3 Try not to give away [ ].
4 Dale is not aware that he comes across [ ].
5 At the family reunion, Gloria picked up on [ ].
6 The expert was quick to point out [ ].

| A |
| --- |
| • well on video<br>• as a bit arrogant<br>• that way |

| B |
| --- |
| • an important topic<br>• the issue of paid leave<br>• politics |

| C |
| --- |
| • the flaws of the system<br>• that there was an error<br>• their shortcomings |

| D |
| --- |
| • a lie<br>• a bogus story<br>• a lame excuse |

| E |
| --- |
| • the ending of the play<br>• too much information<br>• your secrets |

| F |
| --- |
| • the fact that I was sad<br>• the vibe in the room<br>• something I said earlier |

**D Complete the sentences with the phrasal verbs in parentheses in the correct tense. Some verbs are in the passive voice. The first one is done for you.**

1 As a psychologist, over the years, I *have picked up* (pick up on) a number of subtle changes in people's body language when they are lying.

2 I can't believe I ________________ (talk into) buying another pair of shoes at the store yesterday! Salespeople can be really persuasive.

3 Jennifer was fired when they found out she ________________ (give away) confidential business information for years.

4 I've known the twins for thirty years, and Richard ________________ (always/come across) as the quieter, more thoughtful of the two.

5 We're more than two hours into the meeting, and no one ________________ (bring up) the issue of sexual harassment yet.

6 A number of weaknesses ________________ (point out) in the report last week, so the company decided to revamp the system.

Answer key:

| Exercise A | Exercise B | Exercise C | Exercise D |
| --- | --- | --- | --- |
| 1 A | 2 talked me out of it | 2 D | 2 was talked into |
| 2 B | 3 gave it away | 3 E (C fits, too.) | 3 had been giving away/had given away |
| 3 B | 4 made them up | 4 A | 4 has always come across/always comes across |
| 4 B | 5 picked up on it | 5 F | 5 has brought up |
| 5 B | 6 pointed them out | 6 C | 6 were pointed out |
| 6 B | | | |

# 85 FIGURE OUT

## 1 WHAT IT MEANS

**1 When you figure out the answer to a question or the solution to a problem, you manage to understand and/or solve it:**

trying to figure out how the app works

▶ It took me hours to figure out how the app works.
= It was really hard to understand how the app works.

**2 When you figure someone out, you finally understand them:**

▶ I can't figure her out at all.
= I can't understand what kind of person she is or why she acts the way she does.

## 2 HOW IT WORKS

**1 *Figure out* takes an object (i.e., what or who you figure out). If the object is a noun, it tends to go at the end:**

☑ I couldn't figure out the instructions. (more common)
☑ I couldn't figure the instructions out. (less common)

**2 If the object is a pronoun, it always goes in the middle:**

☑ I couldn't figure them out.
☒ I couldn't ~~figure out them~~.

**3 You can use *if/whether*, a *wh-* word or a *that* clause after *figure out*:**

☑ I couldn't figure out if I was tapping the right button.
☑ It was hard to figure out what I was doing wrong.
☑ I soon figured out that I was doing something wrong.

## 3 HOW YOU USE IT IN REAL LIFE

**1 *Figure out* + *wh-* words:**

▶ He spends a lot of time trying to **figure out what** to do and far less actually doing anything.
▶ Once you've **figured out why** you should invest, the next step is to learn how.

▶ She's smart enough to **figure out how** to get things done and brave enough to make them happen.

2 *Figure out* + **phrases with** ***way*****:**

▶ I have just over 1,000 followers on Instagram, and I'm always trying to **figure out ways to** get them more engaged.

▶ We are a week away from Christmas, and I'm trying to **figure out a way of** explaining to my five-year-old why Santa is not coming.

3 **Common expressions:**

▶ Don't worry! We'**ll figure something out**. (= find a solution)

▶ Just when you think **you've got it all figured out** (= you have all the answers), life proves you wrong.

## 4 MORE REAL-LIFE DATA

***Figure out*** **often attracts words and phrases expressing difficulty:**

▶ She looked at me as if she **was trying to figure out** a puzzle.

▶ When I heard the news, I **couldn't quite figure out** what to do.

▶ If you're **having trouble figuring out** how to take the first step, then this article is for you.

▶ Richard was Mary's first and only love, and she **struggled to figure out** how to move forward without him by her side.

## 5 CONVERSATION TIP

**Imagine you are struggling to set up a new printer. Here's how you can ask for help:**

**I can't figure out how to make this thing work. Can you talk me through it?**

# 86 GET AWAY WITH

## 1 WHAT IT MEANS

**1 When you get away with (doing) something wrong or risky, you manage to do it without suffering any serious consequences:**

▶ I was lucky to get away with only a small fine.

= I did something against the law, but, luckily, the only punishment I received was a small fine.

**2 After you finish this lesson, turn to page 252 for an additional meaning of *get away with*.**

## 2 HOW IT WORKS

**1 *Get away with* takes an object (i.e., what you get away with). The object always goes at the end, whether it is a noun or a pronoun, so never separate the verb (*get*) from the particles (*away, with*):**

☑ I got away with a small fine.

☑ I got away with it.

☒ I ~~got away a small fine with~~.

☒ I ~~got it away with~~.

**2 If you use a verb after *get away with*, put it in the *-ing* form:**

☑ I got away with paying a small fine.

## 3 HOW YOU USE IT IN REAL LIFE

**1 *Get away with + it*. Notice the ideas that the pronoun *it* refers to:**

▶ We have a president who believes he can lie and **get away with it**.

▶ She's beat the system before, and she's **gotten away with it** [UK: got]. What makes you think she wouldn't try again?

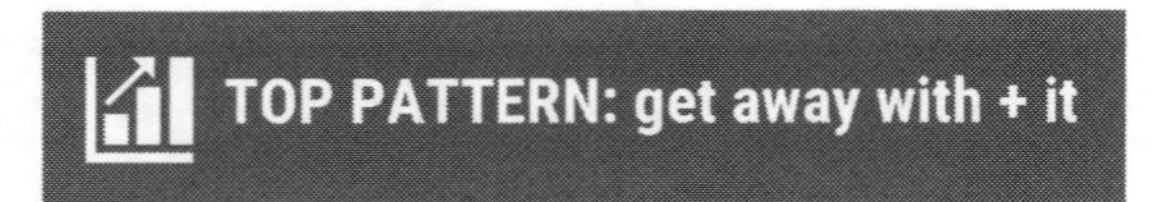


**2 *Get away with + anything*:**

▶ He's a strict teacher who doesn't let the kids **get away with anything**.

3 *Get away with* + **words related to legal and ethical matters:**

▶ She lied about what happened in an attempt to **get away with** the **crime**.

▶ New evidence surfaced at Senate hearings yesterday that more and more Americans are **getting away with** tax **fraud**.

▶ Did you really think you could **get away with stealing** from me?

▶ No one has ever **gotten away with lying** to me, and you certainly won't be the first one.

▶ You shouldn't let them **get away with treating** you like this.

4 **Common expression –** ***get away with murder*****:**

▶ This is a comedy about three people who killed someone and tried to **get away with murder**. (= literally kill someone without being punished)

▶ The guy they hired was lazy, arrogant, and felt that he could **get away with murder** (= figuratively speaking, do something wrong and not be punished) because of his good looks.

## 4 MORE REAL-LIFE DATA

***Get away with*** **tends to follow words expressing ability and permission:**

▶ Sadly, there are things that my male colleagues say and do that, as a woman, I **could** never **get away with**.

▶ This is unbelievable. I wasn't expecting the governor to **be able to get away with** tax evasion.

▶ We shouldn't **let** the media **get away with** protecting either candidate.

▶ It really is shocking what drug companies **are allowed to get away with**.

## 5 CONVERSATION TIP

**Imagine you are talking to a close friend who did something wrong but didn't expect to get caught. Here's what you can say:**

**What made you think you would get away with it?**

# 87 GO THROUGH

## 1 WHAT IT MEANS

**1 When you go through an experience, especially a challenging or unpleasant one, it's something that you live through or something that happens to you:**

▶ I had no idea you were going through a divorce.

= I didn't know you were in the middle of a divorce.

**2 After you finish this lesson,** **turn to page 252** **for additional meanings of *go through*.**

## 2 HOW IT WORKS

***Go through* takes an object (i.e., what you go through). The object always goes at the end, whether it is a noun or a pronoun:**

☑ I'm going through a divorce.

☑ I'm going through it.

☒ I'm ~~going a divorce through~~.

☒ I'm ~~going it through.~~

## 3 HOW YOU USE IT IN REAL LIFE

**1 *Go through* tends to attract words describing difficult moments:**

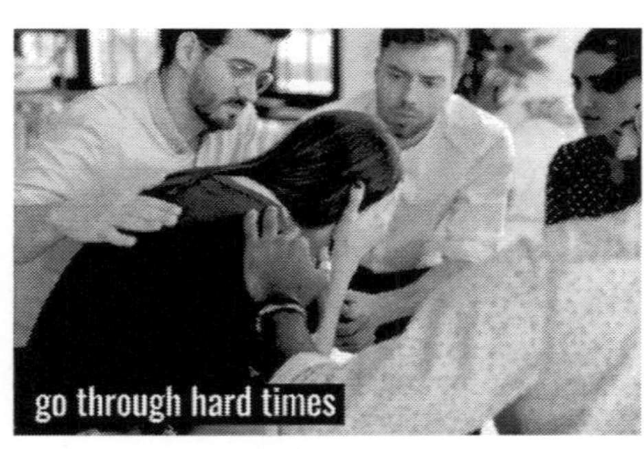
go through hard times

▶ Self-help books are great, but if you're **going through hard times**, you should surround yourself with family and friends.

▶ In my speech, I recalled the words of Winston Churchill: "If you're **going through hell**, keep going."

▶ In 2019, I **went through** a personal **crisis** after losing my job.

▶ As a rebellious teen, I was a little withdrawn and would sometimes **go through** bouts of **depression**.

▶ If you knew me and understood the **struggles** some disabled people **go through**, perhaps you wouldn't be so judgmental.

▶ It's tough to watch your own child **go through** the **pain** of young adulthood.

▶ Everyone **goes through difficulties** in life, but for some people, the difficulties go beyond what's usually considered acceptable.

2 **Common expression – *go through the motions*:**

▶ Mike's teaching seems really mechanical, as if he's just **going through the motions**. (= teaching without much enthusiasm)

## 4 RELATED MEANINGS

***Go through* can be used to talk about:**

1 **Phases or time periods:**

▶ In the book, Ron is a successful advertising executive who **goes through life** in a zombie-like state after his son dies.

▶ Unlike George Harrison and John Lennon, Paul McCartney never **went through** a **phase** of disparaging the Beatles.

▶ My three-year-old is **going through** a **period** in which her language skills are changing rapidly.

▶ Most relationships **go through stages** where one person is more emotionally generous than the other.

2 **Slow or challenging processes:**

▶ The central idea in this lesson is that, throughout life, our bodies **go through changes** that are caused by many factors.

▶ You don't have to **go through the process of** buy**ing** a house alone. Have you considered hiring a realtor [UK: estate agent]?

## 5 CONVERSATION TIP

**Imagine you are talking to a close friend about the struggles you are facing in your personal life. Here's what you can say:**

**You have no idea what I'm going through.**

# 88 MAKE UP FOR

## 1 WHAT IT MEANS

**When you make up for the loss/lack of something or for a bad experience, you try to compensate for it:**

▶ I believe that nothing can make up for the loss of a child.

= If you lose a child, I believe that there is nothing you can do to ease the pain.

## 2 HOW IT WORKS

***Make up for*** **takes an object (i.e., what you make up for). The object always goes at the end, whether it is a noun or a pronoun, so never separate the verb (*make*) from the particles (*up, for*):**

☑ It's impossible to make up for the loss of a child.

☑ It's impossible to make up for it.

☒ It's impossible to ~~make up the loss of a child for.~~

☒ It's impossible to ~~make it up for~~.

## 3 HOW YOU USE IT IN REAL LIFE

1 ***Make up for*** **+ things you lose or miss:**

▶ Our local newspaper had hoped that online advertising would **make up for the loss of** traditional print ads, but that hasn't been the case.

▶ Sorry, I can't make it. I've got some stuff to finish up tonight to **make up for missing** work tomorrow.

▶ Skipping meals increases sugar cravings, and it can cause you to overeat to **make up for missed** calories.

2 ***Make up for*** **+ things you lack:**

▶ Sleeping late on Sundays will relieve part of a sleep debt, but it will not completely **make up for the lack of** sleep.

▶ We should try to move away from an educational system that tries to **make up for deficiencies** and embrace one that really teaches.

▶ Professional photographers know how to adjust the exposures of their prints to **make up for shortcomings** in the negatives.

3 *Make up for + the fact that*:

▶ The staff is so nice that it **makes up for the fact that** the hotel itself has seen better days.

4 **Common expression** – *make up for lost time*:

▶ I didn't travel much in my thirties, but now I'm **making up for lost time.** (= traveling more now that I have the opportunity)

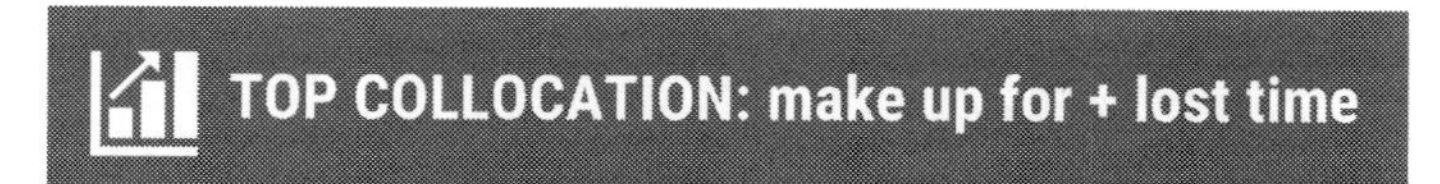


## 4 MORE REAL-LIFE DATA

1 **The use of *more than* to emphasize *make up for* is very common:**

▶ I don't have the perfect job, but the good days **more than make up for** the bad ones. (= The good days make the bad days seem far less important.)

2 ***Make up for* is often used with the verb *lack*. Notice the pattern in bold:**

▶ **What** the performance **lacked in** subtlety and precision, **it made up for in** passion.

▶ **What** I **lack in** experience, I more than **make up for with** a willingness to learn.

3 **Notice the use of *by* + an *-ing* verb to provide more details:**

▶ Even if you eat a lot, you can **make up for it by** be**ing** physically active.

## 5 CONVERSATION TIP

**Imagine you are recommending a restaurant to a friend because of the food, *not* the service. Here's what you can say:**

**The service isn't that good, but the food more than makes up for it.**

# 89 PUT UP WITH

## 1 WHAT IT MEANS

**When you put up with unpleasant things or people, you try to tolerate them:**

▶ I swear I won't put up with his lies anymore.

= I swear I won't continue to accept his lies.

## 2 HOW IT WORKS

1 ***Put up with*** **takes an object (i.e., what or who you put up with). The object always goes at the end, whether it is a noun or a pronoun, so never separate the verb (*put*) from the particles (*up, with*):**

☑ I won't put up with his lies.

☑ I won't put up with them.

☒ I won't ~~put up his lies with~~.

☒ I won't ~~put them up with~~.

2 **If you use a verb after *put up with*, put it in the *-ing* form:**

☑ No one should have to put up with being lied to.

## 3 HOW YOU USE IT IN REAL LIFE

1 ***Put up with*** **+ words describing bad behavior** [UK: behaviour]**:**

▶ In this day and age, no employee should have to **put up with bullying** in the workplace.

▶ Remember you don't have to **put up with abuse** from anyone – and that includes your family and friends.

▶ There is no reason why you should **put up with** any form of **harassment**. If I were you, I'd reach out to HR.

▶ Her attitude shows a total lack of respect for you, so let me ask again, why are you **putting up with** his **crap***?

*Crap* may sound vulgar. Be careful when and where you use it.

2 *Put up with* + **words related to the senses:**

▶ To be honest, I don't think I could have **put up with** the **pain** without some very powerful painkillers.

▶ As long as you're willing to **put up with** 24-hour **noise**, London's West End is a really great place to live.

▶ If you like horses, you have to learn to **put up with** the **smell**. You can't have one without the other.

## 4 MORE REAL-LIFE DATA

1 **You often use *put up with* after expressions of obligation and willingness:**

▶ I am so sorry that you've **had to put up with** this, and our staff will see to it that it never happens again.

▶ Nobody should **be forced to put up with** someone they dislike, for any reason.

▶ Be kind to our planet. It's the only one left that **is willing to put up with** us.

2 ***Put up with* often attracts the words *anymore* and *no longer*:**

▶ The polls suggest that the electorate is **no longer** willing to **put up with** lies and broken promises from politicians.

▶ The way you treat me is not acceptable, and I will not **put up with** it **anymore**.

3 **Notice the pattern *put up with someone's doing something*:**

▶ Sandra couldn't **put up with** her husband's cheat**ing** and finally worked up the courage to leave him.

## 5 CONVERSATION TIP

**Imagine you are talking to a friend who has a difficult boss. You admire your friend's patience. Here's what you can say:**

**Honestly, I don't know how you put up with (her).**

# CHECK YOUR PROGRESS 15

**A Complete each sentence with a phrasal verb. Check your answers before doing exercise B.**

| figure | get | go | make | put |
|---|---|---|---|---|

| away with | out | through | up for | up with |
|---|---|---|---|---|

1 I'm sorry I was late. To ______________________ it, lunch is on me today.
2 I tried to use the software but couldn't quite ____________ it ____________.
3 Don't think you're going to lie to me and ______________________ it.
4 It's a bad experience, but you don't have to ______________________ it alone.
5 That noise is unbearable. I don't know how you ______________________ it.

**B Go back to exercise A. Underline the word(s) or idea that *it* refers to in each sentence. Read the examples below first.**

Example 1: Politics is a sensitive topic at home, so we never bring it up when we're together.
Example 2: The ending of the book is a happy one, but I don't want to give it away!
Example 3: I was feeling sad, and my mother picked up on it when she saw me.

**C Complete the sentences using words from the first, second, and third columns, without changing the order. The first one is done for you.**

| | | |
|---|---|---|
| • figure out | • abuse | • from your boss |
| • get away with | • a way | • in my life |
| • went through | • lots of changes | • of sleep |
| • put up with | • the lack | • to solve it. |
| • make up for | • treating | • you like this |

1 Stand up for yourself! Don't let him
*get away with treating you like this.*
2 This is a serious problem. We need to
______________________________________________
3 I didn't sleep a wink last night, so this morning I had three cups of coffee to
______________________________________________
4 There are plenty of good jobs out there. You shouldn't have to
______________________________________________
5 I was married for 20 years. After the divorce, I
______________________________________________

**D EXTRA CHALLENGE! Rewrite the sentences without changing the meaning. Use the bold words to create phrasal verbs. The first two are done for you.**

1 The teacher didn't notice that the students were not interested in the lesson.
**PICK**
The teacher didn't *pick up on the students' lack of* interest in the lesson.

2 He didn't mean to reveal how the book ends.
**GAVE**
He accidentally *gave away the ending of* the book.

3 I'm struggling to make more people follow me on Twitter.
**FIGURING**
I'm having trouble ________________________ get more Twitter followers.

4 She only paid a small fine for driving too fast.
**GOT**
She broke the speed limit and ________________________ a small fine.

5 Dave's teaching is very mechanical.
**GOING**
In class, it feels as if Dave is just ________________________ motions.

6 When you lose someone you love, nothing can compensate for it.
**MAKE**
Nothing can ________________________ of a loved one.

7 It is hard to tolerate customers who have no patience.
**PUT**
It is not ________________________ customers.

Answer key:

Exercise A
1 make up for
2 figure/out
3 get away with
4 go through
5 put up with

Exercise B
1 I was late
2 (use) the software
3 lie to me
4 (a) bad experience
5 (That) noise

Exercise C
2 figure out a way to solve it.
3 make up for the lack of sleep.
4 put up with abuse from your boss.
5 went through lots of changes in my life.

Exercise D
3 figuring out a way to/how to
4 got away with (paying)
5 going through the
6 make up for the loss
7 easy to put up with impatient

# 90 COME UNDER

## 1 WHAT IT MEANS

**1 When you come under something, you experience (and often suffer from) it:**

▶ The government has come under attack for being too slow to respond to the crisis.

= The government has been criticized [UK: criticised] for not dealing with the crisis quickly enough.

**2 After you finish this lesson, turn to page 253 for additional meanings of *come under*.**

## 2 HOW IT WORKS

***Come under* takes an object (i.e., what you come under). The object always goes at the end, whether it is a noun or a pronoun:**

☑ The government has come under attack.

☑ The government has come under it.

☒ The government ~~has come attack under~~.

☒ The government ~~has come it under~~.

## 3 HOW YOU USE IT IN REAL LIFE

**1 *Come under* + *attack* and other related words:**

▶ British diplomats in Benghazi **came under attack** from suspected Islamist militants. (literally)

▶ Freedom of the press is **coming under attack** in a number of countries. (figuratively)

▶ The app has **come under fire** after news that it may be collecting user data automatically unless users specifically opt out. (figuratively)

▶ In many ways, the pandemic can be expected to result in globalization [UK: globalisation] **coming under assault** like never before. (figuratively)

▶ The president has **come under** a lot of **criticism** for joining protesters calling for military intervention.

▶ When communities **come under pressure**, they sometimes look for scapegoats they can blame for whatever is going wrong.

2 *Come under* + *control* **and other related words:**

▶ In Orwell's *1984*, every aspect of our lives eventually **comes under** state **control**.

▶ Different parts of India **came under** British **rule** in different periods.

▶ Farsi is an Iranian language primarily spoken in Iran, Afghanistan, Tajikistan, and countries that historically **came under** Persian **influence**.

3 *Come under* + *investigation* **and other related words:**

▶ The governor has **come under investigation** for accepting bribes linked to construction projects.

▶ The company has **come under scrutiny** recently due to questions about the viability of its business model.

▶ No one should ever **come under suspicion** because of their appearance or their last name.

## 4 MORE REAL-LIFE DATA

1 **Notice the <u>patterns</u> after the nouns in bold:**

▶ Each of these measures should **come under scrutiny** <u>from opposition parties</u> and the media. (*from* + noun)

▶ The newspaper has **come under fire** <u>for its lack</u> of reliability. (*for* + noun)

▶ The app has **come under** a lot of **criticism** <u>for being</u> beautiful, but not very functional. (for + -*ing* verb)

2 **The adjectives in bold below are commonly used:**

▶ The role of the U.S. Federal Reserve has **come under increasing** scrutiny in recent years.

▶ The company has **come under heavy** criticism for its privacy policies.

▶ The U.S. drone program [UK: programme] **came under intense** scrutiny after the news report.

▶ Journalists trying to cover the uprising have **come under severe** pressure from the authorities.

## 5 CONVERSATION TIP

**Imagine a friend from another country is asking you about the local government. Here's something you can say:**

**The government has recently come under fire for (its handling of the economy).**

# 91 GET OVER

## 1 WHAT IT MEANS

**1 When you get over a problem, a negative feeling, or an unpleasant experience, you manage to overcome it:**

▶ I think we can get over this problem without too much difficulty.

= I don't think it will be too hard to overcome this problem.

**2 When you get over someone you used to have a relationship with, you start to forget them and move on with your life:**

▶ It took me a long time to get over my ex-wife.

= It took me a long time to forget my ex-wife and move on with my life.

## 2 HOW IT WORKS

**1 *Get over* takes an object (i.e., what or who you get over). The object always goes at the end, whether it is a noun or a pronoun:**

☑ I can't get over my ex. ☑ I can't get over her.

☒ I can't ~~get my ex over~~. ☒ I can't ~~get her over~~.

**2 *Get over* can be followed by *wh-* words, most commonly *what* and *how*:**

☑ I can't get over what my ex did to me.

☑ I can't get over how badly she treated me.

**3 Verbs are relatively rare after *get over*, but if you do use a verb, put it in the *-ing* form:**

☑ I still can't get over losing her.

## 3 HOW YOU USE IT IN REAL LIFE

**1 *Get over* tends to attract words describing negative feelings and experiences:**

▶ I **got over** my **fear** of big dogs when we adopted a Rottweiler.

▶ We've made a lot of progress, but there are still some **hurdles** to **get over**.

▶ I never thought I'd have such a hard time **getting over** a **breakup**.

▶ I want to **get over** my **anger** and release the rage so I can get on with my life.

▶ Mine was a really bad **breakup**, and I'm still **getting over** it, so I'm just not ready for a new relationship yet.

2 **Notice the use of phrases with *the* + negative word + *of*:**

▶ People ask me how long it takes to **get over the loss of** a loved one. My response is, you never get over it.

▶ After **getting over the shock of** the diagnosis, I faced my mortality head-on and decided to live life to the fullest.

▶ Children have a hard time **getting over the death of** a pet, and it's up to parents to help them deal with the loss.

## 4 RELATED MEANINGS

**Common expressions with *get over*:**

▶ How do I **get over the fact** (= learn to accept) that I'll never be good at basketball, no matter how hard I try?

▶ I hate to break it to you, but she will never win the presidency. **Get over it.** (= Accept it and move on.)

▶ **I can't get over** (= I'm surprised at) how good the book actually was.

## 5 CONVERSATION TIP

**Imagine you have not forgotten someone you broke up with. Here's what you can tell a close friend:**

**It's no use fooling myself. I still haven't gotten** [UK: got] **over (him).**

# 92 GO ABOUT

## 1 WHAT IT MEANS

**The way you go about a situation, problem, or task is how you deal with it:**

▶ How do you go about creating your marketing strategy?

= How do you deal with the task of creating a marketing strategy?

## 2 HOW IT WORKS

**1 *Go about* takes an object (i.e., what you go about). The object always goes at the end, whether it is a noun or a pronoun:**

☑ How do you go about this task?

☑ How do you go about it?

☒ How do you ~~go this task about~~?

☒ How do you ~~go it about~~?

**2 Verbs are very common after *go about*, and they are always used in the *-ing* form:**

☑ This is how I went about creating a marketing strategy.

## 3 HOW YOU USE IT IN REAL LIFE

**1 *Go about* + *task* and other related words:**

▶ Setting up an online business is easier said than done, and there is no one right way to **go about** this **task**.

▶ As we **go about the task of** design**ing** products and services, we should keep the end users in mind at all times.

▶ There has to be a better way to **go about** this **process** without letting the entire financial system collapse.

▶ While people **go about the process of** writ**ing** in their own unique way, four different steps are usually involved: pre-writing, drafting, revising, and editing.

▶ As I **went about the business of** writ**ing** my autobiography, I found all sorts of avenues for understanding and forgiveness.

▶ Frankly, I don't see any other way of **going about** this **problem** other than revamping the entire process.

2 **Phrases with *how* and *way* + *go about*. Notice the frequent use of action verbs:**

▶ I really have no idea **how to go about** doing something like this.

▶ If you're not sure what your weaknesses are, **how will you go about** getting feedback that will help you improve?

▶ I love the suggestions in the book, but **how do you go about** trying to make all those major life changes?

▶ **The best way to go about** creating a loyal customer base is to focus on user experience.

▶ By "business method," I mean **the way** a company **goes about** making products or services available.

▶ In my talk, I shared some of my thoughts on **different ways to go about** building social and political capital.

## 4 RELATED MEANING

**You can also use *go about* to talk about your normal day-to-day activities. In this case, it is usually followed by *my, your,* etc.:**

▶ I had absolutely no idea what was happening around me as I innocently **went about my business**.

▶ Patricia **goes about her work** with a great deal of enthusiasm and a tremendous sense of pride. I can recommend her wholeheartedly.

▶ The tragedy hasn't stopped the population from **going about their lives**.

## 5 CONVERSATION TIP

**Imagine you are giving a school presentation. Here's how you can explain how you collected data:**

**First, let me tell you how I went about the data collection process.**

# 93 PULL OFF

## 1 WHAT IT MEANS

1 **When you pull something off, especially something challenging, you succeed in doing it:**

▶ I doubted they were going to be able to do it, but, somehow, they pulled it off.

= I didn't think they were going to be able to do it, but, for some reason, they succeeded.

2 **After you finish this lesson, turn to page 253 for an additional meaning of *pull off*.**

## 2 HOW IT WORKS

1 ***Pull off* takes an object (i.e., what you pull off). If the object is a noun, it usually goes at the end:**

☑ They pulled off a deal.

2 **If the object is a pronoun (usually *it* in this case), it always goes in the middle:**

☑ They pulled it off.

☒ They ~~pulled off it~~.

## 3 HOW YOU USE IT IN REAL LIFE

1 **The most common way to use *pull off* is with the pronoun *it* as object:**

▶ Williams took on the challenge and **pulled it off**. Frankly, I'm not surprised. That's what champions do.

▶ I have this great idea for a new app, but I don't have the knowledge yet to **pull it off**, and this is where you come in.

▶ The Roborock S4 is one of the most affordable robot vacuums, and when it comes to vacuuming, it **pulls it off** better than most.

2 *Pull off* **often attracts words related to competition, especially in sports and politics:**

▶ If the Hokies* can **pull off** that **win**, they'll return home on Saturday, August 14 to face the Cavaliers*.

▶ That evening, the Titans* **pulled off** an **upset** (= a surprising victory), beating the Steelers* 26-23.

▶ Donald Trump triumphed in North Carolina, while Joe Biden **pulled off** a surprise **victory** in Arizona.

3 *Pull off* **+ words describing major achievements:**

▶ It doesn't sound like an easy **feat** to **pull off**, but Streisand makes it all work splendidly, leaving the audience speechless.

▶ The **trick** Spielberg needed to **pull off** was to make the characters' moral choices dramatically compelling.

▶ Unless the singer's lawyers can **pull off** a **miracle**, he is expected to be in jail before the week is over.

## 4 MORE REAL-LIFE DATA

**Notice how** ***pull off*** **often attracts words and expressions describing ability:**

▶ Despite a few technical glitches, he **managed to pull off** a thrilling presentation.

▶ Finding a pair of jeans that appears well-worn is the key to **successfully pulling off** this look. (= You need old-looking jeans to look good in this particular style.)

▶ This is a hard task to accomplish, and even GM **couldn't pull it off**.

▶ The three roles **are** incredibly **difficult to pull off**, and, despite a few minor glitches, the cast excelled.

▶ No matter how well organized [UK: organised], a huge event like this **is** always **hard to pull off** without problems.

## 5 CONVERSATION TIP

**Imagine you managed to do something you never thought you could. You tell a friend about it. Here's what you can say:**

**I still can't believe I managed to pull it off.**

*These are all American football teams.

# 94 TURN AROUND

## 1 WHAT IT MEANS

**1 When you turn around a plan, business, or system that was unsuccessful for a period of time, you fix it:**

▶ Turning the economy around won't be easy.

= It will be hard to fix the economy.

**2 You can also use *turn around* in a general sense:**

▶ Mindfulness has turned my life around.

= Mindfulness has changed my life completely – for the better.

**In both cases, notice the connection to the basic physical meaning of *turn around*, which is to move in order to face the opposite direction.**

## 2 HOW IT WORKS

**1 *Turn around* can be used with or without an object (i.e., what you turn around). Without an object, you can simply say that something turns around:**

☑ The economy won't turn around.

**2 If you use an object, and if the object is a noun, it tends to go in the middle:**

☑ It'll be hard to turn the economy around. (more common)

☑ It'll be hard to turn around the economy. (less common)

**3 Longer objects usually go at the end:**

☑ It'll be hard to turn around a post-recession economy.

**4 If the object is a pronoun, it always goes in the middle:**

☑ It'll be hard to turn it around.

☒ It'll be hard to ~~turn around it.~~

## 3 HOW YOU USE IT IN REAL LIFE

**1 *Turn around* + words related to business and the economy:**

▶ Reagan won in a landslide because he **turned around** a struggling **economy** and restored the country's confidence.

▶ Thohir is a well-regarded businessman, with a good track record of **turning companies around**.

▶ Some homeowners are holding on to their properties and renting them out until the **market turns around**.

2 *Turn around* + **words related to fate:**

▶ From the looks of things, my **luck** has finally **turned around**, and I'm not getting fired after all.

▶ Carl's savings will keep him afloat for a few months until his **fortunes turn around**, and he finds a job.

3 *Turn around* **often attracts the word** ***things:***

▶ The housing market needs to hit rock bottom before **things** can finally **turn around**.

▶ In this episode, Mia and Richard tell us how they **turned things around** after a disastrous first date.

## 4 RELATED MEANING

***To turn around and do or say something*** **means to do or say something unexpected or unreasonable, without worrying about the consequences:**

▶ This was your idea, remember? So, don't **turn around and** say you don't know what we're talking about.

▶ The company has **turned around and** blamed an app developer for the data breach.

## 5 CONVERSATION TIP

**Imagine you are telling a friend about big changes you want to make in your life. Here's what you can say:**

**I think the time has come for me to turn my life around.**

# CHECK YOUR PROGRESS 16

**A Write (S) if each underlined phrasal verb has a similar meaning in both sentences. Write (D) if it has a related but different meaning.**

1 _____

A Media companies have <u>come under</u> a lot of criticism in recent years.

B The government has <u>come under</u> fire for not acting quickly enough.

2 _____

A It took me a while to <u>get over</u> the shock of the news.

B I need to learn how to <u>get over</u> my fear of butterflies.

3 _____

A How is your company <u>going about</u> the process of interacting with customers on a global scale?

B I was <u>going about</u> my business when the police stopped me for no reason.

4 _____

A This is not an easy feat to <u>pull off</u>. Congratulations!

B Despite his lack of experience, he managed to <u>pull off</u> a great presentation.

5 _____

A It's often hard to <u>turn around</u> a struggling economy.

B It's too late now. Don't <u>turn around</u> and say I didn't warn you.

**B Read the sentences. Which phrasal verb from exercise A completes all the sentences in each group? The first one is done for you.**

**group 1:** *turn around*

- Don't give up. Your fortunes will eventually ____.
- Don't ____ and blame me for your problems!
- Instead of waiting for life to ____, do something to change it!

**group 2:** ______________

- The company has ____ attack because of its new ad.
- The documents have ____ scrutiny in recent weeks.
- The president has ____ pressure from the opposition.

**group 3:** ______________

- The team has managed to ____ a win at the last minute.
- Unless we can ____ a miracle, this is a lost cause.
- You look amazing. Not many people can ____ this look.

**group 4:** ______________

- There are still some hurdles to ____.
- It took Mary a long time to ____ her husband's death.
- I can't ____ the fact that I was laid off.

**group 5:** ______________

- What's the best way to ____ this problem?
- There's no magic formula to ____ the writing process.
- How you ____ your work says a great deal about you.

C **EXTRA CHALLENGE! Complete the second sentence without changing the meaning. Use the words in parentheses. You may have to change some words in the first sentence and add others. The first one is done for you.**

1 I didn't feel angry anymore, and I finally forgave her.
I *got over my anger* (get / anger), and I finally forgave her.

2 This is how we created a marketing strategy.
This is how we ________________ (go / task / create) a marketing strategy.

3 It looks as if things are going well for me again.
It looks as if my ________________. (luck / finally / turn)

4 It was challenging project, but we succeeded.
It was a challenging project, but we ________________.
(able / pull)

5 The company was criticized [UK: criticised] because it is not environmentally friendly.
The company ________________ (come / criticism / not / be) environmentally friendly.

Answer key:

| Exercise A | Exercise B | Exercise C |
|---|---|---|
| 1 S | 2 come under | 2 went about the task of creating |
| 2 S | 3 pull off | 3 luck is finally turning around/has finally turned around |
| 3 D | 4 get over | 4 were able to pull it off |
| 4 S | 5 go about | 5 came under criticism for not being |
| 5 D | | |

# 95 DO AWAY WITH

## 1 WHAT IT MEANS

**When you do away with something, you get rid of it:**

▶ They should do away with all these stupid rules.

= They should eliminate all these stupid rules.

## 2 HOW IT WORKS

**1 *Do away with* takes an object (i.e., what you do away with). The object always goes at the end, whether it is a noun or a pronoun, so never separate the verb (*do*) from the particles (*away*, *with*):**

☑ They should do away with these rules.

☑ They should do away with them.

☒ They should ~~do away these rules with~~.

☒ They should ~~do them away with~~.

**2 *Do away with* can be used in the passive voice:**

☑ These rules should be done away with.

## 3 HOW YOU USE IT IN REAL LIFE

***Do away with* can be used with a wide range of nouns, from *plastic bags* and *cash payments* to *free parking*. It tends to attract words describing laws, rules, and regulations:**

▶ The committee is considering **doing away with** the **rule** prohibiting players under 19 from being hired.

▶ In 1817, the U.S. Congress **did away with** all internal **taxes**, relying on tariffs on imported goods to run the government.

▶ Over the years, more than 60 countries have **done away with laws** that made adultery a crime.

▶ Airlines are entitled to **do away with** their frequent-flier **programs** [UK: programmes], but they risk alienating a lot of customers if they do so.

▶ The minister announced plans to **do away with** visa **restrictions** for the citizens of 66 countries.

▶ The government has decided to **do away with** the **requirement** for TV channels to renew their license [UK: licence] annually.

▶ The proposed changes are supposed to **do away with** the **system** currently in place in order to provide universal healthcare for all.

## 4 MORE REAL-LIFE DATA

1 **Notice the different patterns with the noun *need*:**

▶ Net banking and ATMs [UK: cashpoints] have virtually **done away with the need to** visit brick-and-mortar banks. (*need* + *to* + verb)

▶ YouTube essentially **did away with the need for** illegal downloads by making all the music in the world available at the swipe of a finger. (*need* + *for* + noun)

▶ The new system will **do away with the need for** users **to** have multiple logins for different departments. (*need* + *for* + noun + *to* + verb)

2 ***Do away with* often attracts adverbs that mean *in every way possible*:**

▶ This bill was partially repealed in the 1980s and then **completely done away with** in the late 1990s.

▶ Several hotel chains have announced plans to change the "Do Not Disturb" sign or **do away with it altogether**.

▶ Wi-Fi Direct works well, and it **does away with** your router **entirely**.

## 5 CONVERSATION TIP

**Imagine the school principal is meeting with your class, asking for suggestions. Here's something you can say:**

> **I know it's a long shot, but I think (formal tests) should be done away with.**

# 96 FALL APART

## 1 WHAT IT MEANS

**If something such as an institution, system, agreement, or relationship falls apart, it has so many problems that it can no longer exist or function:**

▶ The deal fell apart, and we had to start from scratch.

= The deal had so many serious problems that we had to start all over again.

**Notice the connection to the basic physical meaning of *fall apart*, which is to be in bad condition or breaking into pieces.**

## 2 HOW IT WORKS

***Fall apart* takes no object. You simply say that something falls apart:**

☑ The deal fell apart.

☒ The deal ~~fell it apart~~.

☒ ~~We fell apart the deal~~.

## 3 HOW YOU USE IT IN REAL LIFE

1 *Everything, things + fall apart*:

▶ Don't lose hope. Just when you think **everything** is **falling apart**, that's when everything is actually falling into place!

▶ I'm glad I stayed in the UK. If I'd gone to Chicago, **things** would have **fallen apart** after a couple of years.

2 ***Life* and *world*, often preceded by *whole* + *fall apart*:**

▶ Suzanne's **whole life** appears to have **fallen apart** in the past six months, and she's feeling pretty lost.

▶ Sometimes I wonder if Patricia knows that if she ever leaves me, my **whole world** will **fall apart**.

3 **Words describing interpersonal relationships + *fall apart*:**

▶ Elvis' **marriage** to Priscilla **fell apart** as his career started to fall back into place, some people say.

▶ American scientists have developed a new method to assess whether a romantic **relationship** is going to **fall apart**.

▶ How can you tell if your **friendship** has **fallen apart**? Are there any signs to look out for?

4 **Words related to business and politics + *fall apart*:**

▶ It was a really long negotiation, with the **deal** almost **falling apart** in the final stretch. But they pulled it off in the end.

▶ Although no deal has been agreed on so far, and the **talks** could still **fall apart**, insiders remain optimistic.

▶ A quarter of a million jobs have been lost this month, and it seems as if the **economy** is quickly **falling apart**.

5 **Common expression – *fall apart at the seams*:**

▶ The president insists that the country is not **falling apart at the seams** (= failing completely), but his administration seems to be.

## 4 RELATED MEANING

**When people fall apart, they lose control of their emotions and can't deal with their personal or emotional problems. Notice the bold words and phrases before *fall apart*:**

▶ Lucy **completely fell apart** when her husband died.

▶ I'm under so much stress that sometimes I **feel as if I'm falling apart**.

## 5 CONVERSATION TIP

**Imagine you are giving a school presentation on a celebrity who had a difficult life. Here's something you can say:**

**(Whitney)'s personal life began to fall apart when (she married Bobby Brown).**

# 97 RUN OUT (OF)

## 1 WHAT IT MEANS

**1 When something runs out, there is no more of it left:**

▶ Time is running out, and we must act now to save the planet.

= We don't have much time left to save the planet, so we must do something now.

**2 You can express a similar idea in a different way, adding *of*:**

▶ Hurry up! We're running out of time.

= Hurry up! We don't have much time left.

## 2 HOW IT WORKS

**1 *Run out* takes no object. You simply say that something runs out:**

☑ Time is running out.

☒ Time is ~~running it out~~.

☒ ~~It is running out time~~.

**2 *Run out of* takes an object (i.e., what you run out of). The object always goes at the end, whether it is a noun or a pronoun, so never separate the verb (*run*) from the particles (*out*, *of*):**

☑ I'm running out of time.

☒ I ~~ran out time of~~.

☑ I'm running out of it.

☒ I ~~ran it out of~~.

## 3 HOW YOU USE IT IN REAL LIFE

**1 You can use *run out (of)* with many different words. Here are a few very common uncountable nouns:**

run out of water

▶ How dire is the situation? How close are we to **running out of water**?

▶ With transportation [UK: transport] systems down, hospital generators will **run out of fuel** after weeks, or maybe even days.

▶ The survey suggests that people's **patience** is all but **running out**. When will the local authorities stop and listen?

▶ My sister keeps saying that my **luck will run out** sooner or later, and that people will wise up to my tricks.
▶ The start-up saw its sales plunge after it **ran out of money** to invest in online marketing.
▶ Sometimes I feel that our **time** on Earth is **running out** because of global warming.

2 **These countable nouns are commonly used, too:**
▶ During the war, food **supplies** quickly **ran out**, and people were reduced to eating leaves and grass.
▶ When I asked cartoonist Gary Larson if he ever **runs out of ideas**, he said no.
▶ When the crisis hit, the company had **run out of options** other than bankruptcy.
▶ Is it true that I should let my **battery** completely **run out** every so often before recharging?

3 **Common expression –** ***run out of steam*****:**
▶ The demand for new housing has been met, and the market seems to be **running out of steam**. (= losing energy/strength)

## 4 RELATED MEANING

**When an official document runs out, it is no longer valid:**
▶ Negotiation of Silva's **contract**, which **runs out** next month, seems to have stalled.
▶ Eventually her **visa ran out**, and she was deported.
▶ I am selling the car because the **warranty runs out** this year.

## 5 CONVERSATION TIP

**Imagine you are brainstorming ideas for a team project. You are tired and can't think clearly anymore. Here's what you can say:**

**I'm running out of ideas. Why don't we take a quick break?**

# 98 SHUT DOWN

## 1 WHAT IT MEANS

**1 When a business shuts down or is shut down, it stops operating:**

▶ The company plans to shut down three plants and cut thousands of jobs.

= The company plans to close three factories and cut thousands of jobs.

**2 You can use *shut down* to talk about machines and vital organs, too:**

▶ I don't understand why my computer shuts down on its own sometimes.

= I don't understand why my computer turns itself off sometimes.

## 2 HOW IT WORKS

**1 *Shut down* can be used with or without an object (i.e., what you shut down). You can simply say that something shuts down:**

☑ The computer shut down automatically.

**2 If you use an object, and the object is a noun, it tends to go at the end:**

☑ I shut down the computer. (more common)

☑ I shut the computer down. (less common)

**3 If the object is a pronoun, it always goes in the middle:**

☑ I shut it down.

☒ I ~~shut down it~~.

**4 *Shut down* can be used in the passive voice:**

☑ The computer was not shut down properly.

## 3 HOW YOU USE IT IN REAL LIFE

**1 *Shut down* + words related to business and politics:**

▶ My employer has **shut down operations** temporarily because of the hurricane. Am I eligible for unemployment benefits?

▶ The company has announced plans to begin **shutting down production** in the U.S. next week.

- My father was laid off when the paper **plant** was **shut down** for good after a strike.
- Under the proposed plan, private **businesses** will **shut down**, and people will lose their jobs.
- Miami International Airport is **shutting down** one of its **terminals** next weekend.
- It's not clear why the government has decided to **shut down** the **investigation**.
- In the United States, the **government** can be **shut down** when there is a failure to pass funding legislation to finance it.

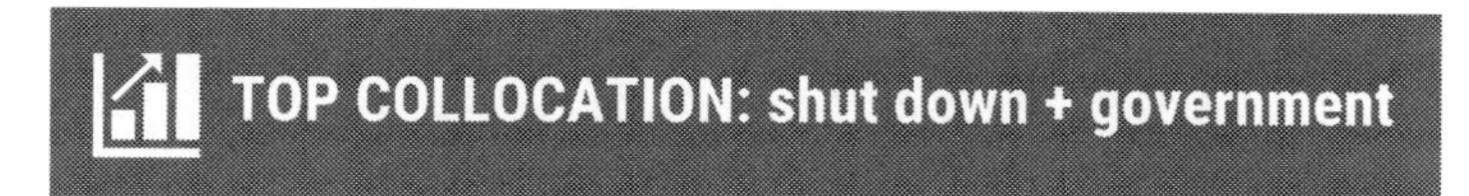


2 **Words related to machines +** ***shut down*****:**

- "Let's make sure that the last nuclear **reactor** is **shut down** by 2028 at the latest," the prime minister said.
- A Canada flight bound for São Paulo had to make an emergency landing today when an **engine shut down** just after the plane took off in Toronto.

3 **Vital organs +** ***shut down*****:**

- When I heard the news, my vision started to blur, and I felt as if my **brain** was **shutting down**.
- By the time Ron suspected that something was wrong, his **kidneys** had **shut down**.

## 4 MORE REAL-LIFE DATA

***Shut down*** **tends to attract** ***completely*** **and other similar adverbs:**

- The president has threatened to **completely shut down** the border. (= close the border between two countries)
- On November 13, all subscriptions will be canceled, and the service will be **shut down entirely**.
- It seems likely that sooner or later a larger company will purchase the start-up and either change it or **shut** it **down altogether**.

## 5 CONVERSATION TIP

**Imagine a friend is asking you about COVID-19 restrictions when the pandemic hit your area in 2020. Here's what you can say:**

**Most (local businesses) had to shut down.**

# 99 TEAR DOWN

## 1 WHAT IT MEANS

**When you tear something down, you destroy or remove it:**

▶ They're tearing down the old buildings to make way for a park.

= They're demolishing the old buildings so they can build a park.

**Remember that the verb *tear* rhymes with *there*, not *ear*.**

## 2 HOW IT WORKS

1 ***Tear down* takes an object (i.e., what you tear down). If the object is a noun, it tends to go at the end:**

☑ They're tearing down the buildings. (more common)

☑ They're tearing the buildings down. (less common)

2 **If the object is a pronoun, it always goes in the middle:**

☑ They're tearing them down.

☒ They're ~~tearing down them~~.

3 ***Tear down* is often used in the passive voice:**

☑ The buildings were torn down.

## 3 HOW YOU USE IT IN REAL LIFE

1 **Literal uses of *tear down*:**

▶ The company apologized [UK: apologised] after accidentally **tearing down** a **house** that had stood in a historic neighborhood [UK: neighbourhood] for almost a century.

▶ Canadian researchers estimate that a quarter of Vancouver's **homes** could be **torn down** by 2030.

▶ One in five Germans wishes the Berlin **Wall** hadn't been **torn down**, according to a recent survey.

▶ Critics, while acknowledging the need for a new park, say that **tearing down** the historic **building** would be a mistake.

▶ Big animals can be extremely destructive in the winter as they demolish haystacks and **tear down fences**.

▶ The protesters threw stones, damaged cars, **tore down** street **signs**, and demanded constitutional reforms.

2 **Figurative uses of *tear down*:**

▶ Leadership isn't about **tearing people down** but building them up.

▶ If you're going to create an argument to **tear down** your **opponent**, make it believable.

▶ If you want to **tear down** my **argument**, you should present valid points and a strong counterargument.

▶ Prosperity requires **tearing down walls** that stand in the way of progress.

▶ The secretary of state is calling for countries everywhere to **tear down barriers** that keep women out of the workplace.

▶ If you're an Aquarius, your job is to challenge authority, **tear down** existing **structures**, and replace them with something better.

▶ Sometimes I wish we could just **tear down the government** and start from scratch as a nation.

## 4 MORE REAL-LIFE DATA

***Tear down* often attracts the verb *replace*:**

▶ The house was in such rough shape that officials discussed **tearing** it **down and replacing** it with a new building.

▶ The library will be **torn down and replaced** by a church.

## 5 CONVERSATION TIP

**Imagine you have been elected to be your class representative. Here's something you can say in your first speech:**

**Together, we will tear down the walls between students and faculty.**

# 100 WRAP UP

## 1 WHAT IT MEANS

**1 When you wrap up something such as a task, meeting, etc., you complete it successfully:**

▶ The CEO wrapped up the meeting by laying out the next steps.

= The CEO concluded the meeting by saying what should be done next.

**2 After you finish this lesson, turn to page 253 for additional meanings of *wrap up*.**

## 2 HOW IT WORKS

**1 *Wrap up* takes an object (i.e., what you wrap up). If the object is a noun, it usually goes at the end:**

☑ She wrapped up the meeting. (more common)

☑ She wrapped the meeting up. (less common)

**2 If the object is a pronoun, it always goes in the middle:**

☑ She wrapped it up.

☒ She ~~wrapped up it~~.

**3 With certain nouns, you can use *wrap up* without an object:**

☑ The final season of the show wrapped up on Sunday.

## 3 HOW YOU USE IT IN REAL LIFE

**1 *Wrap up* + words related to communication:**

▶ To **wrap up** our **conversation**, I asked Professor Duncan to share his personal teaching philosophy.

▶ We hope to **wrap up negotiations** by the end of the week.

▶ Do you have any last-minute tips or suggestions before this training **session wraps up**?

**2 *Wrap up* + words related to the entertainment industry:**

▶ I love *Big Little Lies*, but I think it feels too soon to **wrap up** the **series**, especially with so many unanswered questions.

▶ *This is us* **wraps up** its fifth **season** next week.

▶ It's becoming increasingly rare for authors to **wrap up** a **story** in one single book instead of dragging it out.

▶ The **tour** is set to **wrap up** with a series of shows in Latin America in January.

3 *Wrap up* + **words related to law and politics:**

▶ After the jury left, the prosecutor told the judge that she expects to **wrap up** the **case** tomorrow.

▶ The police department's internal affairs division is close to **wrapping up** its own **investigation** into the shooting.

▶ Today, the president **wraps up** his three-day **campaign** swing, with stops in Maryland and Michigan.

▶ The prime minister **wraps up** his **visit** to Washington today with a speech to Congress.

## 4 RELATED MEANING

***To be or get wrapped up in something* means to give it so much attention that you end up ignoring the rest:**

▶ Ethan, we need to talk. You'**re** so **wrapped up in** your **work** you don't even look at me anymore!

▶ It is all too easy to **get wrapped up in** the **idea** that we are not good enough, so keep reminding yourself that you're a winner!

## 5 CONVERSATION TIP

**Imagine you are about to finish a talk. Here's something you can say:**

**So, before we wrap up, can I just make a quick announcement?**

# CHECK YOUR PROGRESS 17

**A Complete the sentences with the correct phrasal verbs. The first one is done for you.**

| do | fall | ~~run~~ | shut | tear | wrap |
|---|---|---|---|---|---|

| apart | away with | down (x 2) | ~~out of~~ | up |
|---|---|---|---|---|

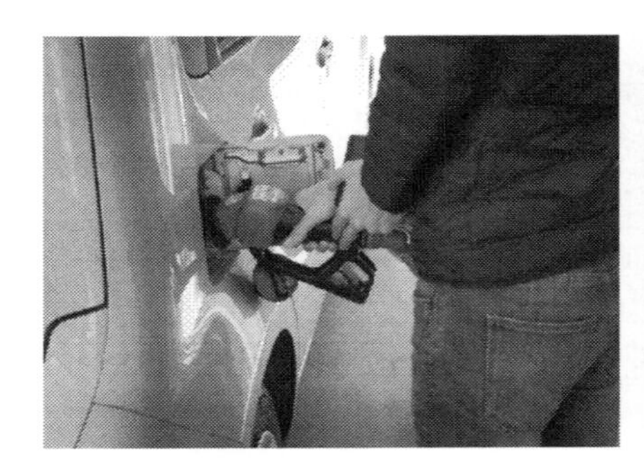

He was about to (1) *run out of* gas when he found a station.

He wants the government to (2) ______________ payroll taxes.

A lot of businesses had to (3) ______________ in 2020.

He is about to (4) ______________ the talk and thank the sponsors.

He is wondering what to do if things (5) ____________ at home.

I can't believe they've decided to (6) ______________ the building.

**B Cross out the option that is illogical, unnatural, or ungrammatical.**

1 I believe [cash payments / outdated laws / these requirements / this system / time] should be done away with.

2 [Beth's career / my whole life / our friendship / the deal / the solution] is falling apart.

3 We are running out of [contract / good ideas / steam / sugar / time].

4 Apparently, they have decided to shut down [production / the border / a deal / the investigation / the nuclear reactor] early next week.

5 She talked about the importance of tearing down [barriers / jobs / old houses / walls / other people's arguments].

6 It's time they wrapped up [negotiations / the house / the investigation / the meeting / the session].

**C Some of the sentences below have either an extra word or a mistake in word order. Correct the mistakes. Ignore the sentences that are correct.**

1 They should do these rules away with.

______________________________

2 It feels as if my marriage is falling apart.

______________________________

3 Hurry up! We're running it out of time.

______________________________

4 My phone was overheating, so I had to shut down it for five minutes.

______________________________

5 The buildings were torn down to make way for a new shopping mall [UK: shopping centre].

______________________________

6 The tour is set to wrap it up with a series of shows in Japan.

______________________________

**D EXTRA CHALLENGE! Choose the correct options.**

1 It's easy to get so ___ up in your work that you forget about your loved ones.
A wrap B wrapped C wrapping D wraps

2 Critics of the project say that ___ down the historic building would be a huge mistake.
A tear B tore C tearing D tears

3 The plane had to make an emergency landing when one of its engines ___ down.
A shut B shuts C is shutting D has shut

4 Some hospitals are close to ___ out of masks for doctors and nurses.
A run B ran C running D runs

5 Guy completely ___ apart when his wife passed away.
A fell B had fallen C has fallen D had been falling

6 It's about time the government ___ away with plastic bags in supermarkets.
A do B did C doing D to do

Answer key:

| Exercise A | Exercise B | Exercise C | Exercise D |
| --- | --- | --- | --- |
| 2 do away with | 1 time | 1 ...do away with these rules | 1 B |
| 3 shut down | 2 the solution | 2 Correct | 2 C |
| 4 wrap up | 3 contract | 3 ...running out of time | 3 A |
| 5 fall apart | 4 a deal | 4 ...to shut it down for... | 4 C |
| 6 tear down | 5 jobs | 5 Correct | 5 A |
|  | 6 the house | 6 ...to wrap up with... | 6 B |

# ADDITIONAL MEANINGS

## 2 COME UP WITH

**When you come up with something, especially money, you find a way to provide it (informal):**

▶ We need to come up with the rent money soon, or we are going to be evicted.

## 4 OPEN UP

1 **When you open up a building, you unlock the door:**

▶ Who will open up the school so we can hold our meeting here?

2 **When a place or area of interest opens up, more people can travel or do business there:**

▶ With the downfall of communism, new markets opened up in Asia.

3 **When you open up, you express your intimate feelings:**

▶ We have been friends for years, but I feel she has never really opened up to me.

4 **In sports, *open up* means to increase a difference in your favor** [UK: favour]**:**

▶ The South African racer had opened up a two-minute lead.

## 6 SET UP

1 **When you set up home somewhere, you start living there, usually by buying a home:**

▶ They first met in Italy but set up home in France.

2 **When you set up or you set yourself up, you start your own business:**

▶ I decided to leave the company and set myself up as a consultant.

3 **When you set yourself up as something you are not, you make people believe you have that characteristic:**

▶ Some coaches set themselves up as therapists, but they have no formal training in the field.

4 **When something sets you up for an experience or an event, it provides you with what you need:**

▶ A healthy breakfast sets you up for the day.

5 **When you are set up by someone else, the person makes others believe you did something wrong when you did not:**

▶ I swear I was set up. Someone must have put your phone in my bag. I don't steal!

6 **To set two people up means to help them meet so they can become romantically involved:**

▶ A good friend of ours set us up, and we asked her to be our maid of honor.

## 7 CARRY ON

1 **When you carry on, you continue moving in the same direction:**
▶ I knew I was lost, but I carried on anyway.

2 **When you carry on in a certain way, you behave that way:**
▶ From the way she carries on, you would think she is a princess.

## 9 HOLD UP

1 **To hold up an object in your hand means to raise it:**
▶ Can you hold up the book so everyone can see the picture?

2 **When an object holds something up, it supports it:**
▶ I don't have a tripod, but I can use these books to hold up the camera.

3 **When you hold someone up, you make that person late:**
▶ Sorry, I didn't mean to hold you up. Were you going somewhere?

4 **When you hold up a process, you delay it:**
▶ In a domino effect, a thunderstorm in the vicinity of an airport can hold up flights at several other destinations.

5 **When a criminal holds up a place, such as a bank or a store, the criminal threatens people there and demands money, often with a gun:**
▶ The robbers held up the bank but were unable to break into the safe.

6 **When your behavior** [UK: behaviour] **is held up as an example, it is exposed for people to criticize** [UK: criticise] **or admire:**
▶ Being a very responsible student, she was held up as an example to the whole class.

## 10 KEEP UP

**When you keep someone up, you don't let them go to bed:**
▶ I hope I haven't kept you up. I know it's a little late to call.

## 19 BUILD UP

1 **When you build someone up, you make them feel better and more confident:**
▶ A good coach can build up the players before a game.

2 **When you build things or people up to yourself or others, you make them seem more important than they actually are:**
▶ I've built him up in my head, but he's only disappointed me.

## 20 PICK UP

1 **To pick something up means to lift it from a surface:**

▶ The baby picked up the toy and bit it.

2 **When you pick up the phone, you answer it:**

▶ Why did it take you so long to pick up? I need to talk to you.

3 **When you pick yourself up, you stand with difficulty after falling:**

▶ Sue was run over by a bike, but she managed to pick herself up and walk home.

4 **When you pick up the check or the tab, you pay for it:**

▶ Let me pick this up. It's your birthday!

5 **In U.S. English, to pick up a room or objects in the room, means to clean and organize** [UK: organise] **it:**

▶ Pick up your room, or no dessert for you!

6 **In the entertainment industry, to pick something up means to win or get it:**

▶ The movie [UK: film] picked up quite a few Oscars.

7 **To pick something up means to buy it:**

▶ If you pass the supermarket, can you pick up some milk, please?

8 **When you pick someone up from somewhere, you go there to collect them, usually by car:**

▶ I've really got to go now. I promised I'd pick my sister up from the airport.

9 **When you are picked up by the police, you are taken to the police station:**

▶ My nephew got picked up by the police, but they didn't press charges.

10 **To pick up an illness means to get sick from it:**

▶ I must have picked up a virus when I was away on business.

11 **When you pick up a skill, you learn it without making much effort:**

▶ I picked up some French from listening to Piaf.

12 **To pick someone up means to meet someone new in the hope of having a sexual relationship:**

▶ The book is a collection of tips on how to pick up someone you're attracted to.

13 **When you pick up a task or a conversation, you return to it after being interrupted:**

▶ Let's pick up where we left off yesterday.

14 **When something picks up the color** [UK: colour] **in something else, it enhances the color, and both things look nice together:**

▶ This new wallpaper really picks up the purple in the sofa.

## 26 ACCOUNT FOR

1 **To account for something means to give a complete explanation:**

▶ Her alibi couldn't account for all her movements on the night of the murder.

2 **When you account for something like a policy, you are responsible for it, and you have to justify the actions taken:**

▶ The president will have to account for the country's response to the pandemic.

3 **To account for money means to keep track of it in your budget:**

▶ When you set up a new business, it is important to account for small expenses, such as transportation.

4 **When you account for people, you know they are safe:**

▶ After the landslide, over 30 people who lived on the hill were never accounted for.

## 29 LIE IN

**When you lie in, you stay in bed for longer:**

▶ I love to lie in and do nothing on Sundays, but there is usually so much housework to do.

## 33 STAND BY

1 **When you are standing by, you are available to help if needed. In this case, the verb is usually in a continuous tense (i.e., verb +** ***ing*****):**

▶ As per state regulations, we need at least one ambulance standing by because the event will attract more than 1,000 people.

2 **When something bad happens, and you just stand by, you are present but do nothing to stop it:**

▶ I'm not going to stand by and watch her die. I need to do something!

## 34 STAND FOR

**When you do not stand for a behavior** [UK: behaviour] **or a situation, you refuse to accept it. In this case, the verb is usually in the negative form:**

▶ This whole situation is ridiculous. I will not stand for any of this!

## 38 BACK UP

1 **To back up means to move backwards:**

▶ Back up a little, so I can get the whole of you on camera.

2 **When you back up a vehicle, you drive it backwards a little. This meaning is more common in American English:**

▶ I passed the entrance, so I had to back up.

3 **When a liquid or a liquid container backs up, it is blocked by something and gradually starts collecting in one place:**

▶ My toilet keeps backing up. It's a nightmare!

4 **When traffic backs up, the vehicles form a long line:**

▶ Traffic is backed up for miles on the way to the coast.

## 43 TURN TO

1 **To turn to a page in a book means to go to that page:**

▶ Turn to page 94 for more information.

2 **When you turn to something, you direct your attention to it:**

▶ Let's now turn to the issue of financing.

3 **When you turn to a task, you start working on it:**

▶ They turned to the task of finding a nursing home for their widowed father.

4 **When you turn to a new activity or career, you start to do that, instead of what you used to do:**

▶ The actor turned to singing after his musical success.

5 **When something turns to something else, it changes its substance or form:**

▶ Our laughter turned to tears when we realized [UK: realised] it was not a joke.

## 47 LAY OUT

1 **When you lay things out, you put them on a flat surface so they become easy to see:**

▶ Let's lay the books out first, before we reorganize [UK: reorganise] the shelves.

2 **When you lay out an area or a building, you plan or design it:**

▶ A formal garden is often laid out in a geometrical pattern.

3 **When you lay out a person for burial, you prepare the body before the funeral:**

▶ Mummies were laid out in their tombs with their personal objects.

4 **When you lay out some money to buy something, you spend a lot of it (informal):**

▶ I can't lay out $1,000 on a prom dress. I'm not a millionaire!

## 48 MAKE OUT

**1 When you can't make someone out, you can't understand their character or how they behave. The verb is usually in the negative or question form:**

▶ My new boss is a mystery to me. I can't make her out at all.

**2 When you make someone or something out to be something, you make people believe false information about the person or situation:**

▶ The situation was not as volatile as the media made it out to be.

**3 When you ask how someone is making out, you want to know if they are succeeding:**

▶ How's your son making out on his new job?

**4 To make out a document, such as a check or a receipt, means to write all the information on it:**

▶ Let me make out a receipt for you.

**5 To make out with someone means to kiss and caress them (informal):**

▶ They made out on the sofa.

## 50 COME OUT

**1 When a star or the moon comes out, it becomes visible in the sky:**

▶ I've been waking up before the sun comes out.

**2 When flowers come out, they open:**

▶ These flowers start to come out in early May.

**3 When dirt or a stain comes out, it is removed from the fabric:**

▶ The wine stain on the sofa never came out.

**4 When a photo comes out, it is clear:**

▶ Your wedding photos came out really well!

**5 When something comes out, it is easy to notice:**

▶ The passion she had for her art came out clearly when she spoke.

**6 When something you say comes out in a certain way, people understand it that way:**

▶ Sorry, that came out all wrong. I didn't mean to offend you.

**7 When people come out to go somewhere, they go somewhere for a social event:**

▶ Would you like to come out for a drink?

**8 When workers come out (on strike), they stop working in protest:**

▶ Air traffic controllers came out on strike demanding better working conditions.

## 53 PAY OFF

1 **To pay off a debt means to finish paying back the money you owe:**

▶ After 10 years, I finally paid off my student loans.

2 **When you pay off an employee, you pay that person for the last time when they stop working for you:**

▶ As expected, the CEO was paid off. He got US$ 10 million when he left.

3 **When you pay somebody off, you pay that person, often illegally, to prevent them from telling a secret or doing something:**

▶ The witnesses told a different story in court, so it is believed they had been paid off.

## 55 TURN OUT

1 **When people turn out for an event, they are present:**

▶ Voters turned out in record numbers this year.

2 **When you turn somebody out, you force the person out of a home:**

▶ The landlord threatened to turn her out if she didn't make the payment by the end of the week.

3 **When a business turns out products, it produces them:**

▶ Volkswagen has begun turning out electric cars in its Chinese factory.

4 **To turn out a light or the gas means to switch it off:**

▶ They turned out the lights and went to bed.

## 69 TAKE ON

1 **When a business takes somebody on, it gives that person a job:**

▶ Amazon is taking on 7,000 new staff to cope with the Christmas demand.

2 **When you take on a person or an institution you consider more powerful than you, you fight or compete against them:**

▶ Erin Brockovich took on the energy corporation PG&E and won.

3 **When a vehicle takes on passengers, goods, or fuel, it stops so it can be loaded:**

▶ This bus will stop here exclusively to take on passengers. Do not disembark.

## 70 TAKE UP

1 **To take up a job or a position means to start doing it:**

▶ She will take up her duties as the school principal next term.

2 **When you take up a story or activity, you continue it after an interruption:**

- ▶ Let me take up the story where I left off.

3 **To take up an issue with someone means to pursue it, often with a higher authority:**

▶ When you do not agree with your grade, you are welcome to take it up with the principal.

4 **When you take up clothes, you make them shorter:**

▶ Because I'm short, I always need to take up the hem on my skirts.

## 71 TURN DOWN

1 **When you turn down something like sound or lights, you reduce the volume or the level:**

▶ Can you please turn down the TV? I can't hear myself think!

2 **When the rate of the economy turns down, it decreases:**

▶ With the economy turning down, unemployment may rise in the next quarter.

## 74 COME ALONG

1 **When someone comes along with you to an event, they accompany you:**

▶ Can my husband come along with me, or is it going to be just us girls tonight?

2 **When something is coming along, it is making progress. In this case, the verb is usually in a continuous tense (i.e., verb + *ing*):**

▶ How are your music lessons coming along?

## 75 COME UP

1 **When a star or the moon comes up, it rises:**

▶ The sun came up as we were walking back home.

2 **When someone comes up, they approach you and stand next to you:**

▶ The teacher came up to me and asked if I was OK.

3 **When an opportunity comes up, it presents itself:**

▶ Soon after I finished my internship, an opportunity came up in the same department, and I was hired.

4 **When something comes up for sale, it becomes available:**

▶ The house of my dreams has just come up for sale!

5 **In legal terms, a case comes up (for a hearing) when it is time to judge it in court:**

▶ Unfortunately, in some countries, most rape cases never actually come up for a hearing.

## 77 RUN INTO

1 **When a vehicle runs into another vehicle or thing, it collides with it:**
▶ That motorcycle came out of nowhere and ran into the back of my car.

2 **To run into a certain number means to reach it:**
▶ There were rumors that the company's debts were running into the billions.

3 **When things run into other things, they become mixed:**
▶ It was hard to follow what he was saying because his words ran into each other. I think he might have been drunk.

## 78 BRING UP

1 **When you were brought up in a place, you lived there as a child:**
▶ I was born in Brazil, but I was brought up in Argentina.

2 **When you bring up children, you are responsible for them, and you take care of them until they become adults:**
▶ She brought up her five children on her own.

3 **When you bring up children in a certain way, you teach them to behave that way or have certain beliefs:**
▶ I was brought up to believe that money is not the number 1 priority in life.

4 **When you bring something up on a computer screen, you make it show:**
▶ Could you please bring up that slide with the QR code again?

5 **When you bring someone up on charges, you make them go to court to be judged:**
▶ He was brought up on charges of public indecency.

6 **When you bring food up, you vomit:**
▶ Seeing all that blood made him bring up his lunch.

## 80 GIVE AWAY

1 **When you give things away, you give them to other people because you do not need or want them anymore:**
▶ Every spring, I separate clothes to give away.

2 **When a company gives things away, it gives them for free, often as a marketing strategy:**
▶ The perfume store always gives samples away to the customers.

3 **When you give away an advantage to an opponent, you lose the game by accident:**
▶ The captain of the team admitted that they had given some goals away.

4 **In certain types of wedding ceremonies, you give away the person who is getting married if you enter the ceremony with that person:**

▶ It is customary for the father to give the bride away, but she chose to walk down the aisle with the grandmother who raised her.

## 81 MAKE UP

**When you make up with someone after an argument, you become friendly with them again:**

▶ They argue a lot, but, in the end, they always kiss and make up.

## 86 GET AWAY WITH

**When you steal something and get away with it, you manage to escape with it:**

▶ The burglars got away with $40,000 worth of electronic equipment.

## 87 GO THROUGH

1 **When you go through some objects, you look at them to find something, or to sort them:**

▶ Every spring, I go through my clothes to decide what I don't need any more.

2 **To go through a text or a list means to check it from beginning to end:**

▶ Let's go through the checklist again and make sure we haven't forgotten anything.

3 **When you go through information, you discuss it in detail, often to make sure it is correct:**

▶ We don't need to go through the details now.

4 **When you go through something artistic, you rehearse it before a performance:**

▶ Let's go through this scene again from the top!

5 **When you go through your resources, you use all you had available:**

▶ We had planned to travel for six months, but after two months we had gone through our savings, so we went back home.

6 **When ideas or thoughts go through your mind, you think of them:**

▶ We had known each other for years, but I never knew what was going through his mind.

7 **When you go through a standard procedure, you follow the official system for dealing with problems:**

▶ We had to go through all the proper channels, yet we never got our refund.

## 90 COME UNDER

**1 When something comes under a title or a heading, it belongs in that category:**

▶ I guess her fiction nowadays comes under the heading of “self-help.”

**2 When a section comes under an official organization** [UK: organisation] **or department, it is subject to its authority:**

▶ In Brazil, all three Armed Forces come under the Ministry of Defense.

## 93 PULL OFF

**When a vehicle of a driver pulls off a road, they stop by the side of the road or turn into a smaller road:**

▶ Can you pull off at the next gas [UK: petrol] station, please? I really need to use the restroom [UK: toilet(s)]!

## 100 WRAP UP

**1 When you wrap up an object, you cover it in paper or another material:**

▶ This one is a gift. Can you wrap it up for me?

**2 When you wrap up or when you wrap someone up, you put on enough clothes to stay warm:**

▶ I wrapped the baby up in a warm blanket.

# A-Z INDEX

# BY THE SAME AUTHOR

If you know the basics of academic writing but still struggle to express your ideas using the right words, *The Only Academic Phrasebook You'll Ever Need* is a lifesaver. This book is a short, no-nonsense, reader-friendly bank of academic "sentence templates" written for both graduate and undergraduate students who need help with their essays, dissertations, and theses. Students preparing for the TOEFL and IELTS exams will find this book useful, too.

*The Only Academic Phrasebook You'll Ever Need* contains 600 sentence frames organized around the typical sections of an academic paper, as well as 80 grammar and vocabulary tips for both native and non-native speakers.

*The Only Academic Phrasebook You'll Ever Need* will help you find the best way to say what you want to say so you can ace that academic paper and get the grade you deserve!

Available on Amazon. To purchase the paperback edition in Brazil, go to bit.ly/3mGcI6h.

E-book/Paperback - Worldwide:

Paperback – Brazil:

Made in United States
Orlando, FL
28 February 2022